OWN
ME

OWN ME

The Wolf Hotel #5

K.A. TUCKER

ISBN 978-1-990105-45-6 (paperback)
ISBN 978-1-990105-44-9 (ebook)

Edited by Jennifer Sommersby

Cover design by Shanoff Designs

Published by K.A. Tucker Books Ltd.

one

"**A**nd were any of *them* trapped in that mine?" Henry's jaw is tense as he paces around the plane, knuckles white from his grip on his phone. "Let me help you with that answer, Mick. *No*, they weren't. They were in their beds with their high-priced escorts sucking their dicks—"

I wince. Whichever corporate lawyer Mick is, he can't be enjoying this tongue-lashing.

"If I want suggestions from *the board* on how to manage *my* company, I'll ask!" He ends the call and tosses the phone onto an empty seat.

"Everything okay?" I dare ask.

"Yes," he snaps, then sighs, as if catching his temper. He pushes his hands through his thick mane of chestnut-brown hair, revealing the small scrape he earned in the mine collapse. His only injury, thankfully. "Just Scott still trying to fuck me from his grave."

Mention of his conspiring, murderous brother has me reaching for my forehead, where bruises still linger from my last run-in with him. Scott has already almost succeeded in taking Henry from me once, thanks to that old mine he'd been funneling company money into, unbeknownst to everyone. Henry made a terrible mistake going into it. He could've died in there.

What else has Scott done?

Henry sees my reaction and the anger radiating from him dissolves instantly. He settles into the cream leather seat across from me and pitches forward, collecting my hand. "He can't hurt either of us anymore." He kisses my knuckles, his beautiful blue eyes catching the engagement ring he slipped on this morning. The gold band is thin, the pearl centerpiece perfectly round with an iridescent luster, surrounded by a cluster of tiny diamonds. It's simple, and nothing like one might expect from the owner of Wolf Enterprise. It was his grandmother's ring.

Who knew the hard-nosed billionaire tycoon who once intimidated me would be so sentimental?

I smile. *I* did. At least, I figured it out somewhere along the way to falling madly in love with him.

And now Henry Wolf is all mine.

He leans into his seat and rests his head, showing off a protruding Adam's apple and that delicious cleft in his chin. Absent is the tailored suit I've grown accustomed to seeing him in. Today, he chose dark blue jeans and a soft charcoal gray cashmere shirt that hugs his powerful torso in all the right places.

While I can't decide which version of Henry I love more, this casual one always gets my blood flowing, especially when his legs are splayed, drawing my attention to a part of him that has brought me so much pleasure over these past months.

"I was thinking about this meeting with Margo's Nordstrom friend next week."

"Yeah?" My eyes divert from their intent focus.

Henry is smirking at me. His hand slides to rest on his thigh, his fingers drumming inches away from the prize. "What are you thinking about, Abbi?" His eyebrow arches. "Being *full* last night?"

My cheeks flush upon mention of our depraved evening. Never would I have expected Henry to share me with another man—let alone Ronan. I can still feel both of them deep inside me. "What about the meeting?" I ask, steering the conversation away from one I'd never want anyone overhearing.

His knowing gaze lingers on me for another few beats before relenting in his teasing. He opens his mouth but then stalls. "Are you nervous about meeting with this buyer?"

"Terrified," I admit with a laugh. "Like, come on! I make homemade soaps in my parents' barn using herbs from their garden, wrap them in plastic, and sell them at the Christmas bazaar and the farmers' market. I don't know the first thing about this whole big business world. I'm going to make a fool of myself. I don't even understand what a buyer does."

Margo wasn't much help when I asked her. "She chooses all the wonderful things they carry in store!" she exclaimed with glee. But when I asked how and why this Nordstrom buyer chooses what she does, Margo winked and said, "As long as she picks *your* wonderful thing, what does it matter?" A predictable answer from the enigmatic supermodel who has people falling at her perfect, beautiful feet wherever she goes.

"I can help prep you if you want." Henry's lips twist in thought. "But it might not be the right move for you."

"What do you mean? It's *Nordstrom*." Where's he going with this?

"This is your company, Abbi. Your brand. No one else's. You get to call the shots. But do you want my opinion?"

"Of course. Always." Henry runs a multibillion-dollar empire. There's no one's advice I value more, even if it's for my little soap business.

"Don't be so quick to hand it over to anyone."

I frown. "But I thought landing distribution in a department store is *the* end game."

"Maybe. But in today's retail world, maybe not. You clearly have something people want. You're only just starting out and look at all the demand you're already stirring up."

"You mean that Margo is stirring up." She's been tapping into beauty industry connections that even Henry doesn't have.

"She knows who to talk to, I agree." Henry leans forward, resting his elbows on his knees. "But you don't want to lose control too quickly by signing contracts that handcuff you. Besides, a contract like that means you have to find a production facility, which means you risk manufacturing a subpar product because you can't possibly make that much by hand. That's something you want to work up to, instead of getting thrown into."

"So you don't think I should pursue this."

He hesitates. "It's *your* company."

I groan with frustration. "Henry, you've been involved with *my* company since this all started. *Now* you've decided to stay out of it?"

"Fine. I don't think you should take the deal." His voice has shifted to that typical commanding tone. "You can have a highly successful business without your product ever touching a shelf inside a store, at least for now. My advice is to stay the course. Build your name on your own first. Retail store contracts will be worth that much more later."

I weigh Henry's words. "Zaheera seems to know what she's doing." In the time since Henry hired and paid for Nailed It to step in and help me make something of my hobby, I now have stylish packaging, a website, and a basic but perfect new name—Farm Girl Soap—for my legal company.

"They're the best at what they do. That's why we went with them."

"*We*?" There was no "we" in that decision the day I got the phone call from Zaheera.

Henry ignores me. "She'll make sure it grows at a healthy rate that you're comfortable with, so you're not overwhelmed. Besides, you still have a degree to finish, right?"

I wince at the reminder. "I'm *so* behind." After my father's accident, when I knew I couldn't head back to Chicago to finish my last year full-time because my parents needed help, I enrolled in correspondence courses. I've barely touched the assigned work for this semester, too wrapped up in life with Henry.

"You'll get there." He takes my hand in his, his thumb sliding over the pearl. "And now you have a wedding to plan too."

A thrill radiates through me as I admire the ring again. My wedding to Henry. Because Henry will be my *husband* soon. It still doesn't feel real, and I doubt it will until I'm walking down the aisle. "If I can wrestle it away from Mama." I held my breath when I announced the good news over the phone just before leaving Wolf Cove, not sure what to expect from a woman who has done everything in her power to keep Henry and me apart, including ingesting caffeine pills to fake a heart attack.

The whoop of glee that escaped her had my mouth hanging. According to her, Henry is doing the honorable thing ... finally. We've only been together a few months.

Henry chuckles. "At least she's not knitting a Henry doll to burn in effigy."

"Have you met Bernadette Mitchell? She'd be afraid God himself would strike her with lightning for something so sinful as black magic."

His laughter grows, his eyes twinkling. "Do you think she'll keep it quiet—"

"Not a chance." There won't be a soul in Greenbank, Pennsylvania, who won't have heard about my engagement by the end of the day, which means the media will find out shortly after. With all the interest in Henry these days, that's likely to cause a stir. Will the headlines be kind or judgmental? Worry gnaws at my bliss, threatening to damper it.

"And did you tell her it would be in Alaska?"

"One hurdle at a time." Though I suspect *that* will be a monumental one to overcome. Mama will have her heart set on including the entire church congregation, and we can't possibly be expected to fly them all up there.

Henry's wry smirk says he guessed as much. "Wolf Hotels has a special events planner for big occasions. I'll have Miles contact her to call you next week to start the ball rolling. She's good. Her name is Jill, and she'll organize anything you want."

"*We* want," I correct him. "It's your wedding too."

"Abbi, if it were up to me, we'd be driving to the courthouse from the tarmac as soon as we land, and I'd be fucking my wife by nightfall."

"How romantic," I tease, but my stomach flips with nerves. There is something swoony about his sudden impatience to marry me.

A dangerous glint lights in his eye as his grip tightens. "You want romance, Abbi?"

"I want *you*."

"You already have me." He yanks me forward and onto his lap, my legs straddling his thighs. "Every inch of me." Heat from his strong, skilled hands seer my skin through my black leggings as they slide around to cup either side of my ass, pulling me forward until our torsos are flush against each other and that delicious hard ridge is pressing into the apex at my thighs.

I wind my arms around his neck, my wrists entwined behind his head. "I've never been happier in my life," I whisper, a bubble of exhilaration stirring as I lean in to capture his plump lips.

"Same," he murmurs against my mouth before our tongues meet in a slow, seductive dance that quickly spirals, his hand seizing a fistful of my hair, angling my head back so he can get closer.

Jack, the co-captain, slips out from the cockpit. "Sorry to disturb. We're about to start our descent, and we'll have you on the ground shortly. Is there anything you need in the meantime?"

"Draw the privacy curtain," Henry demands in a gruff voice.

Could he make it any more obvious?

Heat crawls up my neck as I catch Jack's sly smile.

"Yes, sir." He taps his ring finger and mouths "Congratulations" before shutting us out with the thick gray curtain.

I let out a yelp as Henry stands and spins us around, releasing me into the seat he just vacated. He drops to his knees.

"What are you doing?"

"You need to ask that?" He tugs my shoes off and casts

them aside, and then his fingers curl around the waistband of my leggings, peeling them, along with my panties, past my ankles, leaving me bare from the waist down.

Moisture pools at my core as he pushes my thighs apart, exposing me to the setting sun that streams in through the portal windows. "We were rough on you last night." His index finger slides along my folds before easing inside.

I wince at the intrusion. "I'm okay."

"No, you're not." He hooks his arm under my thigh and pulls my body toward him, halfway out of my seat. "But you will be."

I barely bite back the moan at the first swipe of his tongue, but I can't stop from crying out as he licks my sensitive flesh. From this angle, I can see everything he's doing, and I watch intently as he seals his mouth over my clit.

Two fingers plunge in and find that spot deep inside. He puts pressure on it, stirring a flood of warmth.

"No one but me will ever taste you again, Abbi," he purrs, his voice vibrating deep within me.

"No one," I pant, my breath ragged as pressure builds low in my belly.

He slips his fingers out and his hands find the backs of my thighs, making my skin slick. He pushes them farther apart, stretching my body as far as it can go as his eyes flip to meet mine.

I see the truth in his hooded gaze, how much he enjoys doing this.

That tongue is *mine* for the rest of our lives ...

His mouth seals over my clit, sucking hard.

My orgasm hits suddenly and unexpectedly. I stifle my cries and grab the back of his head, my fingers digging into his silky hair as I buck against his mouth, trying to get closer, to draw it out.

I haven't even settled before Henry is unfastening his jeans and pushing them down his thighs. I cry out as he shoves his hard length into me in a single thrust.

"Wait!" I gasp.

He stalls his hips. "Are you *that* sore?"

"No, I just ..." I *am* that sore, but I'm also desperate to have Henry come inside me. "I just need a minute. *Please*," I say, even as I roll my hips against his, urging him to keep moving.

He smiles as he slides his cock out and back in, much slower this time, giving my body time to adjust to the intense, almost unbearable fullness of him. Over and over again, Henry pulls out and pushes back in with gentle thrusts, until my hips are lifting to meet his eagerly, begging for more.

"Fuck, Abbi," he growls. "Sweater off, now." He helps me tug it off and tosses it aside. Slipping a hand beneath my back, he has my bra unfastened with one expert flick of his fingers. In a split second, that's cast aside, too, leaving me naked.

He peels his sweater off, giving me a delicious view of his sculpted chest.

"Please don't let us crash," I pant, my body flushed from being so exposed, especially with two men in the cockpit who know exactly what we're doing.

"What a way to go, though." Henry guides my legs over his shoulders and plunges harder into me, his hips slamming against my thighs. The angle is ideal, hitting me deep with each thrust. Soon, all discomfort has faded from thought, my body eager to welcome his. I revel in his touch as he fills his hands with my breasts, the pads of his thumbs teasing my pebbled nipples with merciless strokes.

Slipping my fingers between us, I rub circles around my clit.

"Fuck," he hisses, his eyes filled with raw desire. "You're about to come again, aren't you." It's not a question.

"Yes." That familiar warmth is spreading through my middle, a tingle creeping along my spine. He knows my body so well.

"Let me hear you this time," Henry forces out through gritted teeth, picking up the pace. My slickened body accepts his hard thrusts. Not even the jet's engines can drown out the wet sounds of our bodies enjoying each other. *Everything* about Henry—the feel of his hands on me, the scent of his skin, the sound of his voice, his cries— makes my body sing, and I fall deeper into the endless pit of love for this man.

"I want to hear you, Abbi." His fingers clamp down over my nipples, just shy of the point of pain. "I want *everyone* to hear how fucking good my cock feels, how much you love having it inside you." He punctuates his words with his thrusts.

A surge of blood rushes to my core with his dirty words and his illicit touch, swelling the flesh between my legs. I don't mute myself this time, letting my cries sail as an orgasm rips through me, my muscles contracting around Henry's hard length. He follows seconds later, his face contorting with the guttural sounds that escape his parted lips. I feel him pulse inside me as he unloads in wave after wave until all that's left is our ragged breaths and spent, slick bodies.

"Kiss me," I demand softly.

He leans down, his lips soft and pliable as they touch mine. Affectionate.

"Was that loud enough for you?" I tease.

He grins. "Yes, much better. Thank you."

"Well, I understood the assignment, Mr. Wolf."

Henry chuckles and, peeling away, steals a glance out the portal window. "We're about to land." He pulls free and then does something unexpected by slipping a finger between my legs, coating it in a mixture of us. He holds it against my lips.

With a grin, I open my mouth and suck hard, tasting the saltiness.

A sexy smirk curls Henry's lips. "How far my innocent little farm girl has come."

two

"Remind me why we didn't stay at Wolf Cove, Victor?" Henry calls out, stirring me from slumber. I'm still nestled against his chest where I settled in, his arm slung over my shoulder. I drifted off, listening to his heartbeat and his deep voice as he caught up on business calls.

"That's a good question, sir," our driver responds cordially.

I blink away the sleep and refocus on the countless streetlights outside, blurred by drizzle. Horns blare from every direction. "Are we almost home?"

Henry brushes stray hairs off my forehead before pressing a kiss against my temple—such an uncharacteristically sweet gesture, especially compared to the filthy things he did to my body an hour ago. "Two blocks away. You'll be in bed within ten minutes."

"So will you." I smooth my palm over his curved chest before my fingertips crawl across the ridges of his abdomen.

Henry's sigh is full of contentment as he weaves his fingers within mine, and we wait quietly for our car to navigate the city's gridlock. Finally, Wolf Tower comes into view ahead, a grand looming edifice, the tallest mixed residential and hotel building in the city.

Henry's body tenses. "The reporters are already here?"

"I don't think they ever left," Victor says.

Sure enough, a small horde lingers beneath umbrellas near the entrance, armed with cameras.

"Not when the Wolf name keeps gifting them such lucrative headlines," Henry mutters bitterly. Between William Wolf's sudden death and then Scott Wolf's involvement in it and his subsequent demise, Henry has been caught in a media swirl for weeks. The mine collapse was the brittle on the crème brûlée. And now there are highly publicized pictures of the two of us kissing in the moments after he stepped off the helicopter, covered in dirt and blood, which will stir all sorts of new questions about New York's most eligible bachelor's relationship.

I can feel myself about to get sucked into the swirl.

Henry must feel it, too, because his arm tightens around me in protection. "Take us straight to the underground," he demands, his voice hard.

"Certainly, sir. Already planned on it."

"Please and thank you," I add after a beat.

Victor's eyes catch mine in the rearview mirror, the corners of his crinkled with a smile.

Henry leans in to whisper in my ear, "You wouldn't dare be implying that I don't have manners, would you, Abigail?"

I used to quake when he used that even tone with me. Now I snuggle against his chest. "*Never.*" He has exceptional manners when he chooses to use them, but he's also accustomed to people jumping at his every command.

"I didn't think so." He leans in farther until the light

stubble along his jawline grazes my skin. "But I like those words on your lips. I think you'll be using them later."

His promise stirs a mental image and a memory that ignites my core.

We pull into the valet entrance, waiting for the cars ahead to move. Photographers have their cameras aimed at our windows, calling out Henry's name. It's all a pointless production, thanks to the impenetrable tint.

I fish my phone out of my purse and turn it on for the first time since we landed.

The moment it starts chirping, I wish I hadn't.

"SHE'S ASKED Reverend Enderbey to marry us!" I cry, seeing red as I scroll through Mama's messages. All thirty-two that she sent since I hung up with her before leaving Alaska this morning.

"Sullivan." Henry nods his thanks as the security guard steps aside to allow us into the elevator. The lineman-sized giant was waiting to greet us when Victor parked the car. "Would he fly to Alaska to officiate?"

"I don't know, but she's already booked the church for our ceremony." My thumb swipes at the screen as I speed-read. "And she's called the rental company for our reception *in the barn*! And—oh my God—she's asked three of my cousins to be my bridesmaids!" It keeps getting worse the farther down I go.

Henry's chuckle reverberates.

"This is not funny!"

"Are you surprised? She knows she can't stop you from marrying me, so she's found a new way to try to gain control."

"I knew she'd want to have a say on things, but I didn't think she'd have our whole wedding planned before our plane landed. And all this? This was supposed to be Jed's and my wedding. She's just swapped out the grooms." Which is especially surprising, given Mama was convinced Henry was the devil himself walking the earth until only recently.

"I am definitely not Fuckface," Henry grumbles.

I hold up my phone to show Henry the picture of Mama's wedding dress, pulled from storage and hanging in my bedroom in Greenbank. "Ready to be sized for me."

He frowns. "Is that a bow?"

"One of several."

He shakes his head. "Rethinking city hall yet?"

I groan.

Sullivan whistles before flashing a gap-toothed grin. "Gotta say, I thought *my* mother was demanding, but sounds like you've got your work cut out for you, Ms. Mitchell."

I falter at his use of my name. I've never met this man, though I know Henry replaced the guards who let Scott into the penthouse. But then I remind myself that everyone in Wolf Tower's security staff knows who I am. They're paid to. "She's going to ruin our wedding."

"No, she isn't." Henry wraps his hand around my nape, his thumb drawing small, calming circles against my skin. "It's *your* wedding. Tell her thanks, but no thanks."

"If only it were that easy."

The elevator approaches the lobby level and Henry's chest rises, the only sign that the media attention bothers him. "No reporters inside, right?"

"None, sir. But your niece has been waiting for you for hours."

Henry's face screws up. "My *niece*. I don't have—"

The elevator doors open with a ding, and another massive security guard waits outside to escort us to our penthouse elevator.

Henry's still wearing that look of confusion when Sullivan gestures toward a girl of maybe sixteen sitting on a bench. "Are you saying she's not related to you, sir?"

Henry's mouth opens, but he falters on his answer.

The girl looks up, sees Henry, and jumps out of her seat, smoothing her hands over lengthy ash brown hair as she glances around her. Perhaps searching for an escape? She looks like any regular teenager, with blue jeans and an over-sized gray hoodie and scuffed black and white Chucks.

"Sir, if she's falsely impersonating your niece, we should get you—"

"It's okay." Henry waves Sullivan off, his face unreadable as he approaches her. "Hello. Who are you?"

She takes a deep, shaky breath as she meets his gaze.

There's something so familiar about her. I can't quite place it, though. Have I met her before?

"You told people you're my niece. I only have one brother that I'm aware of. Are you saying Scott Wolf was your father?"

She clears her throat but doesn't speak.

Henry crosses his arms, waiting for an answer. As if she weren't already nervous enough, he will make it tenfold worse.

There's a scuffle at the entrance. A photographer has managed to slide past the doorman and is in the lobby, snapping pictures of us as security guards close in. The distraction gives the girl time to bolt. In seconds, she's running, ducking around bodies and out the door as we're ushered to the elevator.

"She had to be, what, sixteen? Seventeen at most?"

"Or younger. It's hard to tell sometimes."

Henry stares up at the ceiling, the silky bedsheet pooled around his waist. "Scott would've had to be in his first or second year of college when she was born. He never mentioned anything to me about a daughter."

"Would he, though? You guys weren't close."

"He didn't hate me quite so much back then." His lips twist. "Unless he didn't know about her. That would explain why there's no mention of her in his will. He was a fucking degenerate, but even he would leave something behind for his daughter. I *have* to believe that much about him."

Henry's mind has been spinning over the mystery girl since we got back to the safety of our home. We have no information to go on other than the name she gave to security when they asked her why she was loitering. Violet, she said it was, but who knows if that's true. Henry demanded the security footage. We watched as the girl sat in the lobby for four hours, her foot tapping the marble floor, her fingernails probably bitten down to the quick for how often they ended up between her teeth. She got up and headed for the door at least a dozen times before returning to her seat, as if struggling with her decision to come here in the first place.

"The way she was dressed ... You don't think she was homeless, do you?"

I chuckle. "No, she's just a teenager."

"She looked scared."

"A lot was going on. Security guards, reporters. And it's *you* she was coming to see."

"What's that supposed to mean?"

"You know *exactly* what it means." The indomitable Henry Wolf, who fills a room just by stepping into it.

He smirks because he does know.

"Maybe she'll come back." I press my lips against Henry's shoulder.

"I could send her picture to Dyson to see what he can dig up." He makes a sound, as if disagreeing with his idea. "Likely nothing, unless she's a criminal."

"If she's Scott's daughter, then it's in her blood," I mutter, but then mentally chastise myself. It's not her fault she got the short end as far as fathers go.

He snorts, but the frown marring his handsome face won't relent. "Why would she come here?"

three

I wake to my phone vibrating on the nightstand. I paw for it—torn between answering the call and shutting it off.

"My dear Abigail! Congratulations!" Margo's seductive Parisian accent curls around my eardrum.

"Hmm? For what?" I blink at the alarm clock. Nine a.m., which means it's midafternoon in Paris.

"Your engagement to Henry has made Page Six!"

The way she says Henry's name—the *H* silent—always makes me smile. "Already?"

"Oui. I am sending it to you now. Un moment."

With a soft, sleepy moan, I roll onto my back and stretch. The other side of the bed is empty. I'm not surprised that Henry is already up and gone. He was tossing and turning all night. I doubt he got any sleep. Still, it disappoints me. I didn't get enough time alone with him before rejoining reality.

My phone jolts with an incoming text and I read the headline:

Exclusive: Henry Wolf Survives Alaskan Mine Collapse and Proposes to His Assistant

"Ugh. *Ex*-assistant!" Several screenshots appear and they're full of pictures of the two of us—some as recent as last night, through the glass of Wolf Tower's lobby doors—and others taken weeks ago at William Wolf's funeral. There's even one of us from that dreaded night of Wolf Cove's grand opening in early summer when I was so sure Henry was cheating on me.

"Does it say how they found out?" They've made a point of drawing a red circle around my hand with an added arrow pointing at my left ring finger, but it's impossible to see the ring.

"How they *always* find out. 'An anonymous source close to the family.'"

That could be anyone from a fellow churchgoer to Lucy from the feed store with the way my mother's lips have surely been flapping since yesterday morning. "What else does it say?"

"That you are to marry in that barn of yours."

Damn it, Mama. "We are *not* getting married in Greenbank."

"Well, I must say that is a relief. It is a cute barn on a cute farm, but you two are meant for something far grander. Maybe my place? It could be the unveiling of Wolf Hotel's newest boutique hotel, if your fiancé would commit to me already."

I laugh. Margo is nothing if not relentless about her dream to turn her family's old French castle into a Wolf chain hotel. "We're getting married in Alaska next spring, before the hotel opens for the season." The most important place in the world to Henry and now to me.

She makes an exasperated sound. "I suppose that place

will also do. Now, if you are to marry in spring, that does not leave Emmanuelle Agard much time. We will meet with her when she is in New York in a few weeks."

"Emmanuelle Agard? Who is that?"

Margo's laughter fills my ear. "Oh, my sweet Abigail. You are precious. She is only one of the most sought-after dress designers in the world. She must be booked at least three years in advance and only takes on a handful of clients each year. It is a good thing that one of your dearest friends is also one of her dearest friends."

"You don't have to pull strings for me."

"Too late. They are already pulled! She has agreed to make you the most beautiful dress of the year. *Un pièce de résistance*. Far too nice to get married in the woods with wild animals, if you ask me, but nobody is."

I shake my head. "Thank you, Margo." She's always playing the role of master puppeteer, with nothing to gain out of it for herself.

"What are friends for! Now, I must run. My manager has called me three times to inform me that I am terribly late for a meeting." Unhurried heels click on tile in the background. "Oh! Before I forget, has Sandra reached out to you yet?"

The buyer from Nordstrom. A knot forms in my stomach with the worry of disappointing Margo after all the effort she's put in on that front, but I slept on Henry's words and he's right. I need to take control. "She left a voicemail." I hesitate, but then decide it's best to get this all out in the open. "Look, I appreciate everything you've done for me behind this, Margo, *really* ... but I need to hit the brakes. Not forever, but for now. I still have school, and now the wedding, and everything is moving so fast. I'm going to start with a limited run of soap ahead of the holidays." I end my declaration with a wince. "You're not angry, are you?"

"Me? Angry with you?" She tsks. "Oh Abigail, you never need to worry about that, and you do not need to apologize. Sometimes I get overzealous, but I am only trying to help in any way I can. Sandra can wait until you are ready, and I will make sure everyone knows about your launch."

I smile at the ceiling. "You are such a good friend."

"I could be a much better one if that possessive fiancé of yours would allow it." Her musical laughter rings out. "I will see you in a few weeks."

I HEAR RUSTLING in the kitchen and round the corner to find Henry's housekeeper unloading groceries onto the counter. "Raj!"

The middle-aged man looks up from his task and smiles. "Miss Abbi, it is so good to see you again—oh!" He chuckles as I launch into him with a hug. "I was not expecting that." After a beat, he encloses his arms around me.

I take my time pulling away to meet his big brown eyes. "How are you doing?" The man barely knew me and yet saved me from Scott, but in doing so now has to live with the knowledge that he killed a man.

He hesitates, examining the spot where Scott dropped to the floor and did not get back up. "Better each day, thank you for asking. And you? You seem to be healing well." His gaze flitters to my forehead.

"I am. Honestly, I haven't had much time to think about it with everything else."

"I saw the news about the mine. I'm so glad to see you both here and well. Now you can have a few days of quiet."

"I was hoping for a few *years*?"

He snorts, a brief break from his professional persona.

"Wouldn't that be nice." A moment of silence hangs between us before he seems to snap out of it. "I went for a shop, but I don't know your preferences yet. If there's anything specific you need, just ask, and I'll be more than happy to run out for it." He stoops and pulls out a new cast-iron frying pan from the drawer. "A replacement."

I wince. "Looks heavier."

"Oh, it is." He smacks his free palm against the bottom of it. "Does Mr. Wolf have any more brothers we need to worry about?"

I chuckle, though it's a morbid and terrible joke. "Not that I'm aware of." Maybe a niece, but I can't see her being a danger to either of us. Besides, the way she ran out of here yesterday, I don't know that we'll ever see her again.

He starts loading the fridge. "Have you eaten? Can I make you something for breakfast? Here, let me get your coffee started." He's flipping buttons before I have a chance to answer.

"You don't need to wait on me," I call out over the buzz of the fancy Italian espresso machine.

"Mr. Wolf has asked that I come every day to meet your needs, now that you're living here."

"He didn't need to do that."

Raj's brow furrows. "Will my presence here be an issue for you? Because I can speak to Mr. Wolf—"

"No, of course not." I hold up my hands in surrender, afraid I've offended him. "I just mean I'm self-sufficient. I didn't grow up with all *this*—" I wave around me. "You're going to be bored if you're relying on me to keep you busy."

"One can never be bored with good company." He winks before setting a full mug of coffee in front of me, followed by cream and sugar.

"Thank you." I fix my drink, noting how Raj watches

23

intently, no doubt mentally measuring how much of each I put in so he can make it *for* me next time. It's going to take me a long time to get used to this new life.

My phone chirps and my stomach tenses as I see the name pop up. *What now, Mama?*

Mama: *Look what Celeste found among her dress patterns! She'll sew them for your bridesmaids. Connie and Stephanie have already sent their measurements and I've found the perfect fabric.*

I click on the attached picture. Sure enough, it looks like something Celeste Enderbey would sew—chaste and cotton, circa 1985. "Stop it!" I wail, scrolling to the spool of green-and-white gingham fabric. Mama's favorite.

"Is something the matter, Miss Abbi?" Raj asks.

"Yes, actually." I groan with exasperation. "You know what you can help me with, Raj? Tell me how to deal with a Momzilla who is trying to hijack every single element of my wedding."

He cocks his head, his hand collecting mine to study the ring on my finger. "Mr. Wolf neglected to mention that bit of news."

"Oh." I flush. "It just happened yesterday."

A bright smile fills his face as he squeezes my hand. "Congratulations are in order, then."

His sincerity tempers my frustration with Mama for the moment. "Thank you. It's all come as quite a shock."

He gives my hand another squeeze and then releases it. "To you, maybe. I am not at all shocked that Mr. Wolf has asked you to marry him."

"Really? Why not?"

"He is a different man since he met you."

"How so?"

"Just ... different. In a very good way."

I smile. Raj is so easy to talk to. "Can I help you with all these groceries?"

"And leave me with nothing to do? No, thank you." He flashes a grin.

I sip my coffee and watch him quietly as he goes back to his task, washing berries and filling the fruit crisper.

My phone chirps again. A text from Autumn with the same screenshot that Margo sent me earlier. I imagine I'll see it from various sources several more times before the day is through. "The engagement is all over Page Six already."

"Par for the course, being attached to such a powerful man. I'm afraid it's something you will have to tolerate, to some extent, anyway. And some of those reporters will do anything for a juicy story." Raj empties the carton of eggs into the holder. "One offered me twenty thousand dollars for details on Scott Wolf's death. He wanted to know why he came here."

To rape me. And worse, possibly. "Obviously, you didn't take the payday." Those details have not been leaked by anyone yet.

"Mr. Wolf pays me well for not only my services but my discretion. These people think they can wave dollar bills and get whatever they want. That is not the case. At least, not with me. And some things do not need to see headlines. It is enough that it ended the way it did." Raj wipes the counter of a few errant crumbs. "So, tell me about this Momzilla problem of yours."

I savor my coffee as I download on Raj. It turns out, Henry's housekeeper is an excellent listener. By the time he's heading to collect Henry's clothes for dry cleaning, we've devised a plan of attack to deal with Mama that I think—I hope—will work.

I'm reaching for my phone to message Henry when it rings with an incoming call from an unknown number.

"Hello?" I answer warily.

"Abbi! Hey! Congratulations on the engagement!"

"Uh ... Thanks." I frown, the man's voice unfamiliar. "Who is this?"

"It's Luca, from the *Tribune*."

A newspaper reporter. *Great.* "How did you get this number?"

"Do you mind if I ask you a few questions?"

While avoiding mine, apparently. My wariness grows. "Actually, I need to—"

"With Henry's grandparents, father, and brother dead, and mother long since estranged, the entire Wolf empire sits on his shoulders. He must be feeling especially lonely these days. Could that explain the hasty proposal?"

"It wasn't hasty," I blurt without thinking.

"You've only known each other since May, though."

"Well, I mean, yes, it was fast. But he gave it thought," I stammer. *Hasty* is a terrible word. It sounds rushed and poorly considered.

It sounds like a mistake.

"So you're not worried he'll regret it and break off the engagement?"

"I ... no?" Should I be?

"You're his assistant, correct?"

"*Was.* I haven't worked for him for months." I wish the papers would get that part right, at least.

I hear a page flip. "According to sources, your romantic relationship began while you were working as Henry Wolf's assistant at the Wolf Alaska location, despite a strict corporate policy against it. Is that correct?"

Henry and I figured this question might arise. Now that

his father is gone and Henry owns the hotel, it no longer matters, but I know it'll bother him if his reputation is dragged.

This Luca guy said he has sources. "Who told you that?" Belinda and Ronan know, but neither of them would stoop so low as to sell me out to a reporter.

"My sources wish to remain anonymous. Are you confirming it?"

"No!" Jed knows Henry and I started long before I came home from Alaska. He would definitely spill under questioning. I'm going to strangle him if he fed information to this guy.

"So, you're denying it, then."

"No, I'm ..." I'm flustered, is what I am. Who is this guy, what is his angle, and *why* am I still entertaining his questions? "I have somewhere I need to be—"

"Tell me about your coworkers ... Connor Brien and Ronan Lyle."

My stomach drops at the sudden change in topic and to where it's landed. "What about them?"

"How would you describe the nature of your relationship with them?"

An alarm bell goes off. "They're *friends*." Why is he asking? What does he know?

Luca hums like he doesn't believe me, and I can hear his pen scribbling something. "Sources say your friendship with Ronan Lyle was of a far more intimate nature. If Henry Wolf were to find out about your other partners, would this impact your engagement to him?"

Oh, believe me, he knows. I swallow. "Ronan and I have always been just *friends*." Friends who have fucked, but that is none of anyone's business.

"What about Michael Stern, Henry's private massage

therapist? How would you describe your relationship with him?"

The biggest mistake of my life. I press my hand against my stomach to calm my nerves. This is too specific to be an idle rumor. It's obvious this Luca guy has been digging for dirt on me, but who is throwing him bones to fetch? And why does it feel like he's on a mission, firing off question after invasive question to try to trip me up?

If details about my Alaskan escapades get blasted in the newspapers ...

If my parents and all of Greenbank read about it ...

At least I haven't hidden anything from Henry. But who at Wolf Cove has been airing my dirty laundry?

My hand shakes as I hit the End Call button, something I should have done after the first question.

It trills almost immediately, before my finger has left the phone screen. A wave of anger emboldens me as I answer. "Do not call me again!"

"Abbi?"

"Oh, Miles. Hey." I should have read the number before yelling like a maniac.

"I wanted to say congratulations," Henry's assistant continues. "What's going on?"

"A reporter is poking around."

"About what?"

I shake my head, though he can't see it. "Nothing. So, what's going on with you? How are things there? Does Henry have you running around like a headless chicken?" Miles and I bonded early on. As a boss, Henry isn't the easiest person to work for, something we both know from experience. He doesn't ask, he demands, and he expects perfection. And when he's stressed out, he can be intolerable.

"No, actually. It's weird. He hasn't asked me for *anything*. And when I forgot to send the daily report off to the executive team? I expected him to tell me to get my head out of my ass like he normally does, but he didn't say a word."

"That *is* weird."

"He's been in his office for most of the morning, except for an executive meeting where I took notes for him, and he was completely distracted. It was noticeable. Like, *everyone* noticed it."

"He's been through a lot over the last few weeks."

"I know. I mean, his dad and then his brother. And then he almost died! But still, it's not like him. I thought I'd see if there's anything going on that I should know about," he asks tentatively, as if he might be overstepping.

I'd like to know the answer to that too. Maybe Henry got a call from Luca full of insinuations. How will he react to his new fiancée being painted a summertime whore, which is what I sensed from Luca's tone and manner of questioning. Will Henry be embarrassed?

Too embarrassed to go through with the marriage?

I pace around the kitchen island, studying my ring, as a darker thought invades my mind. *Is Henry regretting his hasty proposal already?*

Damn, that asshole reporter. Now that he's planted the idea in my head, it's going to fester all day, driving me insane. By the time I see Henry tonight, I'm going to be an insecure mess.

I need to talk to Henry now. Better yet, I need to see him, to read his eyes and confirm that I have nothing to worry about. I check the time. "Does he have anything scheduled over lunch?"

"Hmm ... nope. Nothing yet."

"Okay, keep it open for me, would you?"

four

"**M**arcello's. *Smart.*" Miles's green eyes widen with delight as he spies the paper bag in my hand. I stopped by Henry's favorite sandwich shop on my way in and the guy behind the counter ran it out to the car. More sage advice from Raj.

I hope so. I've never surprised Henry at work before, and he's not a big fan of people hijacking his calendar. I follow Miles into the elevator.

Miles waves his key card against the pad, hits the top-floor button, then flops back with an exhale. "I am *so* glad to see you."

I smile despite my worries. Henry hired his lanky male assistant after our breakup midsummer when I transferred to Outdoor Crew and he left Wolf Cove. It was a smart move, given his history with female assistants. I can't lie and say I wouldn't have been insanely jealous had he replaced me with another. "Is he still being weird?"

Miles pushes a hand through his curly mop of brown hair. "I spilled a folder full of paperwork in his office, and he helped me pick it all up without a word."

I burst out with laughter. "So, what you're saying is he's not his usual asshole self."

"Exactly. But don't tell him I said that." His gaze flickers to my finger. "It fits."

"It does." I hold out my hand to admire the ring that apparently Henry sized on me one night while I was sleeping. Another sign that his proposal wasn't *hasty*. But wait … "*You knew* he was going to propose?"

He grins. "Who do you think was fielding all the calls between the jeweler?"

"And you didn't warn me?" I give him a playful shove.

"He threatened to have my balls chopped off if it got out."

I picture Henry delivering on that threat. I'm sure it sounded convincing. "He was only kidding. He doesn't do that sort of thing." I pause for effect. "Dyson, however …"

Miles blinks rapidly. The lawyer and general fix-it guy may be intimidating but he hasn't maimed anyone as far as I know.

The elevator doors open, and Miles leads me down the main hall of the executive floor, lined with assistants' desks and private offices screened by frosted glass. It's simple and clean and quiet, save for the tapping on keys and the odd ringing phone.

"I said *don't* approve that!" a man yells from behind one of those doors.

"That's Sunjit. He's always yelling at someone on the phone," Miles says.

"Fun." Outside Sunjit's office, his middle-aged brunette assistant sits at her desk, staring over her glasses at me. In fact, they're *all* watching. Suddenly, I feel eyes crawling over me from every direction.

"Does everyone know?" I whisper.

"That the big boss is marrying his twenty-one-year-old ex-assistant who he met this summer? What do you think?"

My cheeks flush. Are they saying the same things that reporter alluded to? Is there a tally running for how long before Henry recovers from his near-death shock and dumps me?

I keep my focus ahead, lifting my chin slightly. It doesn't matter what any of them say. Henry and I love each other. That's all that matters. Besides, I may be twenty-one, but he just turned thirty-two, not *fifty*.

We pass a door with the name Scott Wolf etched into it and I stifle a shudder. The assistant's desk outside sits empty.

"Have you been to Henry's new office?" Miles asks.

"Not yet." William Wolf kept it for himself right up until his death.

"That's it there." Miles gestures toward the heavy glazed doors ahead. "I would knock first. He doesn't like being barged in on."

"Yes, I remember." Hotel staff weren't even allowed in the penthouse cabin at Wolf Cove, but that's because he was also living there. My knuckles clunk against the glass.

"Come in," comes the deep voice.

I ease open the door and step through, my stomach fluttering with a mix of nerves and excitement over seeing Henry again. I hope this never goes away.

Inside is nothing short of opulence. I expected a grand office for the man behind all of Wolf, but this is outrageous. It may as well be an apartment. Floor-to-ceiling windows reaching two stories high close off the far side, showcasing the city's skyline beyond. To the left is a sunken living room area with plush caramel leather furniture and lamps.

Behind it is a mahogany and chrome bar with crystal decanters. Henry's posh scotch collection.

Opposite the seating area is a wall of bookshelves filled with spines and, in front of that, a desk large enough to accommodate four guests on one side.

My heartbeat quickens at the sight of Henry slouched in his chair, a pen perched between his lips, his attention locked on something beyond the window.

Oblivious to me, though he granted me permission to enter.

"Henry?" I call out tentatively.

He snaps out of his daze, spinning his revolving chair toward me. "Abbi, what are you doing here?" He frowns. "Is something wrong?"

I hold up the brown bag. "I brought your favorite for lunch."

His eyes drift over the simple black tunic dress and heels I threw on after thirty minutes of questioning how Henry Wolf's future wife should dress for a visit to his office. "Thank you," he offers quietly.

"You're welcome." I have an overwhelming urge to touch Henry, to feel his body against mine. To know that whatever inner turmoil he's facing, it has nothing to do with our future. And if these past few months have taught me anything about Henry, it's how to get answers out of him without asking.

"Nice digs." I close the distance, setting the lunch bag aside.

"It's my father's taste. I'll have to update it at some point when I have time."

I round the desk and perch myself on it, next to him. Toeing off my heels, I rest my feet on his chair between his splayed thighs.

"My fiancée sitting on my desk isn't the most professional start to my week."

My heart swells at the label. He wouldn't use that so freely if he was regretting it, would he? "And you're all about professionalism."

"Always." He traces his bottom lip with his index finger as he studies the sheer black pantyhose I tugged on at the last minute. "I seem to recall a certain assistant despising nylons so much that she peeled them off and flung them across my cabin halfway through her shift."

"Yes, but these are *way* more comfortable." I hike up the hem of my dress, enough to show off the lace elastic band holding the thigh-highs up but also to give him a glimpse beneath, to the fact that I skipped panties for my visit here.

His sharp inhale fills the room, but he doesn't make a move. "As pleasant as this surprise is, why are you here, Abbi?"

Miles is right. Something is seriously off with him today. "I needed to see you."

He hums to himself. "Did Miles call you in a panic to tell you he's worried about me?"

"Why would he do that?" I press my lips together to hide the truth. I don't want him getting into trouble for reporting to me on Henry's mental health.

Henry smirks. "Because I can't seem to focus on anything today."

Focusing is something Henry excels at, even under extreme stress. I scramble for an explanation. "Maybe you have a concussion?" The scrape on his forehead is minor and the doctor at Wolf Cove cleared him, but sometimes these things take a few days to reveal themselves.

"No, that's not it." He looks around aimlessly. "I nearly died a few days ago."

"Yeah, I remember." The worst, longest twenty-four hours of my life, waiting for an answer from the search teams. I smooth my foot along his thigh for comfort.

"And now I'm back here, dealing with this"—he casts a hand toward a stack of reports—"juggling a million decisions as if it never happened."

"You didn't have to come back so soon. You're the boss. You can take time off."

"I wish that were true. But everything is in turmoil. This shit my brother pulled is costing us millions to fix."

I don't know the first thing about what he's up against. "But you don't have to do it all on your own. That's why you have this floor of executives to handle the work. Get Sunjit on it. He'll yell at anyone you want him to."

Henry snorts. "They're all swamped with their own jobs. I need new people. I fired Scott's entire team."

"*All* of them?"

"Everyone at the management level. If they missed what he was doing, I can't rely on them. If they didn't miss it, I can't trust them. HR is scrambling to promote who they can and recruit for the rest, but I need someone competent to run the entire metals business. *I* don't know it. My father knew it, Scott knew it, but I never put effort into it. I was always focused on the hotels." He pinches the bridge of his nose. "It felt more manageable before, when my father was around, as much of a pain in the ass as he was. Now it's just me." His eyes wander out the window again. "And is it even worth it anymore? Is this how I want to spend the next however many years of my life?"

This was not what I was expecting when I decided to come here today. "I think this is what they call an existential crisis."

He barks out a bitter laugh. "That, or a good old-fashioned midlife crisis."

"You're only thirty-two. You still have all your hair." A lush, thick mane that my fingers are itching to crawl through.

"Yeah ..." He doesn't sound convinced. "I keep thinking about that girl that showed up last night."

"Violet?"

"What if she *is* Scott's?"

"Then you have a niece?" I shrug. "That's kind of nice." Though the girl seemed terrified of him. Who knows what Scott's told her.

"She's not Wolf blood."

Because Scott was the product of his mother's affair with William Wolf's accountant. "But she's still blood."

His lips twist and when he speaks, it's in a quiet, forlorn tone. "I'm all that's left of my bloodline, Abbi."

That knot in my stomach flares. Henry *is* feeling the weight of his family's absence, as Luca suggested. I reach down to collect his hand from its resting spot on my knee and squeeze. "For now, yeah. Not forever. We can make as many little Wolfs as you want." We've already talked about having children—enough to know that we both want them —but we've never delved into the specifics. When do we start? How many do we want?

A pensive look flickers through his eyes, but he doesn't say anything. With a heavy sigh, as if dismissing that line of thought, he asks, "So, what have you been up to all morning?"

"Oh, you know ... Dodging a reporter's call, letting my mother plan our wedding."

"What reporter?" Henry's voice turns hard.

"Some guy named Luca from the *Tribune*. He was asking

me questions about Wolf Cove and when our relationship started." I falter. "And he asked about Ronan and Michael."

His jaw clenches. "If those fuckers are selling stories—"

"Ronan's not." I messaged him immediately after I got off the phone with Miles, and he had no idea what I was talking about. I believe him. "And a few people knew I was there that night with Michael. It could have been one of them." Or someone they told. It's impossible to pinpoint. Gossip in the Wolf Cove staff quarters spreads like an army of ants after its hill has been kicked.

Henry knows this as well as I do. "Unknown number?"

"Yeah. I didn't answer any of his questions, but I have a bad feeling."

"Deny everything. It's none of anyone's fucking business. Luca what?"

"Just Luca."

Henry scribbles down the name. "We'll get you a new number today. Don't give it out to anyone but close family and friends. People you know you can trust."

"Okay. Thank you. Speaking of family ..." I steel my shoulders. "We're going to Greenbank for dinner on Saturday."

His eyebrow arches. "Are you *asking* me?"

"No. I'm not." I've never had the nerve to make plans for Henry without his okay, and by the hint of annoyance in his tone, he's not too keen on it. "It's sort of an engagement celebration."

"Will I be setting up picnic tables and fending off frisky church ladies?"

Clearly, he's still clinging to memories of Daddy's homecoming party and all the hens flocking around him. "No, and to be fair, you weren't invited. You crashed that party."

He pushes the hem of my dress upward a few more inches. "If I recall, it was worth it."

My cheeks flush. That's the night Henry fucked me on a hay bale. That's also the night Jed caught us mid-act and then ran off to Mama to tattle. "It'll be us, Aunt May, and the Enderbeys, of course." There's no Saturday night dinner without them. I warned Mama that if she invited anyone else, we'd turn right around and head back to New York.

"Saturday night with Fuckface. Even better," he grumbles.

"Jed's not that bad." Now that he's given up on us getting back together.

"No, you're right. We need to remember to thank him in our wedding speech for cheating on you."

At least Henry is sounding more like himself and not that lost, forlorn man. "Whatever. Jed isn't the problem, it's Mama, and the best way to deal with her is face-to-face, with *witnesses* so she has to weigh her words before she says them out loud." Mama has always been good about keeping her mask on when others are around.

"You're really selling this to me." Henry grins. "Should be fun."

"It's going to be *painful*. But if I don't do this now, our wedding will be in a barn with my second cousins as brides-maids, wearing gingham frocks, and I will be miserable by the time next spring comes. *Please*, Henry."

"Relax. Of course, we'll go. It's your family, and it's the right thing to do."

"Thank you."

He squeezes my thighs before leaning back in his seat, collecting my foot. "What are gingham frocks?"

I revel in the feel of his thumbs working over my heel.

"Remember that dress Celeste Enderbey made for Daddy's homecoming?"

"The one from the set of *Little House on the Prairie* that I ripped off you?"

"Exactly."

"I hated that thing."

"Well, now imagine it made with a picnic tablecloth."

He cringes.

"Right? Nothing I want my bridesmaids in."

"Not even second cousins?"

"Ugh! They are *not* my bridesmaids!" As awkward as having that conversation will be, seeing as Mama's already asked them.

He switches to kneading my other foot. "Who will you ask, then?"

I hesitate. "I was thinking about Margo. Is that crazy?"

A soft smile touches Henry's lips. "No. I think that's a great idea."

"So do I." Despite Henry's—and my—past with her, in the short time that I've known her, she has become a friend like no other. She dropped everything and flew up to Alaska to comfort me during the worst ordeal of my life. If that isn't a grand gesture of true friendship, I don't know what is.

"Who else?"

"Autumn." We text almost every day now.

"The concierge?"

"And my roommate." I pause, unsure if I should broach it. "And I was thinking Ronan?"

Henry's hands stop his ministrations as he glares at me. "That's a joke, right?"

"Maybe?" I bite my bottom lip. "Would it be that bad, though? He is one of my best friends. And he helped save your life."

Henry's jaw clenches as if he doesn't want to be reminded of that.

"I trust him like no one else. Except you, of course."

Henry sighs with exasperation, the pressure returning to my feet with renewed force. "Only if he wears the picnic tablecloth."

I giggle. "Come on ... of *everything* we've asked him to do, having him in our wedding party is what you'd take issue with?"

The corner of his mouth kicks up. "Let me think about it."

"Okay." I pause. "What about you? Who are *you* going to ask?" Even if Scott were alive, he wouldn't be welcome at the wedding, let alone invited to stand next to Henry at the ceremony.

He frowns. "Why did you say it like that?"

"Like what?"

"Like I don't have any friends."

"You mean besides female models you've slept with?" Henry has business associates, guys he golfs with while discussing investment opportunities and takeover strategies. I have never—not once—heard him talk about a friend.

"I have male friends, too, Abbi. Several very good ones that I've kept since boarding school."

"*Really*?"

He smirks. "I'm not the loner you obviously think I am."

"I never thought you were a *loner*. A workaholic with intimacy issues, yes—ow!" I squeal as he pinches my pinky toe. "Why haven't I met *any* of them?" Why hasn't he even mentioned one?

"They live all over the world."

"Didn't they come to your father's funeral?" Isn't that what good friends do?

"Preston was there, briefly. He flew in from London and left the same day. It wasn't the right time to introduce you two, though. Warner and Merrick were in the Australian outback on an expedition. They wouldn't have been able to make it back in time, anyway, but I told them not to cut their vacation short."

Henry is marrying a woman and he's never introduced her to his friends for their seal of approval? Isn't that like a rite of passage? All this proves is that I still have *so much* to learn about my future husband. "Tell me about them."

Henry rolls his chair closer. "What do you want to know?"

I shrug as I nudge my free foot into the crevice between his legs, feeling the weight of his balls against my toes. "Anything."

"*Anything.* Let's see ... Preston is a Brit. He lives in London and runs a two hundred-billion-dollar hedge fund firm—"

"Wow," I mouth. I have no idea what a hedge fund firm does, but the dollar figure is impressive.

"Don't say that to him. His head is already too big for his shoulders. Warner's from Spain, but he currently lives in Dubai, building skyscrapers and chasing after married women."

I wince. "That's ... not charming."

"No, and he's going to pay for it eventually. He wants what he can't have. Though to be fair, he usually gets what he shouldn't be able to have. He's a bit of a rake, but he has always been a good friend to me." He gives my calf a playful squeeze. "Merrick is ... Merrick. He's not the easiest guy to get close to, but once you do, count yourself lucky. He's always had my back, no questions asked."

"Where does he live?"

"California, but he's been in Vegas for a while, opening a new hotel and casino."

"That's not far away. You could have made time for him." And Merrick could have made time for Henry. Alaska is a straight flight north.

Henry's brow furrows. "Yeah, he's been busy with family shit."

"So, basically your friends are like you." Filthy rich, complicated men who sleep around.

"Nobody's like me, babe." Humor dances in his voice.

"True." I giggle. "Are any of them married? Besides Warner, obviously."

"No wives, no kids. No commitments beyond work."

Which means a lot of fuck buddies. I hum with disappointment. It would have been nice to have wives or girlfriends to connect with. "What do they think about you getting married?"

"I doubt they know yet. They're too busy to follow gossip headlines. But, don't worry, they're going to love you." His gaze drifts over my chest, but his hands remain where they are.

Will they approve of Henry settling down, though? "I'd like to meet them before the wedding if that's possible."

"It is. They'll be in town at the end of the month for an annual event we always attend together. I meant to tell you about it."

End of *this* month? "For Halloween?"

"You could say that." Henry's lips twist in thought. "It's not the best place to meet them though. It's loud and busy. And there's a lot going on. Why don't we invite everyone to our place for dinner beforehand?"

"Like a dinner party?"

He smiles. "Sure, call it whatever you want."

A strange mix of excitement and nerves swirls through me. I don't know any of these guys, but if they're like Henry, they don't just order pizza. "What would this involve exactly?"

"*Not* picnic tables and potluck."

I laugh. "Hey, there is nothing wrong with a good potluck." I lift my toe, making his entire body jolt.

He grabs my foot, shifting it away from that sensitive area. "If you're on a farm in Greenbank with two hundred of your closest church friends, sure. Not with this crew. Hire someone. Get Raj to help you. He used to work in catering, so he knows the right people."

I can't contain my grin. Our first dinner party as a couple. "Okay. Yeah ... this is a great idea."

"You know what else is a great idea?" His strong hands slide up the backs of my legs as he pushes my thighs apart. His eyes flare as they take in my bare flesh. "You bringing my favorite meal."

My head falls back with a moan at the first swipe of his tongue.

five

enry parks next to the silver pickup truck he bought me this past summer. It's gleaming from a fresh wash. No doubt it was covered in dust only hours ago, but according to Daddy, Jed's been caring for it like it's his own. It may as well be. Henry bought it for me when I was living on the farm, to replace the old banged-up one with duct tape holding the bumper on.

I step out of the SUV and inhale the fresh, crisp air. The sun is already setting, providing a picturesque backdrop for the double-story farmhouse that's over a hundred years old, built by my great-great-grandfather. I've called it home for my entire life. It's the place that's fostered all my childhood memories, including countless ones with Jed.

And for the first time since February, with Henry by my side, it feels good to be back.

Mama always goes the extra mile in fall, filling bushel baskets with vibrant mums and lining the porch steps with pumpkins from our patch. Stacks of small hay bales throughout the front yard create spots for more flowers and pumpkins. She's added a few new pieces to the porch this year—a colorful doormat and hurricane lanterns as well as bulky blankets on the swing that are begging for someone to curl up under them.

The windows glow with light, and I can make out Aunt May's silhouette in one.

"Can you spare a hand?" Henry calls out, rummaging through the trunk of the sleek black Lincoln that was waiting for us when we landed at the private airfield in Pittsburgh.

He hands me a fall floral arrangement, bursting with dahlias in rich hues of orange, burgundy, and gold. "Where did this come from?"

"A florist."

I give him a flat look as he collects several gift bags.

"I gave Miles a list and he arranged for it." With his arms loaded, Henry hits the key fob and the trunk closes. "Flowers for your mother, cognac for your father"—he holds up a cylindrical box wrapped in black satin paper and sealed with twine—"and wine for everyone."

My heart warms. That he even thought to ask Miles is something, especially when he's neck-deep in running an empire. "That was nice of you." But I already knew Henry was capable of being thoughtful. I cringe, wishing I didn't have to warn him. "They don't drink."

He smirks. "Something tells me they will tonight."

"I have *never* seen a bottle of wine at our dining table in my *entire* life."

"Fine. More for us, then." His polished shoes send loose stones scattering as he follows me toward the front porch, slowing to take in the house with a curious stare.

"What's wrong?" I know our little country hovel is nothing like he's used to. Is he wondering how he ended up here, marrying into country folk?

"Nothing. It reminds me of dinners at my grandparents. My grandmother used to decorate their house like this. Of course, I never paid attention to it at the time. I was a dumbass kid. But I just realized how nice it was." A wistful look skitters across his face. "How much I miss it."

I smile, relieved. "Well, you can look forward to seeing this every year at this time because fall is Mama's favorite season." I add more quietly, "Let's hope her love for it helps her mood after I tell her to butt out of our wedding."

His eyes flicker to the window, where Aunt May is still spying on us. "I guess it's time to do this." He releases a shaky breath.

Wait a minute. It dawns on me. "Are you nervous?" Incredulity fills my voice.

"I don't get nervous." But his jaw tenses.

"You are!" If my hands weren't full, my palm would be slapped over my mouth. "I don't believe this. The unflappable Henry Wolf is flapped!" By *my* family, nonetheless.

"I'll show you flapped." He adjusts the bags in his arms long enough to free a hand that he slips under my dress. I know what he's aiming for.

"Stop it!" I skitter away from his touch with a squeal of laughter.

With a secretive smile, he juts his chin toward the house, silently directing me to go, and then trails behind me.

The second porch step creaks noisily under my weight, as it always does, and a wave of nostalgia hits me. I may not live here anymore, but it'll always be home.

The scent of oregano and roasted tomatoes hits me the moment we push through the front door. I inhale deeply. "Lasagna?" I haven't had my aunt's famed dish in too long.

Aunt May rounds the corner wearing an apron. "You and that nose of yours! I can never surprise you. Come here!"

I set the floral arrangement down on the front table just in time to catch her as she pulls me into her in a tight hug. "Congratulations, sweetheart. I'm so happy for you!"

I sink into her slender yet curvy body, wishing for the thousandth time that Mama was more like her younger sister. "Thank you."

She turns to Henry. "And *you*. I know you love my niece, but are you *sure* you want to join this family?"

"Don't scare him off," I scoff.

"If he hasn't been yet, I think you're safe," she throws back in a mock whisper.

Henry offers a charming smile in return. "It's good to see you again, May."

"Here, let me help you with some of that." She sweeps the larger gift bag out of his arms, her eyes flittering over his ensemble, which he let me choose—a casual but delicious sable crewneck and tailored jeans—ever so quickly before winking at me. It reminds me that Aunt May is only four years older than Henry and no more immune to his looks than anyone else.

She's also the only true ally I have in this house when it comes to Mama. "Listen, before we go in there, I need to talk to you about—"

"There she is, my baby girl!" Mama appears, her hands rubbing at a tea towel. "It's been too long."

"A few weeks, at least." I step into her outstretched arms and she envelops me in a warm, tight embrace. Her hugs are what I remember most growing up. No one can say she doesn't like to give them. "Is that a new dress?" I know without asking that it is. She's worn the same outfits for years.

"Got it yesterday." She smooths the material over her hips. "Nothing fits me anymore."

47

After that stunt with the caffeine pills to keep Henry and me apart, Mama and Daddy had a long, serious talk about her health—from the countless cups of coffee she was drinking every day to her poor diet and sedentary habits, to the fact that her mother died of a heart attack at a young age. I don't know what else he said to her, but since then, she's put in a real effort, cutting out caffeine, taking daily walks, and cooking healthier. "You look good."

"I *feel* good. I can walk all the way to the Enderbeys' place without needing a break." She swings her focus to Henry.

I hold my breath.

"How is my favorite future son-in-law?" She charges forward to throw her arms around him.

Henry's eyebrows twitch as he stoops to return her hug, the only sign that he's shocked by her pleasant greeting. "Hello, Bernadette."

"Oh, call me Mama if you want. Would ya look at that." She scowls at the scab on his forehead, like a mother tending to her little boy's injury.

"It's nothing. Just a scratch." His gaze flickers to me.

My mouth is gaping. Who is this woman?

"Thank the good lord you made it out of there with only that. Roger! They're here!" Mama hollers.

"I'm aware of that." I hear Daddy a moment before I see him, hobbling out of the kitchen, his leg still trapped by a walking cast. "I'm a little slower than everyone else, in case you forgot." His eyes fall on me, and his face splits into a smile that Jed insists is reserved for his daughter and his daughter only.

I dive into his chest, squeezing him tight, inhaling his familiar scent: a mixture of hay and Old Spice, with a hint of tobacco from the occasional cigar.

"What is this?" Mama lifts the floral arrangement to inspect its copper vase.

"Henry picked those out for you." No need to bring Miles into this conversation. It's the thought that counts.

She tsks. "Well, we already knew he had impeccable taste, given his choice of future wife. This'll make a fine centerpiece for our celebratory dinner. Thank you, Henry." She whisks the flowers away.

I shoot a bewildered look at Henry before whispering to my father, "What have you done with Mama?"

Daddy snickers. "I guess she realized this was a battle she wasn't gonna win and decided to make the best of things. She's been like this all week long. Why? Would you prefer the other version?"

"*No.*" I shake my head in emphasis.

"Didn't think so." He limps the few steps to close the distance to Henry and holds out his hand. "Good to see you again."

"Likewise." Henry accepts the gesture.

My father's not a giant, but he's by no means small—a born-and-bred farmer, several generations in, and strong, with a square jaw and broad shoulders. But the tractor accident took its toll on his physique, softening his muscles and hunching his shoulders. Henry's only ever seen him when he was in a wheelchair. Now the two men stand face-to-face, shaking hands for a few beats too long, as if taking measure of each other on more even footing.

This must be weird for Henry. He's only nine years younger than his future father-in-law, who was barely out of high school before he married my mother and they had me.

But I guess it could be equally weird for my father, for the same reason.

The only thing they need to care about, though, is that Henry makes me deliriously happy.

After an awkward pause, they break free.

"A gift for you." Henry holds up the sleekly wrapped box. "A little something for after dinner. A favorite of mine."

"That's mighty kind. You didn't need to do that, but I look forward to it. Thank you." He nods, more to himself. "Now, let's get settled in and say hello to the Enderbeys. They're excited to see you too."

"Okay, but before we do that ..." Aunt May has been my ally when it comes to Henry, but my father has been getting through to Mama more than anyone lately. I drop my voice to a whisper. "This wedding Mama's busy planning for us? It's not what we want, and it has to stop."

His lips purse. "I warned her she was gettin' ahead of herself, but she wouldn't listen."

"We're getting married in Wolf Cove, Daddy. Where I worked this summer."

"That's ... not Pennsylvania."

"I know, but I need you on my side for this."

He makes a strangled sound. "Can ya at least wait until *after* we've had a nice meal to break the news to her?"

"I'll try," I promise. "You know how she can get though."

He holds up the black box Henry gave him. "Sounds like I'm gonna need this sooner rather than later."

JED PEERS AT THE LABEL. "SANG-EE-O-VEES?"

"*Sangiovese.*" The grape name rolls off Henry's tongue and, while I've never heard it before, I am one hundred percent sure he's pronouncing it correctly. "From Montepulciano, a medieval town in Tuscany."

"Can you get it at Walmart?"

Henry falters on his answer, likely biting back the one he *wants* to give. He's on his best behavior tonight, even with my ex-fiancé. Still, his smile is smug when he explains with forced patience, "No, it's a reserve from one of my favorite wineries in Italy. My sommelier at our Pittsburgh Wolf location imports it for me." I can hear the unspoken "You idiot" in his tone.

"Seems like a whole lot of effort for foreign red wine when we have plenty here in America." Jed snorts.

"And yet you're enjoying it," Henry fires back.

Jed certainly is. Thank goodness Henry brought several bottles.

With a small grunt, Jed refills his glass for a second time to near brimming before setting the bottle down.

The softest sigh escapes Henry—too soft for anyone but me to hear—and then he lifts the bottle. "More wine for you, Laura?"

Jed's pretty blond girlfriend's cheeks ignite with a furious blush. I've caught her staring unabashedly at Henry at least a dozen times since we sat down, and each time she notices me watching her, she ducks her head and reaches for Jed's hand. "Yes, please. Thank you."

Henry refills her glass, then tops up mine without asking. "Celeste?"

"Thank you, but I will pass," Celeste declines softly. She accepted a "splash" for a toast. It's more than I've ever seen her drink.

Henry goes around the table. "Bernadette?"

"Oh, maybe just a smidge." Mama holds up her glass, her cheeks rosy. "Don't judge me too harshly, Reverend. This *is* a special occasion, after all."

"I would have to be a pot calling a kettle black, now, wouldn't I." Reverend Enderbey takes a sip of his wine.

Aliens *must* have landed in Greenbank, Pennsylvania, recently and possessed bodies because Henry was right —*everyone* accepted wine with dinner.

Henry stands to refresh Mama's glass before setting the bottle down and retaking his seat.

Jed glowers, processing the lesson in gentlemanly manners Henry just gave him without saying a word.

Beneath the table, I smooth a hand over my man's muscular thigh. "By the way, if anyone gets a call from a reporter about me or the wedding or Henry, please tell them 'No comment.'" I shoot a warning look Jed's way. He's already promised that he hasn't said anything and he won't.

"Have they been bothering you?" Daddy asks.

"A little. Nothing I can't handle." I force a smile. Henry had his people check, and no one by the name of Luca works as a reporter at the *Tribune*, which is both a good and bad thing. He can't be with a reputable news source if he misidentified himself.

Autumn set alerts on her phone for anything to do with Henry—which is both endearing and creepy—and nothing has appeared online yet.

"Before I forget, Abigail!" Mama helps herself to another heap of Caesar salad. "I convinced Chester Fry to lend us his carriage."

"You mean that dilapidated *wagon* he uses to get around?" Chester Fry is Amish. That's his only mode of transportation. What on earth does Mama need with Chester Fry's wagon?

"It ain't dilapidated. It catches everyone's notice when he's out and about."

"That's because they're afraid the wheels will fall off."

"It's gonna happen any day now," Jed agrees.

Mama chortles. "It only sounds like that, but it's good and sturdy, promise. Big enough to fit you and the girls in it."

Me and the girls. It dawns on me. She means for the wedding. I should have known that was what this was about.

"Oh! And you need to give Angela a call so she knows what she can get started on planning for you. She's who you want for your maid of honor. Good head on her shoulders. Joy and Diana are sweet and they sure are pretty, but they couldn't organize a lemonade stand if they were given step-by-step instructions."

My fist clenches around my fork. Now she's telling me who my maid of honor will be?

"May, what kind of cheese is in the lasagna?" Henry asks, rubbing my forearm.

"Oh, do you like it? I make the ricotta myself. I find it much creamier than anything I can find from a supplier. Every time I serve this dish at the restaurant, it sells out, so I must be on to something." She grins. "I know this isn't the same caliber as those meals your Michelin Star chefs make you, but folks around here seem to like it."

"No, you're right, it's not." Henry winks. "It's better."

The key to Aunt May's heart is complimenting her cooking, and Henry seems to have figured that out. She beams. "You'll have to come into the Pearl to try my cheesecake, then. I use the same ricotta."

"You would not have to twist my arm. That is a favorite of mine."

"It is?" I rack my brain thinking back on meals we've had together. Has Henry ever ordered dessert? "How did I not know that?" Is he telling the truth or is it part of a game to win May over?

"Because you've only been together for two minutes," Jed mutters under his breath.

I frown. Jed and I have been on much better terms over the last few months. I've even started considering him a friend. But he seems gloomy tonight. If I didn't know better, I'd say news of my engagement might be too big a pill for him to swallow.

I dismiss his sulking and focus on Henry. "So if our wedding cake is made of cheese, you'll eat it?"

"Oh, I'll definitely eat it," he teases, with a wicked glint in his eye that tells me he's not talking about wedding cake.

I give his ankle a playful kick as my face flushes. "Good, I'll tell Jill." I spent two hours on the phone with Wolf Hotel's event planner yesterday. It was overwhelming, to say the least, and I think she sensed it because she gave me an easy and fun homework assignment—set up a Pinterest board with wedding ideas.

"Who's Jill?" Mama asks.

Here we go. "Our wedding planner."

"You don't need one of those pretentious fussy bodies," she scoffs, waving me off. "They cost a fortune and all she'll do is take over your wedding."

"Imagine that," I force out through clenched teeth.

Daddy clears his throat, and Henry presses his lips together to smother his smile.

"No need, anyway. I've already got Peggy Sue's niece lined up to make the cake—"

"Let's leave all that wedding business for *after* dinner," my father cuts in, his uneasy gaze on me as I silently fume.

But, as usual, Mama's not listening to anyone but herself. "She's making you a fruitcake. A good, *traditional* choice."

"I *hate* fruitcake!" I snap, tossing my fork down. It lands with a clatter. "Peggy Sue's niece is *not* making our wedding cake." I can't take another minute of this. It has to end now. "Angela, Joy, and Diana are *not* my bridesmaids. And I am *not* riding to my wedding in a wagon driven by the Amish man who lives down the road!" I may as well lay it all out on the table. "We're not getting married in Greenbank, Mama."

Silence hangs like a heavy curtain around the dining table as anxious glances flitter toward Bernadette, waiting for her reaction.

Her face is a mask of shock, as if my words have slapped her across the cheek without warning. As if she couldn't foresee this. "What do you mean, you're not getting married in Greenbank? Of course you are. You're a Mitchell. This is your home. Your family is here, your congregation is here!"

Her congregation, that I've been indoctrinated into from birth, not by choice. I haven't been to church once since I left Greenbank. "We're getting married in Alaska," I say calmly. I don't care if we're married in a church or a reception hall or in a damn field, but I leave that part out for now.

"No way," Jed blurts, his expression filling with excitement. "We're invited, right?"

"Unfortunately," Henry says before gulping back a mouthful of wine.

"Roger!" Mama glares at my father. "Talk some sense into the girl!"

Daddy sighs with resignation and pours himself more wine. "Abbi's got plenty of sense."

A wildness flickers in her eyes as they dart around the table, searching for allies, realizing she has none. At least, not ones who will step in to involve themselves so blatantly.

"I'll start the coffee pot." Celeste is on her feet quickly to collect empty plates.

"I'll help." Laura scurries behind her.

I take deep breaths to try to calm myself. The last thing I

wanted was for tonight to turn into another major blowup. We already had one of those this summer and we barely survived it. "Mama, I am thrilled that you seem to have accepted Henry as my future husband." *Seem to* being the operative words. "Truly, I am. But this is my wedding. *Our* wedding." I collect Henry's hand in mine. "And it's going to be what *we* want."

"What *you* want? Or what *he* wants?" She spits out with that familiar venom from the past. I knew her bitterness still had to be lingering beneath this facade. There was no way it could have evaporated. How long before he's demoted to "that man" again?

I dare glance at Henry.

His expression is peaceful, unruffled. "If it were up to me, Abbi and I would have married at city hall the day we landed back in New York."

Mama gasps, her fearful eyes flittering to Reverend Enderbey as if merely suggesting such an idea has earned our family a one-way ticket to the fiery pits of hell. "You wouldn't dare."

"Oh, believe me, *I* would." A grin stretches across Henry's face. The bastard finds this amusing. He isn't the least bit fazed by Mama's antics. "But that's not what Abbi wants, and I will give her whatever *she* wants as long as in the end, she's my wife."

Mama worries her bottom lip. She's beginning to see she won't win this. "Fine." She throws her napkin onto the table and eases her sturdy body out of her chair. "Seeing as you don't care if your family is a part of your wedding day—"

"I never said that," I cry.

"—then you'll be happy getting married without your father and me there, Abigail."

My stomach drops in despair at the thought of their absence. "Mama ..."

But she's already storming out of the dining room. Moments later, the kitchen door swings open and shuts with a clatter.

My shoulders drop as tears of anger and frustration prick my eyes.

Henry rubs the back of my neck but remains quiet.

"Give her time." Daddy carves another chunk of his lasagna.

"You think that'll make a difference?" She didn't even try to hide her anger from Reverend Enderbey, which means I miscalculated her need to be on her best behavior for an audience. Clearly, I've caught her off guard. Is she stubborn enough to follow through with this threat, though?

"Yes," Aunt May jumps in. "Bern has a big heart, but she's also used to getting her way. She used to do this sort of thing to me, too, until she learned better. I think this is good for her, to see you all grown up and making your own decisions, even if she doesn't approve of them. It'll make things easier for you down the road."

"Bernadette can be a tad set in her ways." Reverend Enderbey frowns. "Sometimes she needs to ease herself into new ideas, and there have been a lot of *new ideas* in her life lately." He glances at Henry, making his point clear. "Like Roger said, just give her time to digest."

And give the reverend time to talk her off this hill she sounds determined to die on, he doesn't say.

I sink into my chair, dejected. "I never thought you guys wouldn't come."

"I will be there no matter what, don't you worry about that," Daddy promises.

Aunt May reaches over to pat my forearm. "So will I."

That brings me some comfort, at least.

"Reverend, I know Bernadette asked you to officiate." Henry smiles at the kindly man. "Would you still be willing to do that in Alaska?"

Reverend Enderbey opens his mouth but falters, his gaze flittering to me, then to his son. Is it weird for him to marry Henry and me after Jed and I were assumed destined for a life together? Because, honestly, this may be a bit fucked up.

"I'm sure Bernadette would appreciate your role in this," Henry adds. "It would go a long way in helping *everyone* move forward." That last part must be directed at Jed.

Smooth one, Henry. It's an olive branch for Mama, having the reverend there, a way to get something she wants. Maybe it'll help sway her.

"Celeste and I have always wanted to see that part of the country," Reverend Enderbey admits.

"Then here's your chance. Your transportation and accommodations will be covered, of course."

"How do you say no to that, James?" my father murmurs. It's so rare that I hear anyone use Reverend Enderbey's first name. It's a reminder that, beyond the church and my relationship with Jed, our families have been good friends and neighbors for decades.

"I don't think he can, so that settles it. We'd be pleased to have you officiate." Henry reaches for my hand, squeezing it.

The reverend nods, more to himself. "I would be honored to be a part of your day, so thank you."

"Can I get in on that plane too?" Jed, who's been unusually quiet this whole time, asks around a mouthful of lasagna.

six

It's midnight by the time we walk through the front doors of Wolf Tower. The horde of paparazzi have found someone else to harass, making for a quiet entry into the building. Still, I scan the lobby seating area that serves hotel patrons, bracing myself against the chance I'll discover a long lens pointed at me.

"Good evening." Sullivan swipes the key card for our private elevator.

"No, it was terrible," I lament.

The giant security guard winces.

"Oh. You weren't actually asking."

Henry places a hand on the small of my back and guides me into the open elevator. "Good night, Sullivan."

"Good night, sir. Good night, Ms. Mitchell." The guard's sympathetic smile disappears behind the shuttered doors.

I flop against the wall. I can't wait to crawl into bed. "What am I going to do if she doesn't come around?" Our little dinner celebration fizzled quickly, with the Enderbeys and Laura returning home, and Henry and my father venturing into the living room with snifters of cognac while I helped Aunt May clean up in the kitchen.

Mama ambled through the door as we were finishing up and announced in a quiet, worn voice that she was betrayed, broken-hearted, and going to bed. She wouldn't even acknowledge me.

"She could win an Academy Award for her portrayal of the victim," Aunt May had whispered then, rolling her eyes and patting my arm with comfort. "Ignore it."

But ignoring Mama's antics is easier said than done.

"She'll come around," Henry promises as our elevator flies to the very top of the building. We couldn't stop at any of the other floors if we wanted to. This is our dedicated elevator.

"You don't know Mama. 'Hell hath no fury like Bernadette scorned.'"

"I know she cares about keeping up appearances. How will it look to her congregation if everyone, including the reverend and Jed, has accepted this marriage and she refuses to? After she's been running around, planning the entire thing for you?"

"She'll look petty," I agree. She'd be the butt of all the church gossip. They'd see it for what it was—Mama trying to get her way. People know what she's truly like, even if she hides it behind smiles and sweet words. "That was smart of you to ask him to come to Alaska."

"I've handled my share of difficult people in the past. I know how to get my way."

I don't doubt that for a second. Henry has had me agreeing to things I never thought I would. "You know, if she does come, she'll be a pain in the ass the entire time at Wolf Cove."

"That's fine. I'll make Belinda deal with her."

Picturing Wolf Cove's previous manager in her tight, cleavage-bearing dress, facing off against Mama—who would no doubt label Belinda a harlot at first glance—is enough to make me giggle.

"That's better."

The elevator doors open. Henry guides me out while I admire the pearl and diamond ring on my finger, wondering for at least the hundredth time if this engagement is a dream that I'm about to wake from.

The scent of fresh paint tickles my nostrils. It still lingers, weeks after Henry ordered a wall built for added security. No one will ever surprise us again like Scott did, he insisted when the workers showed up.

The phone to the lobby security is ringing as we step into the penthouse.

"Yes?" Henry says by way of greeting, then frowns. "*Again*? What time is it?" He checks his watch as he asks this. "No ... no ... send her up. Please ... That's fine." He drops the receiver on the base.

"Send *who* up?" I ask warily.

"My *niece* is paying me another visit." He gives me a knowing look.

"Violet?"

"Or whatever her real name is."

"*Now*? How did she even know we came home?" I didn't see her sitting in the lobby area. I would have remembered her.

His frown grows deeper. "She must have been watching the building from the outside, waiting for me to come home. Who knows how long she's been sitting there."

Hours, maybe. And what if we had come in through the parking garage? Her efforts would have been all for nothing.

"Is this a good idea?" While the teenage girl didn't

appear to be a threat, looks can be deceiving, and this whole situation reeks of desperation.

"Probably not, but she told security she'd wait outside for the reporters to come back and then cause a huge scene if they didn't let her up to see me."

I groan. "That's all we need."

"My thoughts exactly." Henry sheds his jacket and tosses it on the hook. "It'll be fine. Sullivan's escorting her. How much trouble can she cause with him here?"

A moment later, the elevator dings. I hold my breath as we watch Violet step out, her shoulders hunched within a black hoodie, the hem of her blue jeans dragging across the travertine marble floor. A ponytail gives her a more youthful appearance.

Her wide blue eyes skitter over the grand penthouse foyer with lightning speed before settling on Henry and me.

She looks *so* familiar, but I can't place it.

"Hello again. Violet, is it?" Henry asks cordially.

She lifts her chin as if steeling her nerve and casts a glare at Sullivan. "Do these Neanderthals search *everyone* before they're allowed up here, or is it just innocent girls you're afraid of?"

She doesn't seem terrified of him this time, at least.

Henry's piercing gaze holds her.

I used to shrink under that attention before I got to know him. What I would give to read his mind right now.

"Sullivan, that'll be all," he says smoothly, never releasing Violet from his sight.

The security guard disappears into the elevator.

Henry folds his arms over his chest and takes a casual stance, leaning against the wall. "Do you mean *innocent* girls who loiter outside my building and threaten to cause scenes? Or *innocent* girls who lie about who they are?"

Alarm flashes across Violet's expression. "So you know who I am?"

Henry pauses as if to consider his answer. "I don't think you're Scott's daughter."

"You're right, I'm not." She hesitates. "I'm yours."

Henry blinks several times, the only sign that she's caught him off guard. "So now we're playing this game, are we?" he says, his voice edged with cold calm.

"It's not a game. You're my father."

"And yet I was your uncle only minutes ago."

I study her more closely.

Her blue eyes ...

Her jawline ...

The shape of her nose ...

A sick feeling swirls in my stomach as a voice inside my head confirms what I saw but couldn't see. *She looks like him.*

"Yeah, I ... I lied before," she stammers, the first break in her tough act.

"What's wrong, you realized being my niece wouldn't get you a payday?"

She flinches. "I don't want your stupid money."

"No? Well, that would be a first. Tell me, how old are you, Violet?"

"Fifteen."

"Fifteen," he repeats, the corner of his mouth twitching.

Violet pulls her shoulders back. She seems to be clawing for confidence. "Yeah. Sixteen in January."

Henry barks with laughter, but it's a hollow sound. "Which means *I* would have been, what, sixteen when you were born?"

"Yeah? And your point is?" She glares at him. "You do know how babies happen, don't you?"

He opens his mouth, but stalls. Whatever he was about

to say was likely not appropriate for a fifteen-year-old's ears. "None of the girlfriends I had during that time ever had a baby."

"Obviously, one of them did because I'm standing here," she counters.

"And what's your mother's name?" He goads her.

Violet bites her bottom lip. Either she doesn't have an answer, or she doesn't want to give one.

"I thought so." Henry's mood darkens, his relaxed pose fading as he pulls himself up. "Enough of this shit. How much is Crystal paying you?"

Confusion flickers in Violet's eyes. "Who's Crystal?"

"Your loving *grandmother*, according to you." The title is bitter on his tongue. "Let me guess—she's figured out it'll be years before she sees a penny from Scott's estate, if she ever does, so she's back to trying to get money out of me any way she can."

I hadn't considered that Henry's mother might be involved in this. Would she stoop to this level, though? I recall the conversation I overheard between her and Scott at William Wolf's funeral, about a possible windfall that would make Henry look like a chump.

Yes, she would.

But that doesn't explain the resemblance between these two.

"So, what's her plan, Violet?" Henry asks.

Violet shakes her head.

"There's *always* a plan with her." He steps forward. "There was a plan when she and Scott were conspiring about that mine, when they nearly *killed* me."

Violet swallows. "I ... I don't know what you're talking about—"

"For your sake, I fucking hope you don't." His anger reverberates through the foyer, so sudden that I startle.

"Henry," I warn. Regardless of what game this girl is playing, she's still only *a girl*, and his fury with his mother is getting the better of him.

"I don't know Crystal." Violet blinks furiously against the well of tears forming. "I just wanted to meet my asshole father once, that's all." Her voice cracks with emotion.

Henry's shoulders sink, his rage seeming to evaporate. "I'm sorry, Violet, but you have the wrong man."

"Are you Henry Wolf?"

"Yes, but I am *not* your father."

"Oh, yeah?" She digs into her backpack and pulls out a manila envelope, tears streaming down her cheeks. "*This* says you are!" She throws it at Henry's feet and then spins on her heels and marches to the elevator to jab at the button. Sullivan must have sent the car back up to wait on our floor because it opens instantly and she's gone.

Henry and I steal a glance at each other before he stoops to collect the envelope, sliding a stack of paperwork from it. It's legal size, the bottom section bent in an awkward fold.

"What does it say?" I ask.

Henry shakes his head absently as he speed-reads through the first page.

And then his face blanches.

Oh my God. "It's true?" My jaw drops with my stomach.

He doesn't need to answer me with words. His expression says it all.

seven

Henry charges through our front door to the phone and punches the key to reach security. "The girl who came down the elevator," he barks into the receiver, "is she there?" He listens intently, then curses. "Stop her if you can. *Please*."

For once, our speedy elevator is not a benefit. She must have left the building already.

I edge in closer as Henry waits for an answer, my pulse pounding in my ears. "So, it's true? Violet's your daughter?"

Henry's eyes flitter to me, a look in them that I've never seen before—a mixture of shock, confusion, and possibly hurt. "I don't know."

But *I* know. I saw it in Violet's delicate features. The similarity.

Henry has a child.

Unbeknownst to him, but a woman out there is the mother of his child.

I feel like I've been punched in the stomach, and I'm sure it's nothing compared to what he must feel.

"Yes," he answers in a rush, and then his shoulders sink.

"Thank you for trying. If she returns at any time, keep her there and call me immediately." He drops the receiver and sinks against the wall, the back of his head thumping as he studies the ceiling.

I bite my tongue against the question burning to escape. Who does the love of my life, the future father of *my* children, already share a child with?

He must sense it lingering there. "Her mother's name is Audrey," he whispers, so softly I nearly miss it.

"Was she a girlfriend?"

"I wouldn't call her that." Henry tosses the paperwork on a side table and strolls to the living room bar cart, where he pours himself a scotch.

I trail after him, wanting to give him space but desperate for more details.

He sucks back a mouthful of the amber liquid. "*Ms.* Audrey Campbell," he says, staring out at the panoramic view of Manhattan from the windows. "My sophomore year English teacher at Hartley."

"Your *teacher*? *Henry!*" I gasp, trying to process this. "How old was she?"

"Twenty-nine."

My mouth hangs as I do the math. "She was fourteen years older than you."

"So what? I'm eleven years older than you."

"It's *so* not the same. What that was is ... is ... illegal!" Henry isn't the type to shy away from indiscretions, but she should have known better. "And we're only ten and a half years apart, by the way," I add in a mutter.

He peers over his shoulder, sees my horrified expression, and chuckles. "I know it's not the same." He pours a second glass and holds it out to me.

I accept it wordlessly, downing it in one sip that burns

and makes me cough. I've only ever tasted scotch on Henry's tongue, but tonight's news bomb warrants it.

"She was smoking hot. Sexy and confident."

"And that makes it okay?"

He sighs. "No."

"What would a twenty-nine-year-old, smoking hot, sexy, confident *woman* want with a fifteen-year-old *boy*? There's no way you looked like *this*"—I wave a hand at his chiseled body—"at that age."

"I was a lot scrawnier," he admits. "But I had my charm. And she was a good teacher." A secretive smile touches his lips, as if he's reminiscing.

"She's *sick*." Wait until the media gets hold of this. Another scandal involving Henry, one where he was more prey than predator. It won't matter to them. A juicy story about the Wolf family is a juicy story, nonetheless.

His amusement fades as he wanders over to collect the stack of legal documents again. "Every guy in my boarding class had a massive hard-on for her. We *all* flirted shamelessly. We had bets going to see who she'd flirt back with. But she always laughed us off."

"Apparently not *always*."

He studies the liquid in his glass. "We were on a school ski trip. She was monitoring the halls and caught me trying to sneak back in from somewhere. She'd been drinking. That night, she didn't say no."

My anger flares. While it's impossible for me to picture Henry as anything but who he is—which is far from innocent—at one time, he was. "And after that?"

"We fucked a few times. Once, on her desk, during a detention she gave me"—another smirk as he remembers and I quietly seethe—"and then I left for the summer and when I came back, she was gone. She was no longer on the staff." He shrugs. "I didn't think anything of it, but I should have known."

"You should have known that she was pregnant by her fifteen-year-old student?" Just saying it out loud makes my face twist with disgust.

"No, that my father was somehow involved in her leaving." His face turns sour as he hands me the stack of paper.

I see the familiar name at the top almost immediately. "He knew."

"He liked to keep tabs on us, make sure we weren't fucking up our lives."

"Sounds like he had good reason," I mutter.

"I don't know how he found out about Audrey, but he did, and he threatened to disinherit me if I ever went near her again. William Wolf's favorite pastime—dangling money over his loved ones to control them." Henry sucks back another gulp of scotch.

"Would he have?" That's all I've heard about since I met Henry: William's threat to give Wolf Hotels to Scott if Henry got caught up in another inappropriate relationship; his threat to out Henry's mother as a lying, cheating thief of a children's charity if she didn't leave their lives.

"I don't know anymore. But he made good on his threat to cut Scott out."

I scan the legal jargon but am quickly overwhelmed. "What does all this mean?"

"It's an agreement for financial support as long as Audrey makes no contact with me and I never find out about this child's existence. *Ever*."

"So, all these years, he knew he was a grandfather. He knew *you* were a father, and he never told you." William Wolf looked his son in the eye and lied by omission.

"I'm sure he thought he was protecting me."

A dark thought hits me. Henry's father had cancer and was given only a few years to live. That was cut even shorter by Scott and his accomplice, but had it not been, would William have confessed on his deathbed to hiding this human from Henry, or would he have taken this secret to his grave? The fact that he had a detailed letter included in his will about Scott's true parentage, and about funneling money out of the company in his search for diamonds—just in case something happened to him—but no mention of Violet, makes me think the latter.

The depth of betrayal in Henry's family seems bottomless. "And Audrey agreed to this." Obviously, she did. Her signature is somewhere on these pages.

"My father wouldn't have given her a choice," Henry says, suddenly somber. "It was this or the end of her life as she knew it."

Because Audrey slept with her fifteen-year-old student and William Wolf would ensure she landed in a prison cell. Babies aren't allowed in there. She'd have lost her child.

If it were me, I would have taken the deal too. "Maybe she thought she was doing you a favor."

"Maybe she was." Henry grimaces, as if he realizes how harsh his words sound.

"Why come to you now though?" I answer the question myself a moment later. "Because your father's gone." It was all over the news.

"Knowing him, I'm sure there are still provisions here in the event of his death, but it would mean someone acting on them. Who's going to do that?" Henry collects the contract again and flips through the pages. There are a lot of them.

"Do you think Audrey is after more money?" How much did her silence cost the Wolf family?

"He matched her boarding school salary for eighteen years. The agreed-to payment schedule is right here."

"That's a lot better than what she would have made in prison, but it's nothing compared to what you're worth." I don't even know how much Henry is worth. I've never asked, and honestly, I don't care. When I told him I'd love him if he gave all this up and worked alongside my father on the farm, I meant it.

"That's what's in writing." His lips are pressed in thought. "I can't see my father not taking good care of them. Violet *is* a Wolf."

"So he may have paid her more? Or meant to, but then he died."

"There's nothing about either of them in his will. No paper trail anywhere."

Because he had no intention of Henry ever meeting Violet.

Eerie silence hangs throughout the penthouse. And here I thought planning a wedding around Mama's demands would be my biggest challenge in the coming months. Now it seems I'm about to become a stepmother, and to a girl who is only six years younger than me, no less. "What are you going to do?"

"What am I supposed to do? I can't have a daughter."

And yet you do.

Henry looks at me, and for the first time since I've met him, through all the trials he's faced—Scott trying to sabotage his takeover of Wolf Hotels with a threat of fake rape charges by his ex-assistant, Scott manipulating my insecurities opening weekend to destroy Henry and me, Henry's father's death, which turned out to be murder, his near-death experience in the mine—he looks genuinely lost.

Henry wanders over to the window to stare out into the

night sky, his back to me, the contract dangling from his fingertips.

This is jarring—the invincible Henry Wolf, who always has a plan, who moves forward at breakneck speed, hurdling over problems to get to his destination, is facing something he doesn't know how to tackle.

A fifteen-year-old girl.

"Why would Audrey let Violet show up here unannounced like this? And in the middle of the night?" he asks, but I'm not sure he's looking for an answer.

"Maybe she doesn't know Violet came."

"Which would mean Audrey had no plans to break the deal with my father. Maybe she doesn't want me in Violet's life."

"What do *you* want?" I'm sure teenage Henry never imagined he'd be revisiting his indiscretions later, in the form of another human being. Is he looking for a way out of it now?

His jaw tenses, but he doesn't answer the question. "There's a Philly address here."

"That's a long way for her to travel, alone."

"This contract was signed sixteen years ago. I doubt they still live there."

"Dyson could help you track them down, if that's what you want."

"It's not about what I want, is it? It's about what's right." His shoulders drop as if weighed down. "I could do without a life-altering shock for a week or two. Is that too much to ask?"

I close the distance and curl my arms around his waist. He smells delicious—of cedar and spice. "We'll figure it out."

Henry rests his chin on top of my head, allowing me to hold him in silence while his thoughts sink into the depths.

Finally, he sighs, breaking the spell. "I need to comb through this in detail, see how my father's lawyers tied her up so I know what I'm dealing with. I'll see you in bed."

A dismissal. He wants time alone to absorb and think. "Don't stay up too late," I warn him, but it's futile. If I know Henry at all, he won't come to bed until he has every answer he's looking for.

"DYSON FOUND THEM."

I blink against the daylight slipping through the crack in the curtains, taking a moment to gather my bearings. Henry stands in the doorway to the bathroom, a white towel wrapped around his waist, his hair damp. I'm not sure he even made it to bed.

Last night's sleep was restless, my mind toiling as I drifted in and out of consciousness, my insecurities feeding on baseless worries and my dreams painting terrible scenes —of Henry's *smoking hot teacher* and the mother of his child invading our lives.

Of Henry rethinking his future with me.

"They're still in Philadelphia." He disappears into the closet, and I hear the towel flop to the floor. My blood stirs with a mental image of Henry's perfect naked form.

Now is not the time for those thoughts. I pull myself up to a sitting position, searching for the will to get out of bed. "How did Violet get here from Philly?"

"Train, I imagine. Unless she stole a car. With that kid's attitude, I wouldn't be shocked." A moment later, Henry emerges with pants on.

I admire his torso as he tugs a black sweater over his head. "What are you going to do?"

"There's only one thing to do. Talk to Audrey."

The version of Henry I know well is back—calm, take charge, unruffled. "And you're sure Violet is yours?" I ask, though I already know the answer to that. I saw it in her face.

"Yes, she's mine. My father insisted on a paternity test as part of the contract. He probably gave them my toothbrush as a sample."

"Of course he did." If William wanted the test and didn't want Henry to know, then the test would run and Henry wouldn't be the wiser.

"It doesn't matter what my father did or didn't do in the past. He's gone and I'm here, and I have a child I now know about. I can't ignore that, even if I might want to." Henry collects his wallet and watch from the dresser. "I'll be back later."

"Wait, you're going *now*?" I check the bedside clock. It's a quarter to ten on a Sunday morning.

"It'll be noon by the time I get there."

"Right." Of course, he wouldn't waste time. This is Henry, after all. But a twinge of worry pricks me. Henry is running out the door to meet the mother of his child, his horny teenage conquest.

And he's doing it without me.

No, he's not.

"Give me fifteen minutes to get ready."

His jaw tenses. "I think it's best if—"

"I'm coming with you, Henry. Don't you dare try to tell me otherwise." I force as much confidence in my voice as I can muster, sliding out of bed.

He tracks my body—clad in a tank top and panties—as I stroll past him into the closet.

But he doesn't argue.

In fact, from the corner of my eye, I think I catch a smile.

~

MY FACE BLANCHES as I read the email. "Zaheera is recommending a first batch run of *five thousand* soaps for mid-November."

"It's a small start," Henry says, his focus on the business section of the newspaper.

"A *small* start?" I gape at him. "I haven't sold that many bars in all my years of making soap, combined."

"And I'm sure you'll be sold out in under a day. They would have run the numbers. They know what they're doing. Trust them."

"I do. Of course I do. This marketing campaign they're going out with is insane." I flip through the presentation deck, filled with taglines and graphics, and Farm Girl Soap product reviews they've collected from Margo and her high-society friends, as well as a list of influencers they're targeting.

"Then what's the problem?"

"Nothing. I'm nervous." What if everyone is wrong? What if they think too highly of my product? Of me?

Victor turns onto a quiet street where quaint houses line each side, their lawns sprinkled with fallen leaves and the odd bicycle. I count six basketball hoops and two hockey nets as we creep along. Speaking of being nervous ... "Mrs. Robinson found a cute little neighborhood to hide in."

Henry's eyebrow arches, but there's no amusement in

the look. "I didn't agree to you coming so you could attack her. If you can't be civil—"

"I'll be on my best behavior." I cross my finger over my chest, drawing his interest downward over the fitted poppy red V-neck sweater I chose. One of his favorites. I'd be lying if I said I didn't choose it because I wanted to look especially good next to his teenage paramour.

His eyes settle there, and I can almost read the split second of depraved thoughts flittering through his mind. At some point, this tension is going to get the better of Henry, and I know how he likes to manage his stress levels: with me pinned against a wall or bent over a table.

I can't wait.

"Did Dyson say if she was married?" Audrey would be about forty-six now. Is she still *smoking hot* by Henry's standards?

He folds the newspaper and sets it on the seat beside him. "No, she's never been married from what he could see."

"Because her boyfriends still have a curfew."

"Abbi ..."

"Best behavior! I swear." I hold up my hands in surrender.

"Yes, I remember your best behavior with Kiera at my father's funeral. I believe you tried to crush her hand."

"After what she put you through, she deserved it."

"Regardless, this is not like that."

No, it's far worse. Kiera was an enamored assistant who cheated on her husband, hoping for a life with Henry. She's out of our lives for good. Audrey, on the other hand, was a high school teacher who did a very bad thing and is now forever connected to Henry—and me, by default—for life.

That's a sobering thought.

Victor makes a right turn onto Acorn Way. It's a cul-de-sac lined with six adorable houses. He slows in front of a one-and-a-half story with a covered porch and a solid red door. An oak tree fills the front yard, its fallen leaves raked into piles but uncollected. Several bushes around the side could use a healthy trim, but otherwise, the house is cute and well-maintained. "This is it, Mr. Wolf," he declares.

A large white van is parked in the driveway, its rear doors propped open. A logo on the side names a medical equipment company.

"What's that about?" I ask.

"There's only one way to find out." Henry climbs out, holding the door open for me to follow. He stalls at the base of the stone path.

"You okay?" I ask softly.

"I will be once this is over. I never expected to see her again." He slips his hand within mine, and I note the clammy feeling of his skin.

We take the stone path up toward the front porch steps as two men are wheeling out a hospital bed.

"Excuse me, can I help you?" A middle-aged woman in a sage green velour tracksuit stands in the open doorway, her wispy brown hair pulled back into a bun that highlights the gray at her temples.

Is this her?

"We're looking for Audrey Campbell," Henry says, answering my unspoken question. "I was told she lives here?"

"Oh." The woman's face falls. "Yes, but I'm sorry to be the one to inform you that Audrey passed away."

eight

Henry's body stiffens beside me. "When?"

"The day before yesterday. She went peacefully, at least."

The two men who carried out the bed trot up the stairs, murmuring, "Excuse me."

"Just the last bit over there in the corner," the woman tells them, pointing to somewhere unseen, before returning her attention to us. "I'm Rhonda. I was Audrey's hospice caregiver."

Henry looks like someone's slapped him.

I step in. "Hi, I'm Abbi and this is Henry. If you don't mind me asking, what did Audrey pass away from?" Hospice only ever means one thing.

"I guess it's no secret, given the obituary," Rhonda says, more to herself. "Audrey had ALS."

"Oh my gosh." My eyes flitter to Henry and find a stony expression.

"One of the youngest patients I've had pass from it." Rhonda's face pinches. "How did you know Audrey?"

"She was an acquaintance of mine," Henry says, finding his voice. "I haven't seen her in a very long time."

"Oh." Rhonda nods. "She was only diagnosed a few years ago. It progressed quickly. I'm sorry you didn't get a chance to reacquaint yourself with her."

Henry's eyes dart past her, into the house. "Where is Violet?"

"With her grandparents. They moved the last of her things out yesterday morning."

"And where is that?"

Rhonda hesitates. "I don't have the address handy."

Henry crosses his arms. "You don't have it, or you don't want to give it to me?"

Rhonda clears her throat. "I'm not permitted to share my patient's personal information."

"Audrey's no longer your patient," he says calmly.

"*Or* their family's information," Rhonda adds, throwing him a look of disgust.

Henry's jaw clenches. "Do her grandparents allow her to travel to Manhattan by herself at night?"

"Heavens, no, they wouldn't allow that. She's only fifteen!"

"And yet it happened," he snaps, his patience vanishing. He's so used to people asking how high when he demands they jump. "I have concerns over Violet's care, and I need to find her. *Now*."

"I can't just—"

I cut in before Henry erupts. "If you have a way to reach her grandparents and ask for permission to pass along their address, that would be okay, wouldn't it?"

"I suppose," she admits reluctantly but doesn't seem too eager to help.

"Violet showed up at our place in Manhattan last night

and then took off. She was upset," I explain. "We would like to meet her grandparents and make sure Violet is okay."

"I have people who can get me the address within the hour, but if Violet is in any danger and we've wasted time finding her ..." Henry lets the unspoken threat hang in the air, his teeth clenched with frustration.

I give his biceps a warning squeeze. He's usually smoother than this.

Rhonda's wary gaze flickers between the two of us, then to the shiny black SUV parked at the curb, Victor sitting in the driver's seat.

I see the instant her resistance fades. "Give me a moment."

AUDREY'S PARENTS live three blocks away, their street equally quiet and quaint.

"Don't have the address handy, my ass," Henry grumbles as we approach the porch. "I could have had this address with one phone call to Dyson."

"She was just doing her job."

"By risking the girl's safety?" Henry is rattled—by Audrey's death, by Violet's existence, by all of this, who knows—but he certainly isn't himself.

"But she gave it to us and now we're here." I collect his hand. "These people just lost their daughter, and you have no idea what story Violet gave them about where she was last night, so *be nice*."

"I'm always nice." He shoots me a look of exasperation before he raps his knuckles against the door.

The blinds in the front window move and a moment later the door opens with a creak. A shrunken woman with snow-white hair hides behind the glass storm door, gripping her cane. "Rhonda told us you'd be coming," she says by way of greeting. "You were old friends of Audrey's?"

I plaster on as wide a smile as I can to make up for Henry's stony face. "I'm Abbi. This is Henry."

"Hello, I'm Gayle." The woman's aged eyes flitter over us both as if sizing us up a moment. "Please, come inside. It's chilly out there." She hobbles out of the way.

Henry and I step into the cramped foyer. It's what one might expect of an elderly couple's home—cozy and lived in, with decades-old furniture, a small television in the corner of the living room, walls that were painted sage at the height of the color's popularity and not painted since. Nothing that says they have plenty of disposable income or that they care about the latest decorating craze.

There's no doubt someone died recently. Arrangements of fragrant white lilies and red roses of varying size clutter the table surfaces, each bouquet with a little card poking out to express condolences.

"We're very sorry for your loss." I may have arrived on Acorn Way with ire bubbling in my veins, but it has quickly fizzled, replaced by a melancholy—for a girl who has lost her mother, for an elderly couple who have to bury their child. Even for Audrey, who may have done something terribly wrong but didn't deserve a cruel death because of it.

Gayle's wrinkled face pinches with a sad smile. "We had almost three years to prepare for Audrey's death, but it wasn't enough time."

"I can't imagine." Framed photographs line the walls, of two girls—one, I recognize as Violet, at different ages and stages, from gymnastics, to ballet, and dressed in costume. The other girl is from a different era, sporting everything from puffy bangs to crimped hair, her sequin figure-skating costumes competing with the electric blue eyeshadow when she isn't sitting primly in front of a piano. That must be Audrey.

"Howard?" Gayle calls out.

"In the kitchen, fixing a pot," comes a scruffy voice.

"We don't drink coffee, but would you like a cup of tea?" Gayle asks.

"We'd love one," I answer, looping a hand around Henry's arm, squeezing gently. We have no idea what her parents know about their daughter's past or Henry, but I imagine this will be a hard conversation, regardless.

He clears his throat. "Thank you."

The kitchen is much like the rest of the house—outdated but charming, with golden oak cabinets and a table that seats six. A basket of flowers adorns it that Gayle shuttles to a nearby counter.

An elderly man with a full head of wiry gray hair hovers by a porcelain pot. He's the same diminutive size as his wife.

"Howard, this is Henry and Abbi," Gayle introduces.

He turns to study us over his glasses—first me, then Henry, stalling there a moment too long. Does he recognize Henry's face from the news? God knows Henry's been on it enough lately. Or does he see what I saw when I first laid eyes on Violet? The familiarity? "How do you take your tea?" he asks.

"Doesn't matter. Black," Henry throws out dismissively. I've never seen him drink tea before.

I smile. "Sugar for me, please."

"Make yourselves comfortable." Gayle gestures toward the table.

Howard delivers our teacups, his weathered hands trembling as he sets them on the table. "Rhonda mentioned you had concerns about Violet?"

Henry opens his mouth but then falters. "Where did your granddaughter tell you she would be last night?"

"A sleepover at her friend Alison's." Gayle and Howard exchange cautious glances. "Why?"

I stifle the urge to grunt an "I told you so."

"She was not at *Alison's*," Henry says. "At least, not for the entire night. She showed up at our place in Manhattan around midnight—"

"Manhattan!" Gayle exclaims, her expression filled with genuine panic. "How did she get there?"

"My guess would be the train." Henry's hand curls around the teacup but he makes no move to drink.

"That girl has always loved the city. Audrey would take her once or twice a year. She knows how the trains work, but to do it on her own?" Howard shakes his head as he settles in a free chair. "Then again, we shouldn't be too surprised. Violet has always been headstrong. Just like her mother."

And her father. I purse my lips against the urge to say it out loud.

"Why would Violet come to you, though? How does our granddaughter know you?" Gayle asks.

"She *doesn't* know me."

Gayle frowns. "Then why would she go to Manhattan to see you?"

Howard stirs sugar into his teacup, the silver clanking on the china. "I think it's obvious. He's Violet's father. Aren't you, Henry?"

I guess that explains the lingering look moments ago. Howard saw it straightaway.

Gayle's eyes widen with shock.

The wooden kitchen chair creaks as Henry leans back. "Yes, apparently I am. Something I found out twelve hours ago."

The only sound in the kitchen for several long moments is the slow drip ... drip ... drip of the kitchen faucet.

Gayle studies Henry's face. "If you don't mind me asking, Henry, how old are you?"

"Thirty-two."

"Thirty-two. But that's ..." Gayle is surely doing the math in her head. "Well, that's not possible. Violet is fifteen. That would mean ..." Her voice fades, unable to utter the words. "That's not possible, is it?" Again, she looks to her husband for an answer that explains her fears.

Howard reaches over and pats his wife's hand. There's no anger in his expression, though. There certainly doesn't seem to be any doubt either. It's as if he's already accepted the disgraceful truth. "Audrey never told us who Violet's father was, and she said she wouldn't because it didn't matter, he would never be in Violet's life. At first, we assumed it was a married staff member she worked with at that boarding school, but then she bought the house on Acorn Way with cash, which we knew she couldn't be making at her teaching job." He shrugs. "I thought she must have had an affair with a student's father. There's plenty of wealth at that school."

"I was her student," Henry admits, and none of the bravado that laced his words last night—the boy who bagged his smoking hot teacher—lingers today.

Gayle makes a strangled sound, then covers her mouth with a hand. "Good God, Audrey. What did you do?"

Drip ... drip... drip goes the tap as this elderly couple comes to terms with the giant skeleton that just jumped out of their deceased daughter's closet.

Will they hate Henry for his role in this?

"How did Violet find you?" Gayle asks, her voice strained. "Did Audrey tell her about you?"

"I don't know. I haven't seen or spoken to Audrey since I was a student at Hartley. Violet showed up in my building last week, pretending to be my niece. She ran almost immediately before I could question her. I suppose she was testing the waters, or maybe she was unsure? Then, last night, she came back, declared herself my daughter, and left me with a legal document that all but confirmed it."

Gayle scratches her chin in thought. "We were moving some boxes of Audrey's a few weeks ago. Paperwork and such that Audrey had told us to keep after she was gone. Preparing for what we knew was coming, you know? We put them all in our basement for safekeeping. Violet must have found it in there."

"It doesn't matter. Wherever she found it, she found it. Now she knows who her father is, and now *I* know that I have a child." The look on his face doesn't suggest he's pleased about that, but Henry's never been easy to read.

"We came here to make sure Violet made it back safely after she left us," I say.

"We didn't even know she'd left. With Audrey passing away, we didn't think twice about saying yes when she asked if she could sleep over at her friend's house, and now we find out this? Who knows where she could be!"

"Do you have a way to message her?" I ask gently. "Like, on a cell phone?" A beige receiver for the house phone hangs on the wall nearby.

Gayle's face lights up as if she'd forgotten that option. "I can message her. Howard, where is that thing?"

"I think I saw it by the toaster. Give me a sec." He eases out of his chair and moves gingerly toward the kitchen counter.

"Audrey bought it for us two Christmases ago. We hardly

ever use it, but we've been keeping it on lately, especially with all that's been going on."

Howard ambles back. "Let's see here ... how do I ... Violet taught me how to do this, but ..."

Henry holds out his hand. "I can message her for—"

"Why don't I?" I move fast, before Henry gets a grip of it. I've been at the receiving end of his messages in the past, and I highly doubt a teenage girl in an emotional tailspin will be any better equipped to handle them than I was.

Together, Gayle and I craft a simple, innocuous message, asking Violet when she'll be home.

"There, see? She's already responding." I point out the three bouncing dots for Gayle's benefit. For myself, I breathe a sigh of relief.

Violet: *I'm walking home now. Fifteen minutes?*

"She's on her way. Fifteen minutes," Gayle declares.

Henry's shoulders sink and a soft "good" slips from his lips.

"I'm not sure how she'll handle you being here when she gets home," Howard says between a sip of his tea. "Though I guess she wanted to meet you, so there's that."

Henry's lips purse. "I'm afraid we might have gotten off on the wrong foot last night."

Howard hums. "She's a good kid. Audrey did a decent job raising her, while she could, anyway. But Violet's been through a lot these last couple of years. Watching someone you love die will do that. And now *this* bit of news. If she's done the math in her head and figured out what it means—"

"She has," Henry confirms.

"Yes." Howard scratches his cheek. "Then I imagine she must be confused and angry."

"You said there was a legal document?" Gayle asks.

"Yes, between Audrey and my father. He found out about Violet somehow and ..." Henry's voice trails as he chooses how to describe one of William Wolf's many betrayals. "I supposed he wanted to protect *everyone* involved."

And I guess he did, in his own warped way. Audrey avoided jail and ridicule and kept her child, Henry avoided the burden of teenage fatherhood and focused on his future empire with no obligations, and with Grandpa Wolf's bank account, Violet probably never wanted for much.

Except maybe a father.

"About a year ago when it became clear that Audrey's illness would take her sooner than we had hoped, Audrey told us that there is a trust in Violet's name, for her to receive when she's twenty-five," Howard says.

"For how much?" Henry asks.

"She didn't say. All she said was that Violet would be well taken care of and that Audrey didn't want her daughter knowing anything about it. She was afraid she'd turn into one of those spoiled kids like the ones she taught back in Hartley." Gayle offers Henry an apologetic smile.

He smirks. "Smart on Audrey's part. I don't want Violet turning into that either, especially now that she knows who I am."

Gayle cocks her head. "And who are you, dear?" It's such an innocent and honest question, asked by a sweet old lady. "Are you an actor?"

Henry chuckles.

❧

"THERE SHE IS," Gayle whispers, peeking through the blinds like she did when we approached the house.

I steal a glance over her shoulder to see Violet trudging

up the path in the same black hoodie and jeans as last night, seemingly oblivious to the SUV parked on the street. She clutches a paper coffee cup in both hands and hunches as if the backpack slung over her shoulders weighs a hundred pounds.

My heart sinks for the girl.

The door creaks open. "Gramma! Gramps! I'm home—" Violet freezes in the foyer, her face paling as she sees Henry seated next to Howard on the three-seater couch.

Did she sleep last night? The dark bags lining her eyes suggest not. Did she even go to this Alison girl's house? I doubt it, but then where did she stay all night?

"Hello, Violet," Henry says in a calm voice and stands.

She stumbles back a step. "What are you doing here?"

"We have some things to discuss."

She shakes off her backpack, letting it fall to the floor with a thump. "How did you find me? I thought you had no idea who I was."

"I didn't. But there is *nothing* I can't find out, Violet. Remember that."

I groan inwardly. That sounded like a threat.

"Except that you have a daughter, apparently." There's no lack of bitterness in her tone.

"I didn't know I was supposed to be looking."

Violet's chin lifts. "So you believe me now?"

"I read through that contract, and yes, it appears you were telling the truth."

"Really? You sure this isn't part of some sinister plan to steal all your precious money?" she spits out.

"If you had any idea the things that have been going on in my life lately, you might understand why I jumped to such a conclusion."

"Violet, why don't you come and sit down." Gayle gestures toward the empty wing chair.

But Violet remains where she is, her eyes welling. "Did you two know?" At least her tone with her grandparents is less hostile. "Did you know what Mom did? *He* went to Hartley." She throws a hand toward Henry. "He was her student!"

Gayle flinches. "We didn't know. She didn't tell us."

"But *you* should have before you ran off to go find him," Howard scolds gently.

"Which is one of the reasons I'm here. Do you have any idea the kinds of things that happen to young girls traveling alone in a city that size? Girls who look like you?" Henry steps forward, his tone full of reproach.

"I'm not stupid!" she yells back.

"It has nothing to do with being stupid. Though I wouldn't call it a *smart* decision."

"Where did you stay all night, Violet?" Gayle asks.

Violet opens her mouth and pauses, her eyes falling to the coffee cup in her hand. "A twenty-four-hour diner near the train station. I was fine. It was safe. Mom and I used to go there."

I cock my head to try to read the cup. It has a cute red and blue monster logo that I've never seen before, but there's a New York City address listed along the cup's seam.

"You can't be lying to your grandparents about where you are and taking trains into Manhattan whenever you feel like it," Henry says, his tone sharp.

"Don't pretend you care!" she erupts, tears running freely. "I just wanted you to know that I existed. Now you can leave. We don't want you here." She brushes her cheeks with a furious stroke of her hand. "And I *do* know what's been going on in your life. I read *all* about it. Your psycho brother *murdered* your father because your father was sleeping with his twenty-something-year-old fiancée? As if I want to be a part of that family."

Henry's teeth grind. "You can't trust what you read in the media."

"Really? So you're not marrying your *twenty-one-year-old* assistant after meeting her a few months ago?"

"*Ex*-assistant," I mutter, my cheeks flushing. As if it matters.

"Your fiancée is only six years older than your daughter. Did you do the math on that, huh? The reporters are gonna *love* that."

Henry's nostrils flare. "Have you told anyone about me? Friends, teachers, *anyone?*" he pushes, his tone urgent.

"About your dirty little secret?" Her face pinches with fury. "That's why you're here, isn't it? That's all you care about. Your reputation."

Henry's chest rises with a deep breath. "*My* reputation won't be the one to suffer, Violet. What do you think the media will say about your mother if this story gets out?"

Fear sparks in Violet's eyes. She's been so focused on finding out who her father was, she probably didn't give much thought to that question until now. "She's gone, so it doesn't matter anymore."

"I've lived in the public eye my entire life, and believe me, it *will* matter to you and to your grandparents, the things they'll say about her. They will turn every memory of your mother upside down, invade her privacy in search of more dirt. People you thought you could trust will sell lies about her and you. Within hours of finding out, that cul-de-sac will be filled with vans and cameras." He casts a hand toward the bay window and the street beyond it. "You won't be able to leave this place without cameras shoved in your face. It'll be a nightmare for you and your grandparents.

And the things your neighbors and friends will say about Audrey?" Henry's eyebrows are halfway up his forehead in warning.

If he's trying to scare her, I think he's succeeded. Even *I'm* holding my breath.

Violet's throat bobs with a hard swallow. "I haven't told anyone—"

"Good. Don't."

"I won't!" Fresh tears spill. "You're just the sperm donor. I don't want you in my life. I hate you!" The last words are delivered in a shriek as she storms off down the hall. A moment later, a door slams.

Henry hangs his head.

"That went well." Howard lifts his glasses to rub his eyes.

Gayle takes a step in the direction her granddaughter went, then stalls, as if reconsidering. "Audrey used to lock herself in her room for hours too."

"Just give her time," I say gently. I have no clue how to parent anyone, but it's not too hard to put myself in a fifteen-year-old's shoes. I was that age not that long ago. "This is a lot to handle. She's exhausted. She wasn't expecting to see us here. Let her shower and sleep, and process."

"The funeral is tomorrow. She's been dreading having to put on a brave face, but she hates crying in public." Gayle blinks back threatening tears, which makes me think Violet's not the only one dreading the day.

"We didn't come here to disrupt your lives, especially not while you're grieving." Henry gestures, beckoning me to the door.

Howard pulls himself from his seat. "We appreciate you coming all the way here and checking on Violet."

"Yes, we'll have to be more vigilant with her," Gayle says. "This all feels overwhelming. We were a lot younger and the world was different the last time we parented a teenager. I can't even imagine the kind of trouble she can get into now."

Henry slides his wallet from his back pocket and digs out a business card. "If you need me for anything, please do not hesitate to call." He sets the card on the console table and then turns toward the door but hesitates. "I wasn't trying to scare her, but this must stay between us. If the media catches wind of this story, they will run with it, and they will not be kind to Audrey's memory. That'll only hurt Violet more."

Howard chews his bottom lip and nods. "We'll talk to her. Make sure she understands."

The door creaks behind us as we leave Audrey's family to their grief.

nine

Steam fogs the bathroom, but Henry's naked form is clearly visible through the glass as he stands beneath the showerhead, letting hot water pour down over him.

I lean against the sink and admire the view for a moment. Will I always feel this stir in my lower belly when I look at this man, even as the years pass and age erodes muscle and sags skin, when life has worn us down? Yes, I'm sure I will. All I have to do is close my eyes and imagine the electricity in his touch, the feel of his weight on top of me, the smell of his skin, and my pulse begins to race.

And yet now I see him differently than I did yesterday. Not worse. If anything, more human, more capable of mistakes.

More vulnerable.

Henry is a father.

He was quiet on the drive home from Philly, and when we arrived here, he went straight to the home gym, running on the treadmill for an hour as if running for his life. Maybe he was running *from* it. I still don't know what he makes of this news.

He turns then, notices me standing there. "Get in here, Abbi," he demands. His tone is hard and unmistakable. When he's in this kind of mood, I always end up sore and supremely satisfied.

I slide my robe off my shoulders, allowing it to pool onto the tile floor. I slip into the shower stall behind him.

"I found the obit in the newspaper and sent flowers," I say, ogling his hard ass and web of muscle over his back as he rinses the soap from his chest. "They'll be delivered to the funeral home tonight, in time for the ceremony tomorrow." An enormous arrangement that made me choke when I saw the final bill. "I put our names on it."

"I was going to ask Miles to send them. But thank you." He turns his head to show me his profile. "Should I go to the funeral? Would that be the appropriate thing to do? What do you think, Abbi?"

The word *appropriate* left the conversation sixteen and a half years ago, but I keep that to myself because he's asking for my help to navigate this complicated mess. It's so rare for him to do that. "I think it's best you give Violet her space. Her mom just died. They haven't buried her yet. She has her grandparents. She knows them. She doesn't know you at all."

He snorts. "She *thinks* she does."

Moving in to loop my arms around his waist, I shut my eyes against the spray of hot water and press my lips against his spine. "She needs time, Henry. And then she'll realize how lucky she is to have you in her life." Is that what Henry wants, though—to be in this girl's life? He hasn't hinted where his head is at. "Thank you for letting me come with you today."

"Let?" Finally, I hear a smile in his voice. "You surprised me. You're not usually that forceful."

"And you don't usually give in so easily. Why did you?"

He pauses on his answer. "Because you tend to get insecure about women from my past, and I didn't want to give you time to sit here and create something in your head that doesn't exist."

"I barely slept last night," I admit sheepishly.

"I figured as much. I *know* you, Abbi." He pulls my left hand to his lips, kissing my bare knuckles. "Where's your ring? Having regrets about marrying me already?" he says lightly, but I don't miss the edge in his voice.

"It's on the bedside table." I lay another kiss against his skin. "And don't be silly."

He turns in my arms so we're facing each other, our bare, slick chests pressed together. "Are you sure?"

In his bright blue eyes, I see concern. It's almost laughable, given it was me who was worrying about Henry having regrets just last week. I stretch onto my tiptoes until I can skate my lips against his. "Yes, I'm sure."

He sweeps the damp, clinging hair off my face and leans down to kiss my forehead. "Let's forget everyone and get married tomorrow."

I slide my palms up and down his biceps, memorizing their size and shape. "That would be much easier." With Violet storming into our lives the way she did, I haven't had time to think about last night's disastrous dinner in Greenbank. Mama hasn't called or texted since and, knowing her, she'll wait for me to make the first move. "But I want everyone I care about to be there when I marry the man I am hopelessly in love with." I gaze up at him. God, he really is the most beautiful man I've ever laid eyes on.

His jaw tenses. "And you're not afraid of the next thing that's waiting around the corner?"

"What next thing?"

"I don't know, but there must be one. It's been one fucking catastrophe after another since we met."

He's not wrong about that. Since the night a burly lumberjack collected me from the docks of Wolf Cove, my life has been turned upside down.

The muscle in his jaw ticks. "I wouldn't blame you for wanting to be done with me."

I'm not used to Henry being the insecure one. I hate it. I muster as much confidence as I can because that's what he needs from me right now. "What am I going to find out about next? Your secret foot fetish?"

The hint of a smile creeps out. "Funny."

"There's no need to be ashamed."

"Sorry to disappoint."

"Okay, fine." Humor seems to be working on his mood, at least. "If it's not that, what else could there be ..." I tap my chin in mock thought. "Wait, I know. Of course, it's so obvious." I pause for effect. "Porn."

Henry's eyes twinkle. "You think I've been in porn."

"Honestly? I wouldn't be *that* shocked." Henry's only hinted about his previous escapades but, given there doesn't seem to be much he wouldn't try at least once, it wouldn't be the most shocking discovery. "What would it be called? Let me guess ... *The Wolf of Porn Street*?"

His deep chuckle echoes around the shower stall.

"Too obvious, right? How about *The Big Bad Wolf Gets Pegged by Little Red Riding Hood*? No, that's too long. How about *Little Red Pegging Hood*—ah!" I squeal as he spins me around, his foot sliding between mine to force my stance wider.

"Tell me, where did you learn about pegging?" he purrs, pressing his hard length against the crevice of my ass as he herds my body forward, out of the water stream.

"Can't remember." I fall back against his chest. I don't dare tell him that Connor and Ronan enlightened me one drunken night in their attempts to make me blush. It worked.

He bows his head to graze his teeth against my earlobe "Why don't I believe you?"

"Because ..." My clever comeback fades on a gasp as Henry slides his hand between my legs. I shift to give him better access, which he eagerly takes, slipping two fingers deep inside me as his thumb works against my clit. He fills his other hand with my breast, stroking my pebbled nipple with the soft pad of his thumb.

I close my eyes and revel in his undivided attention, but it doesn't last long before he releases me, coaxing my body forward with a hand pressed against my shoulder blades, forcing me to brace my palms against the tile wall ahead.

I steal a glance over my shoulder to watch Henry stroke his rigid cock several times. "Keep doing that."

"No." Our eyes meet, and heat floods my core when I see his blazing. This isn't going to be gentle and that's fine. I don't want it to be.

I arch my back, taunting him.

With a curse, he lines up the head of his swollen cock and seizes my hips, his fingertips digging into my flesh almost to the point of pain.

I cry out as he thrusts deep into me.

"Did Raj help you get everything set up for next weekend?" Henry's gravelly voice cuts into my focus.

I set my book on my nightstand and track him on his path from our en suite bathroom to his side of the bed, the cotton of his boxer briefs hugging his form. A more physically pleasing man can't possibly exist. "Yes. He's been a huge help."

The moment I mentioned hosting Henry's friends here, Raj's eyes lit up. "*Finally*! Something more interesting than dry cleaning and grocery runs," he'd said and fetched his phone. Within an hour, Sasha, with her thick-framed black glasses and clicky heels, was strolling into the penthouse with a clipboard to size up what she had to work with for the perfect Gothic-themed party. My only contribution to the planning so far.

"I knew he would be." The mattress sinks under Henry's weight. "Make sure you tell them everything has to be wrapped up before midnight."

"And where are we going at midnight?" Henry said the guys fly in every year for this annual event, but he hasn't said anything else.

"We won't know until about an hour before when they text the ticket holders. The location changes every year."

"Why so secretive?"

"Because it's a secret party. Everyone wears a mask with their costume and no one knows who attends."

My jaw hangs open. "*Henry Wolf* wears a Halloween costume?"

"For this party, which also happens to be on Halloween, yes." A roguish smile curves his lips.

"What should we go as? Wait! I know! I'll be Little Red Riding Hood and you can be—"

"No." He settles onto his back. "Merrick's taking care of the costumes for us."

"*What*? Why?"

"Because it's a themed event and the organizers are particular about the quality of costumes people arrive in. Something cheap or half-assed gets you disinvited the following year. That's why Merrick arranges them. He always delivers."

"But he doesn't know my size." Or me, for that matter.

"I told him everything he needed to know."

An alarm bell goes off inside my head. "What *exactly* did he need to know?"

Henry's smile grows wider.

"*Henry*," I huff.

His eyes land on me. "Do you trust me?"

"*Yes*, but—"

"Have I ever asked you to do something you didn't enjoy?"

"I guess not."

He clears his throat.

"No," I concede, my cheeks heating as thoughts of some of the more risqué things Henry has asked me to do flood my mind.

"Okay, then. Trust me. You will be dressed. You will look good. And that's *all* you need to know until Saturday night."

Nervous flutters stir in my stomach. *But I'm with Henry*, I remind myself. He *always* takes good care of me. "What's the theme?"

"You'll find out on Saturday."

"Ugh! I don't like this secret."

"I can tell." He enjoys keeping me in the dark.

I know better than to pump him for more information

when he's using that tone. I'll have to work on him through the week to see if he'll slip up. "I do want to talk to you about the quote for the catering company, though. It's insane."

"It's fine." Henry shuts his eyes, as if ready for sleep.

"But you don't even know how much it is."

"Is it more than five digits?"

"No, but—"

"Then it's fine."

I make a strangled sound. "People have hosted *entire* wedding receptions for the cost of this dinner party for *nine* people." Warner and Preston are coming with dates, and apparently, Margo always comes to this annual event, too, so when she caught wind of dinner at our place beforehand, she invited herself plus Joel.

"Just imagine what our wedding reception will cost. Are you still reading?" Henry's unspoken request that I shut off the light.

"It seems excessive." I flip the switch, throwing the room into darkness. That's fine, I can never read in bed when he's here, anyway. I can't focus on *anything* but him.

"So was picking you up from Greenbank in a helicopter, but you didn't complain then."

I search for a retort but can't come up with a suitable one. Besides, that stunt was so worth it when I saw the look of defeat on Jed's face.

Henry sighs. "You're marrying me, Abigail. You need to get used to a certain lifestyle." He only uses my full name anymore when he's lecturing me. After another beat, he adds, "If it makes you feel better, whatever we spend on Saturday, why don't you donate double that amount to a charity of your choice."

I do the quick math. That *does* help my conscience. "*Any* charity?"

"Any charity your heart desires."

I shift closer to him, pressing my lips against his bare shoulder. "What about something for ALS?"

His chest rises with a deep breath. He's been hiding in work for most of the afternoon and evening, but I sense him hiding even deeper in his thoughts. Just last week, he was mulling over his life, feeling the pressure of being the only Wolf left. And in the last twenty-four hours, he has discovered that's not true.

"Have you ever known anyone with it?" he asks quietly.

"No. Not personally," I admit. "You? Before now, I mean."

"One of my father's best friends. He lived with it for almost ten years before his body gave up. He died five years ago."

"Did you know him well?" I ask softly.

"Yeah, I guess you could say that. We golfed together for years. He was a big man and loud. Deep, booming laugh. It was hard watching his body stop working. I kept expecting to hear that laugh." Henry pauses. "It's unfair that Audrey couldn't have more time with Violet. At least see her grow up."

"It *is* unfair," I agree. "But diseases don't care what's fair. They don't care if you've been a good person, or which god you pray to, or if you believe in one at all. They don't care who you leave behind."

Henry lifts his arm to wrap around me, pulling me up until my body is draped over his.

I inhale the delicious scent of soap still lingering on his hot skin. "I felt terrible for Audrey's parents. Having to bury their child and finish raising a teenager at their age? I mean, they must be in their late seventies or—"

"Eighty-four. Both of them. They had Audrey later in life."

"How do you ..." My question fades as it dawns on me. "You had Dyson look into them."

"Of course I did," he says matter-of-factly. "They're legal guardians of my child. I needed to make sure there weren't going to be any surprises."

Those words—*my child*—stir an odd emotion in the pit of my stomach that I can't quite decipher. "From an eighty-four-year-old couple? Such as?" I struggle to hide my exasperation. Sometimes Henry is too much.

"Debts, criminal records, history of drinking or abuse. Anything that could affect Violet negatively."

Worse than her mother's crimes? No use speaking ill of the dead. "And what did you find out?"

"Howard worked as an electrician, Gayle was a teacher. They paid off their house twenty years ago and don't owe anything else. Howard has had one speeding ticket in his life, neither drink, and they spent a lot of time helping Audrey out around her house."

Dyson's been busy, invading privacy and ferreting out information. I don't know how he finds out half the stuff he does, and it's best I don't. "So, you're saying they're good people."

"Yes. They're good people," he admits. "Who are going to struggle with a teenager who lies and takes trains into Manhattan. Gayle broke her hip five years ago, which is why she walks with a cane now. They were on a waiting list to move into an assisted living center but pulled their names off a year ago. I assume it's because Audrey's condition was deteriorating quickly and they knew they'd have Violet to take care of."

There's only one reason I can think of why people would want to move into one of those places, and it's because daily life is getting too difficult to manage on their own. But that begs the question that's been lingering in my mind and I'm sure has crept into his. "How long will they be able to take care of her?"

"Violet turns sixteen in January, so they just need to hang on for a little over two years, until she's an adult and their legal responsibility is over."

"They're not going to kick her out on her eighteenth birthday. And a lot can change in two years when you're in your eighties."

"I'm aware of that, Abbi, but what am *I* supposed to do?" His body stiffens with tension beneath me. I'm sure he's been dwelling on the answer to that question. "Please, tell me, what's my role here? Because I've been asking myself that all day, and I can't find the answer. I don't know the first fucking thing about being a parent."

"No one does when they start out—"

"This is not starting out. This is having a teenage girl dropped at my doorstep. Is that what *you* want? A fifteen-year-old—a stranger—suddenly living with us?"

No. I open my mouth but can't utter the cruel answer, even if it's the truth. We've only just started our lives together. Adding Violet to it would change *everything.* "This isn't about what I want." I would *never* want Henry to see me as the person coming between him and his daughter.

"Violet clearly doesn't want it. You were there, you heard her."

"She needs time to come to terms with everything." How much time, I can only guess.

"And then what?"

"I don't know. Look, you're both processing. No one expects you to know how to deal with this on day one. For now, Violet has a loving home with her grandparents. She'll be well taken care of, and she can help them. And maybe, once this initial shock is over, she'll be willing to let you in."

His chest lifts with a deep breath. "Children terrify me." He says it softly, like a confession.

"Which children?"

"*All* of them."

My stomach clenches. Is this where he tells me that he's changed his mind, that he doesn't want them anymore? *No.* I stop myself from heading down that path and instead ask, "What's so scary about them?"

He pauses. "The way they can change your life in a heartbeat. One minute they don't exist and then they do, and everything suddenly feels different."

"Different, but not bad, right?" I hold my breath.

"No, not bad," he admits after a moment.

I release the softest sigh of relief. "You didn't have time to ease into the idea of this. There was no nine-month count-down, no cute little helpless bundle." Henry got a furious teenager in muddy Chucks, throwing a contract at his feet before storming off.

"She's been alive for almost sixteen *years* and I had no fucking clue. *Sixteen years.*" His voice grows husky. "How many times did that kid ask about her father? How many times did she wonder why I didn't care?"

My heart aches for him as he struggles with his conscience. "That wasn't your fault."

"She seems to think it is."

"No. She's angry. Probably angrier at her mother than you, but you're here and Audrey's not, so you're going to get the brunt of it."

He seems to consider that, his chest rising and falling in slow, steady breaths, his heart beating hard against my ear.

"This wasn't your fault." I say each word slowly so he

hears them, so they sink in. "And you saw that house, and her grandparents. She wasn't abandoned—she's had a good life." Whatever else Audrey can be accused of, it doesn't seem like she was a bad mother.

He's silent for a few minutes. "She's a stranger to me and yet she's mine. She came from me."

"She won't be a stranger forever." I smooth my palm over his bare skin. "Not if you make the effort to get to know her."

I sense him opening his mouth to respond, but he holds back whatever he was going to say, settling his hand over mine.

ten

"Are you sure this isn't too much?"

Raj stands beside me, hands on hips. "You said you wanted a Gothic-themed dinner party for Halloween."

"I did."

"*This* is a Gothic-themed dinner party."

"It *is*. One hundred percent." The catering company arrived at eight a.m. to begin setting up. Hours later, the dining area has been transformed into a luxurious cave swathed in black—from the silk tablecloths and metal candlesticks to the matte cutlery and stoneware. Even the wineglasses are tinted ebony. The only hints of color come from tiny bronzed pumpkins and centerpieces spilling over with green moss. Elsewhere in the penthouse, candles wait to burn atop their candelabras and exotic floral arrangements grace end tables. When Sasha described the medley of black orchids, tulips, and calla lilies, I had no idea what to expect, but I was right to trust her.

That doesn't mean I haven't been questioning everything, every step of the way. "I'm sorry, Raj." His patience with me *must* be thinning by now.

"You're nervous about making a good first impression on Mr. Wolf's friends."

"No, I am really, really, *really* nervous about making a good first impression. In case you haven't noticed, I don't travel in his circle." I didn't grow up in a city with a rich family, I didn't go to private school. I have nothing in common with them. What if they hate me? What if they tell Henry he's lost his damn mind marrying me, that they don't approve of his choice of a wife?

"I don't think you have anything to worry about. But in any case, Sasha's company hosts the more exclusive parties in the city. They know their clientele, and they know what they're doing."

Given the price tag of this party, I should hope so. "What about the food?" The elaborate seven-course menu is printed on parchment and set at each guest's seat. The chef and his staff have been working in the little catering kitchen all afternoon, the only hints that they're in there the fragrant aroma of roasted meat and the odd clatter.

"Hors d'oeuvres are ready, and the tenderloin is in the oven. It will be a magazine-worthy night," Raj assures me. "Everything is taken care of, and your guests will start arriving in less than an hour."

"What?" I check the clock on the wall, the time escaping me. But he's right. "Where's Henry?"

"I wouldn't worry about *him*." Raj looks pointedly at my sweatpants.

"Right. I should do something about this."

"You *really* should."

I grin. "I'm sorry for being crazy. I'm meeting these guys for the first time, and I just want tonight to be—"

"Perfect, I know." He smiles patiently. "And it will be, unless you start doing that." He playfully swats my hand away from my freshly manicured nails.

"Thank you!" I sprint up the stairs and peel off my clothes. Waiting for me in a garment bag is a fitted black dress and stilettos Margo had couriered from a New York designer when I lamented that I didn't know what to wear. I slip into the full outfit, including the shoes—in a pitiful attempt to break them in before tonight—and study myself in the full-length mirror, satisfied. As usual, she knows what will look good on me. I'm glad someone does.

Thankfully, I snuck away long enough this morning for a blowout, so my hair is sleek and smooth. I wish I'd hired someone to do my makeup. I'm still very much in the learning stages after a lifetime of embracing "a wholesome look" at Mama's and Jed's behest.

I still shake my head at all the ways I've been under my mother's thumb. Aunt May is right—the sooner she learns that the days of having a say in how I live my life are over, the better for everyone involved.

My phone chirps with an incoming text as I'm about to tackle eyeshadow.

Ronan: *A journalist is sniffing around. He's looking for a story about you and the wolf.*

I curse.

Abbi: *Was it Luca?*

I texted Ronan after that guy called.

Ronan: *No. Frank. Or Hank. I can't remember.*

Seeing as there's no Luca at the *Tribune*, maybe he's dropping fake names.

Abbi: *It could be the same guy. What'd you tell him?*

My phone rings and Ronan's name appears on the screen.

"I told him to suck my dick," Ronan's gravelly voice fills my ear before I can say hello.

I smile as I throw the call on speaker. Ronan isn't intimidated by anyone, not even Henry, who could legitimately make his life hell. "Hey."

"Hey, yourself." His tone softens immediately. "I haven't heard your voice in forever."

"It's only been a couple of weeks." My cheeks flush with the reminder of the last time we saw each other, just before Ronan left Henry and me alone in the bedroom of Penthouse Cabin One. He said he'd never forget that night.

The truth is, neither will I.

I would never choose Ronan over Henry. *Never*. You could ask me a thousand times and I would only ever have one answer: Henry is all I'll ever want. And yet Ronan was a lifeline during the darkest months of the summer, when my heart had been shattered, the pain a hundred times more than anything I felt after Jed broke it. Our friendship may be unconventional, but it's ours. Keeping him in my life is important to me.

"How's Miami?" With the Alaska location shut down for the season, the staff has retreated to their previous lives. In Ronan's case, it's back to Florida, where he shares a condo with Connor.

"Boring, but balmy."

"Are you staying out of trouble?"

"Define trouble." There's a hint of teasing in his voice.

"I can't. My imagination isn't that dirty." Henry keeps calling Ronan and Connor deviants. Given the things they got up to at Wolf Cove after I left—namely their little fuck club experiment—the nickname might not be too far off.

"I think your imagination is just fine, Red."

I smile as I blend a smoky shadow at the corners of my

eyelids. He's the only one who calls me Red, and I like it that way. "Did this reporter leave you a number?"

"Nope. Unknown caller. Kept calling back until I answered." Ronan snorts. "The balls he has. How did this asshole get my number, anyway?"

"Probably from whoever's feeding him all this information."

"My money's on Tillie."

"Yeah, I'm thinking the same." It *has to* be her. She's a gossip vampire who feels she's been spurned by me, though I've never done anything to her. Yes, Connor flirted with me while they were hooking up, but Connor flirts with *everyone*. But I think it's all driven by jealousy because I'm with Henry, and she had no idea. If there is one thing Tillie was never shy about admitting, it was how happy she would be to climb into the big bad wolf's bed. "She doesn't know anything, though." Nothing for sure. "Deny everything. We're just friends."

"We *are* just friends, aren't we?"

"You know what I mean." If Henry didn't exist, we might be more. "Are you going back to Wolf Cove next year?"

"Haven't decided yet. Got some time before I have to commit."

"But you'll come for the wedding, right?"

"I'm invited?" I don't miss the shock in his voice.

"Don't be silly. Of course, you're invited." I falter on my second question. Henry and I haven't settled on the bridesman topic yet.

"And that's where you guys are doing it? Alaska?"

"Yeah. We both love it up there."

There's a lengthy pause.

"Ronan? Are you still—"

"Yeah, I'll be there. For you. Not for your asshole fiancé. He doesn't deserve you."

Ronan was the only one who knew the silent agony I was suffering during those weeks, no one else the wiser to my secret relationship with Henry. "I'm happy."

"I know you are, and I'm happy for you." He sighs heavily. "What are you doing tonight?"

"Nothing with you," a deep voice cuts in.

I jump at the sudden interruption and spin around to find Henry standing in the doorway. Even with an annoyed scowl on his face, my heart races at the sight of him.

A loud, aggravated groan carries over the speaker. "I guess this conversation is over."

"It shouldn't have started," Henry throws back without missing a beat.

I glare at him, but all it earns is his smug smirk.

"You still work for me, Ronan." Henry closes in on me, his hands loosening his tie. "Which means I can fire you any damn time I please."

"But then you'd have to answer to your future wife, and I doubt she'd be impressed, seeing as I saved your rich, jealous ass for her," comes Ronan's quick retort. "Talk to you later, Red." He ends the call.

"Do you have to be a jerk?"

"Yes." Henry leans in to kiss my neck. "What did he want?"

I inhale the delicious scent of his cologne. "A reporter's been calling him, digging for dirt."

Henry curses. "Same one?"

"I don't know, but we think Tillie might be the one talking."

"Which one's that again?"

"The other redhead in my cabin. She was in house-keeping."

"Southern accent."

"Yeah." I used to think she was a friend. She was so welcoming at first, but I guess she didn't see me as competition back then. "I'm going to ask Autumn to see what she can find out. They still text sometimes." Autumn is friendly with everyone, but Tillie has no idea how close she and I have become since the summer.

Henry tosses his tie toward the hamper. "Let me know what you find out so I can handle it."

"What does 'handle it' mean, exactly?"

"It means I don't keep employees who are selling stories to the press about me." His hand snakes around my waist to splay across my stomach, his gaze dragging downward over the reflection in the mirror. "This dress is perfect on you."

"Thank you. I was thinking I would wear it to the party—"

"Merrick has your costume." He steps back. "New shoes?"

"Yes." I clench my teeth with irritation. I've been needling Henry all week, trying to get him to slip up and give me a clue—about the theme of this party, my character, *anything*—but his lips are as tight as a Federal Reserve vault.

A low grunt of approval escapes him.

"Will I be allowed to wear them tonight or will *Merrick* be choosing my shoes too?" I can't help the annoyance in my tone.

"These, I think I'll let you keep." He pauses. "Any word from your mother?"

"No." The mention of her sours my mood. She hasn't responded to any of my texts, except for one innocuous message about the weather. "Daddy said he thinks she's starting to come around. He caught her looking up flights to Alaska the other day."

"She will. Don't give it another thought tonight." Henry pulls me flush against him, allowing me to feel him hard against my back.

"People will be here in less than an hour," I warn him, even as my blood rushes.

"Since when do I care about other people's schedules?"

I've barely seen him all week. In typical Henry fashion, he distracted himself with work to avoid dealing with the shock of learning about Violet, taking a sudden two-day trip to Dallas and then spending the rest of his time in the office, arriving home late and leaving early. While I've missed him terribly, between catching up on my two correspondence courses and all the prep for the launch of my soap line, I've had more than enough to keep myself busy.

But now I need to feel a closeness with him again, even if it's just physical. I need to know that what we have is real and deep and can weather anything that comes our way.

So I don't argue when he hikes my dress up to my waist and tugs on my panties until they fall to the tile floor. I don't wait for him to demand that I take them off, gingerly stepping out of them.

"Bend over," he coaxes, his hand pressing against my back. "Elbows on the counter."

Heat explodes in my lower belly as I follow his directions. The vanity mirror reflects the sordid scene as Henry takes several steps back to lean against the wall and admire the lewd display, his arms folded across his chest.

Cool air caresses my bare skin as I wait for him to unzip his pants, but he's torturing me with anticipation.

Two can play at this game.

"While you're deciding what you want ..." I adjust my

stance and arch my back, and then pick up my mascara wand.

Henry watches as I paint my lashes with long, languid strokes, pretending that my pulse isn't racing through my veins, before his gaze drops to the view farther down.

I spread my legs apart to tease him.

"Fuck, Abbi." The sound of his zipper unfastening fills the room.

I stifle my smile, even as my sex clenches with anticipation, and keep my attention on my task as he sheds his clothes, right down to his socks.

Suddenly, he's hovering behind me, his hard length gripped in his hand. "You know how to tease me."

Heat pools between my legs. "I've learned from the best." I gasp as he rubs the smooth, round head of his cock through my slit once, twice ... pressing against my entrance in a gentle intrusion.

I close my mascara and set it down, preparing for the hard thrust into me that is coming. Aching for it.

His dark, blazing eyes lift to meet mine. "You're right, you have."

I yelp as he slaps my bare cheek with his palm. "They'll be here soon. Hurry up." He pulls away and strolls into the shower, turning on the water.

I gape as I watch after him, my cheeks flushed with frustration. "That's it?" He's going to leave me like *this*?

He's under the stream of hot water when he peers over his shoulder to flash a wicked grin.

~

"YOU DOMESTICATED MOTHERFUCKER!"

I observe from the corner of the kitchen as a man with

fair skin and a lush mane of black hair pulls Henry into a hug. Given the British accent, this *must* be Preston.

Henry returns the gesture, roping his arms around his friend.

So, this is the guy with the swollen ego who runs the two-billion-dollar hedge fund firm. No wonder ... Not only is he rich and successful, he is *beautiful.* Tall and fit and stylish, with masculine features and a broad, uninhibited smile that shows off straight, white teeth. The guy surely turns heads in every room he walks into.

How I missed spotting Preston at the funeral is beyond me, but I guess that confirms how many people there were and how solely focused I was on Henry.

When the two men peel away, Preston is shaking his head with disbelief. "Never thought I'd see the day Henry Wolf would be getting married and hosting dinners." Finally, he notices me standing off to the side. Warm hazel eyes skitter over my frame, all the way to my shoes, before rising again. "And now I understand."

It wasn't a leering look, and yet my face erupts with heat.

"Preston, this is Abbi," Henry introduces.

Preston hurries forward, thrusting out his hand. "It's a pleasure to meet the woman who thawed Wolf's cold, black heart." His large hand surrounds mine.

"Same." That didn't make any sense. I clear my throat. "I mean, I'm glad you could make it tonight."

"Oh, I never miss this weekend." His smile is mischievous. "And I'm sure Wolf has told you *everything* there is to know about me?"

"Uh ..." I dare a questioning glance at Henry.

Preston barks with laughter. "He's told you absolutely nothing, right?"

"That's not true. I told her you're an arrogant fuck," Henry retorts smoothly.

"Don't worry." Preston releases my hand to squeeze Henry's shoulder. "He may play the prickly asshole, but we know he loves us."

Henry rolls his eyes but he's smiling. "All right, enough of that bullshit. How was your flight over?"

"Short. Kept myself busy." He winks and then stretches an arm out toward the leggy blond who just emerged from the powder room. "Speaking of ... Kendra, this is my dear friend Henry Wolf and his fiancée, Abbi."

Kendra saunters toward us, covertly tugging at the hem of her fitted black dress before it rides up past her ass.

"Kendra works in accounting at my firm."

"You *work* together." It's just the slightest inflection in Henry's tone, but I catch it.

So must Preston because he smirks, seemingly unfazed by his disapproval. "Not directly."

Henry's eyebrow twitches, but he doesn't say anything else as a server in a crisp black button-down and black dress pants swoops in to deliver a tray of cocktails dressed in blackberries.

Honestly, what could Henry say, considering his own indiscretions?

Preston hands a glass to his date before accepting one for himself. "This is Kendra's first trip to New York."

"I'm excited." She lifts her glass in a toast, showing off the delicate tattoo on the inside of her wrist of three inter-twined hearts.

"And the suite they put you in?" Henry asks. "I asked Miles to arrange something adequate. I hope it's to your satisfaction."

"Oh yes, it's lovely, isn't it, Preston?" She trails a finger along his biceps, a subtle sign of affection that he doesn't react to.

"It'll do." Preston tastes the concoction, pauses, and then takes another sip.

A wave of relief washes over me. One day maybe I'll feel like I fit into this lifestyle, okay with dropping thousands on a catered dinner party. Or maybe I won't care to seek approval. Today is not that day.

I take a large gulp of my drink, hoping the alcohol will calm my frazzled nerves.

"We're two floors down, between Merrick's and Warner's rooms. They've checked in already." Preston peers over his shoulder. "They should be here any second."

"Preston said you own this hotel?" Kendra's bright cornflower-blue eyes shimmer with interest on Henry. She's gorgeous. I can see why she caught the finance tycoon's interest.

"Did he now?" Henry smirks at his friend. "He's being modest on my behalf. I own *all* Wolf hotels."

Preston's head tips back with his booming laughter. "Now who's the arrogant prick?"

"Still you. Always you." Henry slaps Preston's back.

My heart swells as I watch the playful exchange. That edge Henry always wears has vanished, replaced by an easygoing nature I've not seen before. Even in the early days, when I was Henry's assistant taking notes while he charmed executives, I didn't know him at all, but I sensed an air of performance.

Maybe a night with his childhood friends is all Henry needs.

Commotion stirs at the doorway and two more men stroll in.

"Good Lord," I mutter under my breath.

Not quietly enough, apparently, because Henry spears me with an exasperated look.

What? I mouth and shrug, even as my cheeks flush. Seriously, what kind of boarding school produced a group of men that look like *this*?

A swell of hellos, jeers, and laughter bursts in the penthouse.

The taller man on the left—the one with a short beard and lush brown hair that cascades to his shoulders in loose curls—reaches Henry first, embracing him much like Preston did. He mumbles something next to Henry's ear that I don't catch, but his expression is morose.

Condolences, for all that Henry's been through lately, if I had to guess.

Henry pats his shoulder as he steps away. "Warner, Abigail. Abigail, this is Warner."

I don't bother correcting his use of my full name as I offer my hand to the man, all while admiring his tanned, olive skin and deep brown irises.

Warner answers by collecting my fingers and lifting my hand to his lips to kiss my knuckles.

"Not even a wife yet and the Latin lover is already making his move." Preston shakes his head. "And where is ... Tatiana, is it?"

Warner waves off his friend's question with an absent "She'll be here when she's ready." As if he doesn't care one way or another if his date arrives.

Behind Warner is a man with a chiseled jaw and cropped dark ash-blond hair. His lean, muscular body, clad in all black, moves gracefully toward us. This is obviously Merrick.

"How was the Australian Outback?" Henry asks, clasping hands with him.

"Got lost and almost died. Other than that, fantastic." Merrick's voice is deep, his tone cool. His face barely cracks a smile as he peers at me. "So you're the one." It's not a question.

Something peculiar lingers in his crystal blue eyes. I can't explain the look, but I wouldn't call it warm or friendly. I can see what Henry meant when he said Merrick is hard to read.

"That's right. Your hopes of playing with Wolf's cock are officially coming to an end," Preston proclaims.

"You mean playing with it *again*," chirps Warner.

My jaw drops. *Wait?* Are they saying ... I asked Henry point-blank if he'd ever been with a man and he told me no. Did he lie, or is this just these two tormenting their friend with typical dumb male jokes?

"Thanks for that. Just couldn't fucking help yourselves." Henry grumbles, "Idiots."

Idiots who are handing me questions I'll need answers to later. He better not have lied. He should know by now that I wouldn't care if he had experimented with a man.

Merrick ignores them, holding up the two garment bags draped over his arm. "These are for you two." If anything, he sounds bored.

Our costumes. *Finally*. I reach for them—

Henry swiftly grabs the bags as my fingers graze the fabric. "Everyone, please make yourselves comfortable. Enjoy the view."

I watch him climb the stairs, likely to hide the costumes out of my reach. "Damn it." I was so close.

"He won't tell you what you're going as, will he." Merrick accepts a drink from the server before she moves toward the living room where the others are heading.

"No, or anything about this secret party we're going to.

It's been giving me anxiety all week," I admit sheepishly. The more I think about it, the more nervous I get. If these guys fly in for it every year, something tells me it won't be like any party I've been to before.

That earns Merrick's smile, and it is a striking one, showing off deep, boyish dimples that soften his initial edge. "It's a good time. There's a different theme every year and specific requirements for costumes. It's very exclusive, invite-only, with lots of security. They don't even disclose the location until an hour before the event begins."

"Yeah, he told me all that." Merrick is talkative, at least, and that cool, bored tone is evaporating. "And the theme this year is ...?"

"Ask Henry," he answers without missing a beat.

· I roll my eyes, earning his laugh.

"If it makes you feel better, the guys don't know who they're going as either."

"How is *anyone* okay with this?"

"That's part of the fun." He sips on the themed cocktail, his full lips lingering on the glass.

He has a beautiful mouth. Has it been on any part of Henry?

I give my head a shake. *Focus, Abbi.* "But *you* know what they're going as."

"I arranged all the costumes, so yes, *I* know," he says, a hint of teasing in his deep voice. "But don't bother trying to get it out of me."

"Can you at least tell me if it's a weird couple thing?" I ask.

"Weird couple thing?"

"You know ... Bonnie and Clyde, Gomez and Morticia. Mickey and Mallory?"

Merrick shakes his head.

"Little Red Riding Hood and the Big Bad Wolf?"

"They were a couple?" He frowns. "That's not the nursery rhyme my mother told me. Look, I wish I could help you out, but I can't. Wolf will kill me."

"At least give me a hint?" I stare up at his handsome face. "Just a tiny hint?"

He studies my features intently. "Red and gold."

"Red and gold?" What characters are red and gold? I draw a blank. "Can I have another hint?"

His stony face breaks with another brilliant smile. "You're a greedy thing, aren't you?"

"No, I'm paranoid." Henry promised I would be dressed, but his idea of what that means differs from mine.

"Yeah, I would be too, given who you're marrying."

"Oh God." I want to ask him what he means by that.

Merrick's throat bobs as he looks around us. "Okay, fine, but this is the last hint, and you can't tell *anyone* I told you. Especially Wolf. Promise?"

My excitement stirs. "Yes."

"*Our* secret, okay?"

"I swear."

He leans down until his face is inches from my ear, and whispers, "The circus."

A shiver runs down my spine as his breath kisses my skin and his cologne teases my nose, but I brush that reaction aside to focus on the clue. *The circus*. Okay, that's something I can work with. "Acrobat?"

He gives a curt head shake. "I told you, no more hints."

"Lion tamer?"

"Damn, you are persistent. I'm not telling you!"

"Clown?"

"We're done here."

But I'm not. I rifle through the characters from *The Greatest Showman*. "The bearded lady?"

The corners of Merrick's mouth twitch.

"Oh my God. Am I right?"

"How could you possibly guess that?"

I gasp. "I'm right?"

"Fuck." He grinds his teeth. "You can't tell him that I told you."

"I know, but ... you're kidding me, right?" I wail. "Henry said I would look good!"

"Hey, who says a woman with a beard can't look good? It's natural."

"So is having it waxed. Couldn't you have chosen something *sexier* than that?"

He shrugs. "Wolf said you'd want a modest costume, and that was the most modest one I could find."

"Because my face will be covered in hair!"

He purses his lips. "I promise, it's not that bad."

I look down at my beautiful black dress in dismay. "What are the other women going as?"

"Acrobats. Sexy costumes too."

"*Seriously*?" I'm beginning to like Merrick less by the second.

Another shrug. "I was just following Wolf's rules."

Henry reappears at the bottom of the stairs.

"Remember, you *promised*." That hardness is back in Merrick's eyes and voice as he glares down at me, as if hiding a threat. How does he change so quickly between warm and cold?

"What's going on here?" Henry's gaze shifts between us, before settling on his friend with a "What the fuck did you do?" look.

"Hello, my dear friends!" Margo strolls in then, her short

black lace dress leaving almost nothing to the imagination. Joel trails a few steps behind her, her trench coat draped over his arm. "Now the party may begin!"

KENDRA LEANS over her place setting on the other side of Joel, who sits between us. "Is it true what I heard? Henry was trapped in a mine recently?"

"Yes. A couple of weeks ago."

She presses her hand against her cleavage. "That must have been *so* scary."

"It was terrifying," I admit, glancing across to where Henry sits. He's not paying attention, deep in conversation with Merrick who, as the only solo guest, is at the head of the table. I'm sure he'd rather bypass a conversation about his recent ordeal.

"Oui, but our Abigail was strong." Margo beams at me from her spot next to Henry.

"I didn't eat or sleep until he came home. I was an absolute mess, and you know that because you dropped everything to be there for me. Because you're a wonderful friend." Who I'm *so* happy insisted on coming tonight. Not that there's been any real awkwardness. It's as if no time has passed since Henry and his childhood friends last saw one another, which I suppose is normal for such a close group.

Margo and Joel fit neatly into the cluster, strangers or not—though it seems Margo has met all the men before. Kendra is friendly and talkative and has been peppering me with questions all evening. Tatiana is the only one I haven't spoken to tonight. Warner's date strolled in ten minutes before dinner, her slender nose in the air, the revealing crisscross front of her cobalt dress covering only half of her breasts. She offered weak hellos before stepping out onto the terrace to fix her crimson lipstick and take selfies. She seems uninterested in dinner, not taking more than a bite of each course. Given how tight her outfit is, she might not *be able* to fit food in there. The vodka, though, that flows freely ...

It seems odd that an outgoing man like Warner would choose to spend an evening with someone like this, but thankfully, her apathetic demeanor hasn't dampened the multiple conversations that buzz around the dining table as the delectable fall harvest-themed courses arrive and easy laughter erupts.

"So, how did you and Henry meet?" Kendra asks.

I guess she hasn't done *all* her homework about us. If she had, she'd know the answer. That, or she's fishing for more information than what she gleaned from the tabloids. "I worked at the new Wolf Hotel in Alaska for the summer."

"*This* past summer? So you two, like, *just* met." I don't miss the inflection in her voice, the words she *doesn't* say.

She seems to eye Henry more keenly.

"I guess when you know, you know." I smooth my finger over the pearl in my ring, doing my best to bury my deepest fears threatening to rise, the ones I wish I could shed.

He'll change his mind. He won't go through with it.

"Henry is a man who knows what he wants and doesn't waste time going after it." Margo winks at me before sipping her wine. Is she saying that for Kendra's benefit or mine? Maybe both. Either way, I could kiss her.

"Have you hired a photographer yet?" Joel asks, changing the topic to one I don't mind being laid out bare on the table.

"Not yet. The wedding planner I'm working with is sending me a list of options."

"Mais non! You cannot hire someone off a list." He grips my forearm, his touch warm. "*I* would be honored to photograph your wedding, Abbi."

"Um ..." My cheeks flush. Joel is famous for close-up stills of the female body during orgasm. He has an entire collection hanging in an art gallery. I accidentally saw him in action once, in Margo's French chateau, and I've seen examples of his work. How do I decline this suggestion politely? "I think we're looking for something more traditional?"

He barks with laughter. "Not *those* types of photographs." He digs his phone from his pocket and pulls up an album. "I also have these in my portfolio."

I watch with fascination as he scrolls through stunning shots of women in elegant dresses and men in suits. "I took these at my dear friend Enrique's wedding. There, see his bride?"

"*Wow*." They're candid and have a glamorous, old-world feel to them. "These look like magazine shots."

"They ended up selling them to a popular French bridal publication, so I guess they are?" He shrugs as if it's no big deal.

"Joel has photographed the most famous models for the biggest brands in the world," Margo jumps in, smiling at him. "He is a superb talent. You would be very lucky to have him capture your special day. *I* will hire him one day, if I ever decide to marry."

"See? I have an eye for more than what you think I do." Joel smiles mischievously. "Though I have an excellent eye for that too." If it fazes Joel that his current girlfriend is talking about a future without him, he doesn't let on. But I already knew these two weren't committed to each other. Monogamy isn't in Margo's vocabulary.

I bite my bottom lip. "Let me talk to Henry about it before I give you an answer." But, looking at these pictures, I already know I'll be begging him to agree.

"Of course. But, again, please know that it would be an absolute honor for me to be a part of your day." He collects my hand and kisses the back of it as if to emphasize that claim.

"I am somewhat of an art connoisseur. I would *love* to see your portfolio, Joel," Kendra gushes, her cheeks flushed from wine.

"Is that so?" A devilish grin flashes across his handsome face. "Let me show you what I am most famous for ..."

I move my attention to Henry before I get an eyeful of women's magnified clits at the dinner table.

"... why the fuck would you get into business with *them*?" Henry scolds Merrick in a low voice, their heads turned for a private conversation. "The Easton name is toxic."

"They've managed pretty well in Phoenix."

"That's a nightclub, not a fucking hotel and casino in Vegas. Do you like the feds up your ass? Because that's where they'll be living for the foreseeable future."

"They can crawl as far as they want up there. They're not gonna find what they're looking for. That, I can promise you. We're a hundred percent legit. And who else are we going to fund this with? You?" Merrick counters.

"You know I would if I could."

"I know, and I would never ask you to." Merrick shrugs. "We've wanted to do this for years, but it's too much risk to go in on our own, and we have challenges finding people who can look past *our* name, forget the Eastons. And they're not that bad." He pauses as if to think about his last words, then corrects himself. "*Gabriel's* not that bad."

"But Gabriel's in Phoenix, running his club. You've got his lunatic brother."

"Yeah. Caleb's a bit of a loose cannon," Merrick admits, smoothing a hand over the back of his neck as if to release tension. "I'm learning how to handle him."

Henry's eyebrow arches in question, earning Merrick's scowl.

"Not like *that*."

Henry carves into his tenderloin. "I'm just saying, guys like that will always cause you problems, and you've had enough of those to last three lifetimes."

"Yeah, maybe. But it's too late now."

The two men realize I'm listening to them, and they both adjust in their seats.

"We'll have to thank the chef personally. This meal is fantastic," Henry says around a mouthful, as if they weren't just talking about lunatic brothers and the FBI up Merrick's ass.

"Raj said they were the best."

A few awkward beats pass. Clearly, I wasn't supposed to be eavesdropping.

"So, Abbi ... looking forward to the party tonight?" Merrick slides a roasted carrot into his mouth.

I force a smile. "I'm sure it'll be great."

"It will," he agrees with an exaggerated nod, but humor dances in those blue eyes. "Especially in your costume."

I grit my teeth. An exclusive, elite costume party and I'll bet every female in there will be wearing something sexy. Meanwhile, I'll be picking hair out of my mouth to get a drink. The more I think about it, the angrier I get. Merrick picked a *terrible* costume for me. He knows it, and the jerk is gloating.

Henry sees right through my act. "What's going on, Abbi?"

Merrick glares in warning.

"Nothing."

"Abigail." There's that tone.

I can't hold it in anymore. Besides, I have no loyalty to Merrick and what's he going to do to me? "You told me I would look good tonight."

"Yes." Henry frowns. "*And*?"

"And Merrick told me it's a circus theme."

"Did he now." Henry glares at Merrick.

Merrick shakes his head at me in dismay. "Sorry, man. She looked up at me with those big, beautiful eyes, and I couldn't lie to her."

"He has me going as the bearded lady!" There's a touch of whine in my voice that I'm embarrassed about.

"To be fair, she guessed that part." Merrick takes a sip of his wine.

Henry purses his lips for one ... two ... three seconds before his head tips back and a loud, booming laugh escapes him.

"She pounced on me the second you were out of the room. Played out just like you said it would, man." Merrick holds his glass up.

Henry clangs his against it in a toast. "Fuck, I missed you, Mer."

Wait a minute. I gape at Merrick. "Were you lying to me? I'm not going as the bearded lady?"

He winks. "I told you not to bother trying."

∼

"That time Dean Warrick caught Preston in his daughter's room?"

Preston groans and covers his face as Warner, Henry, and Merrick burst out laughing.

"I remember looking out my window and seeing a bare, white ass trying to run through knee-deep snow," Merrick manages, gasping for air.

"And then he lost his balance and star-fished facedown," Henry adds.

"Listen, you arseholes! I got frostbite on my dick that night!" Preston yells with indignation.

"Next time grab your clothes before you jump out a window in the dead of winter," Warner throws back, absently keying an upbeat tune on the baby grand piano in the corner. "*Or* don't get caught fucking the dean's daughter."

Dinner is finished and we've moved to the living room where the bartender plies us with drinks and the guys regale us with embarrassing boarding school stories. The only one not laughing is Tatiana, who's parked on the couch, consumed by editing pictures of herself on her phone.

"Come on, I may have fucked the dean's daughter, but Wolf takes the crown." Preston jams a finger toward Henry. "How many times with our English teacher?"

Henry smooths a hand over his mouth as the men explode in a raucous roar.

"In detention once, right?" Warner asks. "Also in the library one night, after it closed."

"Henry!" Margo exclaims. "How old were you?"

"Sophomore year," Preston answers for him.

She tsks, but she's smiling. It's impossible to shock that woman.

"But wait. Isn't that, like ... bad?" Kendra giggles, scrunching her nose as she tries to hide her disapproval.

"Fuck yeah, but Wolf wasn't innocent. I was so jealous of him." Merrick shakes his head. "Remember those heels she always wore?"

Warner moans. "God, yes. You think she still teaches in those?"

Henry's eyes fly to mine, and I see the same unease in them that's cycling through me. This feels wrong, listening to them froth at the mouth over the woman when she's freshly in a pine box.

The mother of Henry's child.

But they don't know any of that because Henry hasn't told them, and now is hardly the time.

"Guys, enough." He gives them a warning look, but they all just laugh harder. No one else seems to notice the way his body has stiffened.

"Come on, that was forever ago. As if anyone would care now." Preston chuckles, but then gasps and points at me. "Wait a minute, did she not know?" As if I'm not listening to this entire conversation.

Henry's jaw tenses. "Abbi knows."

Boy, do I ever. And plenty of people would still care. One of them is a girl struggling with the memory of her mother. I've thought about Violet more than I expected to this week —about how she's feeling, how she's coping. I nearly asked Henry for Gayle and Howard's number so I could call and check up on her, but I decided against it. She needs more time.

A chorus of chirps sounds with incoming texts. The four men and Margo fish for their phones.

"We've got the location!" Merrick announces, the first to read the message.

Henry's shoulders sag, with relief for the change in subject, I'm sure. "And it's a good hour's drive from here, so we better get a move on. See you all there."

"I think he's kicking us out." Preston downs his drink.

"He's definitely kicking us out." Warner pats Henry's shoulder with one hand. "See you soon, buddy." Swooping in to collect my hand, he kisses my knuckles. "I know this degenerate had nothing to do with dinner, so thank you, Abbi, for making the first part of the night perfect." He winks. "See you later." He waves at everyone else.

Tatiana stands and follows him without a word.

"Not the most charming, is she," Joel mutters, his face pinched with distaste.

"What do you mean? She's a fucking delight," whispers Preston—too loudly—and then kisses my cheek, hooks his arm around Kendra's shoulders, and they leave.

Margo offers me her signature two-cheek kiss. "We will look for you," she whispers and then pulls away to kiss Henry's cheek. "Walk with me a moment."

Henry obliges, and Joel trails them out.

Merrick is the last to leave. He towers over me. "You still mad at me?"

"I haven't decided yet." But I struggle to hide my smile. It was a good joke on their part.

"Henry made me do it."

"And do you always do what Henry tells you to do?"

He shrugs. "He can be hard to say no to, as I'm sure you've learned."

I narrow my eyes, searching for meaning hidden within his words.

He laughs at me, and then, with an affectionate squeeze of my biceps, says, "I think you'll forgive me when you see what I've chosen for you."

I watch his back as he ambles toward the foyer, fist-bumping a returning Henry on the way.

"Okay, Raj will see the caterers out and Victor will be downstairs in fifteen minutes to drive us. Let's get upstairs and—"

"Did you and Merrick ever hook up?" I interrupt.

He gives the bartender a salute as he leads me toward the stairs. "No."

"Henry ..."

"Why would I lie? You know I'm not ashamed of anything I've done." His lips twist. "But there *is* a story."

I knew it. "What happened—"

"Not now, Abbi. We have the event of the year to get to." His tone brokers no argument.

eleven

The long row of high-end SUVs and cars crawls forward, each taking their turn at the curb, releasing their patrons before quickly pulling away. The cloaked figures cut through the shadows and vanish through a long, narrow path draped in the typical red and gold fabric of a circus tent.

Never would I suspect this nondescript warehouse of hosting a super elite, invite-only party, but I guess that's the whole point of the clandestine operation. "How many people come to one of these events?"

Henry leans back in the seat, relaxed, his thighs spread, as if he's done this countless times before. "I have no idea. It's hard to say, based on the layout. Hundreds, certainly."

"And they're *all* dressed in costume?"

"They won't be allowed in otherwise." He scowls at a gold button on his jacket that he's concerned isn't stiff enough.

"It's fine."

"It's floppy."

"You look *amazing.*" When Henry stepped out donning the gold and red jacket, my jaw dropped. It looks custom-tailored to his body and sewn with high-end fabrics.

"Yeah?" He smirks. "You have a thing for ringmasters?"

I lean in and whisper into his ear so Victor doesn't hear me, "You still owe me for that tease before dinner."

"The night is young. Careful what you wish for." He weaves his fingers through mine, his gaze dragging down my costume. "You're not the bearded lady, but this will do."

I giggle and smooth a hand over the black-and-white-checkered stockings that reach halfway up my thigh and clip to a garter belt. I'm relieved by Merrick's choice for me. He was right. The second I unzipped the garment bag to reveal the sexy mime costume inside, all bad blood washed away.

"I promised you'd be respectably dressed, didn't I?"

"Depends on who you ask, I guess." Mama certainly wouldn't approve. The frilly little dress is obscenely short, and my breasts have nowhere to hide behind the Lycra material of the bodysuit, but at least it comes with a black bathing suit bottom so I don't show my underwear when I bend over. Paired with my black stilettos, I *know* I look good.

"Just a few more cars, sir," Victor calls out.

"Okay, it's showtime. Give me your wrist." Henry clamps a thin bracelet around it. "This is how you get in and how you pay for drinks. Leave your purse here. Don't worry, Victor will take care of it."

"*What*? But I—"

"No phones, no cash, no wallets. Nothing to record or identify anyone in there. Those are the rules."

I frown as I set aside my little black satchel. What kind of party is this?

"And these stay on at all times unless you're in a designated area," he continues, sliding on a white mask that covers his face down to just above his mouth.

I affix a similar mask, except mine has the traditional black markings of a mime.

Our car comes to a jarring halt and a security guard moves in to open our door for us.

"Ready?" I sense a rush of adrenaline in Henry as he slides out.

With a nervous flutter in my stomach, I accept his hand. Am I?

"OKAY, THIS IS *INSANE*." Music thrums as we move deeper into the warehouse, my focus unsure where to settle. The space has been transformed into an upscale carnival, canopied by a big top tent, and everywhere I look, there's something extravagant to see. A pair of acrobats swing high above us. Ahead, a woman in a risqué red dress stands on a dais, juggling flaming torches. To our right, a female mime sits on a stool in lingerie while a half-dressed man with a dramatic, twirly mustache throws knives at a target directly behind her.

Throughout, cigar girls with tight black skirts and nothing but tassels to cover their nipples strut around with trays of shots.

"I think I know why you guys love this night so much." I give Henry a look that he's likely not able to decipher behind my mask.

His mouth may be the only thing I can see of his handsome face, but when he smiles, it's laced with mischief. He leans down to graze my earlobe with his lips. "And you *will* too."

A shiver slides down my spine. That sounded like both a threat and a promise.

Taking my hand, he leads me farther in, stopping a girl to get us each a shot of something black that tastes like licorice.

Whoever organized this party hasn't spared any expense. Stages that look like circus carts line the outer wall of the massive room. Some are dimly lit in anticipation of the coming act while others have carnival characters in racy outfits on display. A carnival games alley waits ahead, with small crowds and plenty of cheers. Beyond, a lit Fun House sign beckons.

"Where are the guys?"

"Somewhere in here." Henry doesn't seem too concerned as he guides me deeper in.

"How will you find them?" The guests all wear elaborate costumes, everything from mimes to acrobats to lion tamers. Clowns don't look like the typical red-nosed, floppy-shoed hobo version. These men are fit and shirtless, save for suspenders. Most masks are like mine—painted white with exaggerated pouts. It's impossible to tell anyone apart.

"We always seem to find each other." His lips twist. "And with Margo, trust me, you'll know when you see her."

Why am I not surprised? "You said the theme changes?"

"Yes. Last year it was Santa's Village."

I grin. "Who were you?"

"Who do you think? Mr. Claus, naturally."

"Of course." The circus ringmaster runs the circus; Mr. Claus is the boss of the North Pole. Henry always has to be in charge.

"Then there was the murder mystery year. I was the

detective. My favorite year so far has been the Roman Empire. They had a small coliseum, a bathhouse, a market ... It was wild."

"And which Caesar were you?"

"I was Spartacus."

"A gladiator?" I try to imagine Henry in a loincloth. "Are there pictures?"

"Absolutely not."

A carousel churns ahead, the oversized horses painted in iridescent colors and saddled with ornate seats. Several people ride, some individually, others as couples. "I haven't been on one of those in *forever*."

"We can try it later if you want. We have all night."

I watch the couple closest to us—a pair of jesters wearing fool's caps. The male leans back in the seat while the female is positioned over him. The way her hips are tilted ... "Are they—"

"Fucking? Yes."

My mouth drops. "That's allowed here?"

"There isn't much that *isn't* allowed here."

I feel my nose crinkle beneath the mask. "Do they have wipes to clean the horses?"

Henry laughs. "Come on." We veer toward the games alley with his arm curled around my back.

This part reminds me of Greenbank's summer festival, with energetic voices broadcasting scores and bells ringing to announce winners. Small crowds build around the stations, cheering people on.

A smile stretches across my face as I spot a familiar one. "Bucket ball!"

"I haven't played that in I don't even know how many years. Fifteen, maybe?" Henry murmurs.

"Last summer for me."

A female mime wearing a black-and-white-striped jacket, frilly skirt, and strategically positioned suspenders spots us observing her stand and beckons us over with frantic waves of her hands.

"Can we? Please?" I press my body against Henry's arm as I plead.

His blue eyes stare down at me from behind his mask. "Only if you agree to make it interesting."

"And what does that mean?"

"Highest points wins. Three points for the top basket."

"Okay. But, fair warning, I'm a pro. I *always* beat Jed." His girlfriend having better aim than him became a sore spot in our teenage years, in a small farming town where every boy played some form of ball. I had better aim than most of the other boys too.

"Anything involving Fuckface sets a low bar, but I'm game."

"Don't say I didn't warn you," I say in a singsong voice. "I still have this giant dog from when I was fourteen. It's two feet ..." My voice drifts as we get closer to the booth and I discover there aren't any stuffed animals hanging on hooks above. Dangling in their place are an array of dildos, vibrators, plugs, and things I can't identify.

My eyes are wide behind my mask.

"What was that you were saying about a two-foot dog?" Henry hums, pointing at an obscenely long dildo sitting on a display shelf.

"Where would anyone put that?" I exclaim, earning the game host's soundless laughter.

She bows theatrically and then explains the basic process through a series of gestures, pointing to the triangle of wicker baskets, six in total.

"We've got a bet going. Top basket is three points, second row two points, bottom row is one point." Henry taps his bracelet on a machine. "What does sinking all three balls win you?"

The mime points to the top row of elaborate toys.

"Perfect. Let's make this *really* interesting. Winner gets to choose a prize for the loser, and the loser has to use it here, tonight. Sound fair?"

"Of course! I see a plug up there with your name on it," I tease. That shot, coupled with drinks from earlier tonight, has given me some liquid courage.

"Which one?" he asks casually, unfazed.

"The little one with the silver end. I think that'll look good in you." Has Henry ever tried toys on himself? I should know that.

The mime makes a shocked *Oh* face as she sets out six balls on the counter.

Henry smirks but doesn't answer. "Alternating shots?"

"Why not."

He bows and waves his hand, and it's all the more dramatic in his ringmaster costume. "Ladies first."

Collecting a ball, I aim for the top, suddenly wishing I'd asked for a practice shot. It's been a year since I last played. But it's been fifteen for Henry.

The ball lands in the second row, right basket, circling once before settling.

"Two points for me," I declare.

The mime jumps up and down, ringing her bell twice.

Henry collects his ball and drops it in top basket with a graceful throw.

Our game host chimes the bell three times with exaggerated glee.

"I think that's three points to your two, right?" He says.

"Beginners' luck."

He smirks. "Your turn."

I have no choice but to target for the top basket now. I collect my ball, aim, and release with a gentle hand. It swirls several times before settling inside. "Total of five points," I call out as the bell rings. "Good luck getting the top one again."

"Did I ever mention that my high school basketball team won the state championship two years in a row?" Henry tosses his ball, and it lands as lightly as the first one did. "And I was the lead scorer?"

I gasp. "You hustled me!"

"No, you assumed I would be terrible at a carnival game, and I didn't correct you. Excuse me, is that the largest one you have?" he asks the mime, pointing to a strange rainbow-colored toy that reminds me of a unicorn horn.

I'm suddenly nervous. I could lose to Henry. Which of these toys will he make me use? Nothing I wouldn't enjoy, I trust, but I don't see how we could possibly use that anywhere here without attracting a lot of notice.

I get my third ball. "How did I not know you played basketball?"

"The same way I had no idea you've made an Olympic sport out of bucket ball," he counters. "Seriously, have you always been this competitive?"

Gritting my teeth as I concentrate, I aim for the top basket again. It loops inside once before rolling out and dropping down into a first-row bucket. The bell rings once.

"Sorry, what's the score now? I lost track," Henry taunts.

The mime gestures six and six.

"Right ... A tie, and you've used up all your shots. So, I

could put it in *any* of these baskets and win. Even the lowest." His mouth curves into a frown as he tosses with no effort. "Or I could just get another one of these."

For a third time, the ball lands in the top.

"How are you good at *everything*!" I squeal as the mime jumps around, clanging her bell to declare the winner.

With a dramatic bow, she points to the top row.

"What's your suggestion?" he asks her.

She holds up a finger as if to say "One moment" and reaches below the counter to pull out two silver clips.

"What are those?" I ask warily.

Without a hint of hesitation or shame, the mime peels off her suspenders and attaches the clips to her nipples.

I wince. She's a naughty mime.

"I don't think pain's her thing," Henry says.

The mime holds up another finger—she's having too much fun with this. Reaching below the counter again, she pulls out a giant fist-shaped dildo.

I gasp. "Don't you dare!"

He holds up his hands in surrender. "Okay, okay. Seeing as you were so interested in that one, we'll take it." He points to the silver plug.

My stomach stirs with nerves. "Yeah. For *you*, not me."

"I guess *you* should have won, then."

The mime—still wearing the clamps—uses a long metal rod with a hook at the end to retrieve a new one still in its box. She delivers it and a small bottle of lube with a bow, before waggling a finger between Henry and herself, then pointing toward the sign leading to the Fun House.

"Just the game, thanks. But maybe we'll see you there," Henry says pleasantly, leading me away.

"What was that about?" I ask.

"I think she was asking if she could fuck me in the Fun House."

My jaw drops. "Are you kidding me?" I spin around, ready to march back and throw a ball at her head. Or her clamped nipples.

Henry lassos me with an arm around my chest. "Relax, I'm joking. Sort of." He holds up the small package. "This is going to look so good in you—"

I elbow him in the ribs, earning his laugh before he pulls me in close.

I nestle against him as we move on. "You seem different tonight."

"How so?"

"I don't know. Playful. At ease."

"I don't get to be anonymous often. It's a nice change. I can do whatever I want here, and I don't have to worry about reporters or pictures. No one knows it's me. No one cares."

"I guess that's the case for everyone."

"Exactly. Which makes for an interesting night."

Every circus character imaginable surrounds us—magicians, ventriloquists, people dressed as trained animals—and it appears no one has spared any expense for their sophisticated costumes.

"Are there any famous people here? Like actors and singers?"

"I'm sure there are, but we'll never know unless they show us their face. That's the beauty of the rules."

Speaking of famous people ... Up ahead, a sleek female moves through the crowd, her curves visible beneath the sheer black material draped over her body. She's drawing attention from all angles.

"You were right." There's no mistaking Margo in her racy

fortune teller's costume, even with her gold mask. I've seen her naked enough times to recognize her pert breasts and long, svelte torso. The black thong she wears hides little. The tassels on her nipples, even less.

Joel—I assume—walks behind her, dressed as the strong man in a fitted dark red one-piece jumpsuit, the sleeveless top half artfully torn and open to show off his brawny torso. The shorts are tight, revealing runner's thighs and a prominent bulge that would be considered obscene at any other costume party. His mime mask has the added touch of a painted-on handlebar mustache.

"Don't you two look magnifique," she croons in her accent, stretching on her tiptoes to double-cheek kiss Henry as if she didn't just see him.

"How did you know it was us?" I ask.

"You are not hard to pick out." She twirls my red braid in her fingers. "Have you found the others yet?"

"No, but we just got here."

"Perfect timing. A show is about to start." She beckons us to follow.

"THEY'RE AMAZING." I lean back against Henry's chest as we watch two sets of acrobats twirl on aerial rings to sultry music, their outfits nothing more than a thick Lycra ribbon wrapped strategically around their sinewy bodies. The stage is in a structure that reminds me of a giant birdcage, separating the performers from the growing group of spectators.

"I've seen the ones on the left perform before," Margo whispers, peering up at the male and female couple. "They are exquisite."

"How can you tell they're the same people?" Their faces are elaborately painted.

A reserved smile touches her lips. "I just can."

Gasps sound as the performers twirl and the ribbons of material unravel, pooling on the mat below. From that point, the artistry of their performance changes drastically, with naked bodies contorting and stretching to bare revealing angles that tease the crowd.

"I took a few acrobatic classes," Margo muses as her favored couple positions themselves deliberately—the male sitting on the bottom of the ring while the woman curves her body until the apex of her thighs lines up with his mouth. He buries his face against her as his dick swells until it juts out for all to see.

She slides it down her throat, all the way to the base.

This *has* to be the most dangerous sixty-nine ever performed.

I steal a glance at the crowd around us, and while I can't see any faces, the parted lips and little smiles reveal an audience of voyeurs, no one having qualms about watching people have sex. Some are taking it a step further, their hands wandering into their partner's pants and up skirts.

"Some touching is fine, but if they want to keep it going, they have places for that," Henry whispers in my ear, noting my focus. "They don't want people fucking in the middle of the floor."

Just the way Henry says that word, his voice like gravel, stirs my blood.

The female couple is still twirling on their ring, but their bodies are now lined up in the center of it, their legs stretched out with toes braced on either side as they dangle from the top. They meet in a sensual kiss as their lower bodies grind against each other.

I peer over my shoulder at Henry, to see his focus riveted on the people above.

I remember the night I discovered that he liked to watch people have sex. We were at the club with Margo and Joel, and they started fucking in the private room. I was so upset with Henry at the time, assuming he still had a thing for Margo after their brief fling so long ago.

We've come a long way since then.

He breaks his attention to look down at me, and then he circles an arm around my waist and pulls me into his body, letting me feel his hard length against my back. "You're staring at me," he whispers, as his hand slides under my skirt, under the elastic band of the little black bottoms.

I tense—anyone watching will know what he's doing, even if my skirt hides it—but then I remember that no one other than Margo and Joel know who we are. And besides, *no one cares*. Why watch us when there's a live double sex show happening in the air above us at this precise moment?

I force myself to relax as two of Henry's fingers glide past my slit and into my slick entrance.

He leans down to whisper in my ear, "Watching them is making you wet."

I hum in agreement, parting my stance to give him better access.

But he slips his fingers out, earning my grunt of disappointment.

"Good. It'll make this easier." His hand is creeping under again. This time, something cool and hard grazes my flesh, and I realize instantly it's his bucket ball prize. My pulse kicks up a notch as he gently pushes the tip into my sex. At least he chose that spot.

"When did you get that out of the packaging?"

"While you were ogling Margo. I told you we'd use it tonight."

Yes, but I wasn't expecting it so soon. "Until when?"

"Until *I* decide to take it out." His teeth scrape across my earlobe, sending a tremble down my spine.

I turn and try to catch his lips with mine, but he pulls away before I can.

A man in a lion tamer's costume has moved in beside us that I hadn't noticed before, his red jacket parted to show off a smooth, muscular chest beneath. He wears black-and-white-striped pants, and a coiled black whip rests on his hip. His mime-like mask has claw marks painted across its cheek, complete with blood trickles.

He leans in. "I'll have you know, I've seen two *very sexy* bearded ladies so far."

My mouth drops. But of course, there's no way to hide from Merrick either. He chose our costumes. "This one is more my style."

Behind his mask, his blue eyes drop on my cleavage. "I'm glad you like it."

The couples have changed positions—and sexual acts.

"I'm bored." Merrick nudges Henry with his elbow. "I'll see you guys in the Fun House." With that, he strolls away.

"What's in the Fun House?" And, more importantly, what would interest Merrick more than this?

Henry smiles. "Lots of fun things."

"Such as?"

"You'll see when you get there."

I tap my foot with annoyance, my gaze drifting in the direction where Merrick just left. "What's the story with him?"

"No story."

"You said earlier there was a story."

"Really? *This* is happening"—he juts his chin toward the two women contorted at impossible angles, their mouths fixed between the other's legs—"and you'd rather talk about Merrick and me?"

"Yes." I spin around to press my chest against his, my arms tightening around him. The smooth silver toy he slid into me shifts with the movement. It feels somewhat awkward, but it's not intended to go there. "Because I'm completely obsessed with *you*, didn't you know that already?"

He leads me away from the crowd. "What do you want to know?"

"You said you two *didn't* hook up but ..." I let the question linger in the air.

"Things got a bit out of hand once," he admits.

I knew it. "And what exactly is 'out of hand' for you?" Because Henry's threshold for sexual acts would set fire to Reverend Enderbey's pulpit.

"We fucked a woman together."

"You've done that before." Several times, apparently, much to my chagrin.

"Not like that. Let's say it was a *really* tight fit."

My mouth makes an *Oh* shape as I picture that scenario. "You mean, like, the two of you, like ... *together*." I hold my index and middle finger in the air, pressed together. "*Not* like you and me and Ronan."

"Not like that night, no." Something unreadable flickers in Henry's eyes as he watches me closely. "I don't crave dick. Merrick sometimes does. I knew that and I pushed for it, anyway."

"He said you're hard to say no to."

That earns a chuckle. "I guess I was curious, and I trusted him not to take it farther than I was comfortable."

The mental image of Henry and Merrick touching so intimately has heat flooding my lower belly, but it's quickly doused by a different image, one of Henry with another woman. "Was it weird for you two after?"

"What? No. It's Mer." He frowns curiously. "And I might not crave dick, but that doesn't mean I didn't enjoy what we did."

"So ... He's bisexual."

"He's not interested in labels but, yeah, you could say that. I've seen him with mostly women, but he has hooked up with a couple men. He was in a relationship with one not that long ago. It was serious from what he told me."

"What happened?"

"It didn't work out." Henry pauses, his jaw tensing as he decides how much to tell me. "Merrick is one of my best friends. I trust him completely. But he grew up in a very different family from mine."

Given life in William Wolf's household wasn't warm and fuzzy, based on what Henry's told me, it doesn't say much for Merrick. This must have something to do with the conversation I overheard at the dinner table. Something about his name. "What do you mean—"

"Things you don't *ever* need to know or worry about," Henry cuts me off. "But in case you were wondering ... *no*."

I peer up at him, confused. "No, what?"

His index finger traces over my lip. "If you're having any little fantasies about me, you, and Merrick, get those thoughts out of that pretty little head of yours now. I mean it, Abbi."

My mouth hangs. "I don't! I didn't!"

He hums like he doesn't believe me. "I think I've created a monster."

"There you two are." Margo and Joel slink in. "We've seen enough. Ready to move on?"

"Lead the way." Henry slips his arm around me. He grins at Joel. "It looks like you already are. That costume doesn't allow for much discretion, does it?"

My mouth gapes at the tent in Joel's lower half.

Margo's musical laughter rings in the air. "When is he ever discreet?"

twelve

The Fun House in Greenbank was a simple structure made of plywood, fabric, and paint, with an endless loop of ominous laughter playing over a crackling speaker. People in costumes jumped out from behind black curtains to scare you, and then you stumbled through a mirror maze lined with smudged fingerprints until you surfaced on the other side. It was a few minutes of excitement and then it was over.

The moment we step through the sinister clown mouth entrance and into a long curtain-lined corridor lit by black light, I suspect this Fun House will be like nothing I've ever experienced before.

"It's easy to get lost in here. Stay close to me," Henry warns as we move deeper inside, as if I'm not gripping his hand tightly. Plenty of people mill, but it doesn't feel tight except in a few areas where small crowds form. A curtain draws open as we approach, illuminating a small room beyond a plexiglass window. A naked blond woman is strapped to a swinging contraption, bared to the audience, a black ribbon tied over the eye holes of her mask. She can't see us, but we can certainly see *all* of her.

The mime in suspenders from the bucket ball game paces, tapping her thigh with the handle of a black flog, her painted face screwed up as if considering what to do to this woman.

"What *is* this?" I whisper, feeling equal parts fascinated and awkward.

"Guests pay to be participants in these little window displays," Henry whispers. "Some of them are tamer than others."

I peer up at Henry with incredulity. "She *paid* for this?" To be stripped down and strung up?

Henry shrugs. "Everyone's got their thing, and no one knows who she is, so what does it matter?"

I guess, but ... "What will she do to her?"

"Whatever she wants to."

As if answering our question, the mime mouths, "I know!" and then slaps the woman's mound with the flog.

The woman's body jolts with the strike, and her yelp carries through the glass.

The mime grins as she continues her pacing around her subject, tracing the curves of the woman's body with the leather fronds. Each step is like that of a ballerina.

"So when she suggested fucking you in the Fun House, this is what she was hoping for?"

"Or something equally depraved."

The mime strikes the woman between her thighs again and this time her yelp morphs into a moan quickly after. And all around us, people watch with fascination.

But it's not the only crowd forming in this long corridor. "You know who would love this party?" I whisper.

"Don't say it—"

"Connor and Ronan." They would lose their minds over a place like this.

"It's too bad you can't tell them anything about what you see here. *Ever.*" I hear the sharp warning in his voice. "Come on, let's see what else there is."

There is plenty to see, and as wanton and graphic as some scenes are, I find myself unable to look away. People come to this party once a year so they can participate in this? It's like some sort of underground sex house for the obscenely rich.

In one, a woman is strapped into a chair, her legs spread wide as a mime brings her to the edge of an orgasm with a vibrator before pulling away, over and over again. In another, a man is trapped in a pillory that lowly revolves on a platform, giving us a three-hundred-and-sixty-degree view as a mime whips and paddles him.

Not all displays are with people being sexually tortured by mimes in playful costumes, though. We come to three in a row with couples having sex in various positions—on beds, on chairs, standing near the glass. They don't seem to pay any attention to the audience.

I don't think I'd have the nerve to do that, nor do I feel any urge to. And yet I can't deny that watching these attractive bodies convulse and listening to their cries of ecstasy stirs something inside me, especially behind the anonymity of this mask.

"How many of these booths are there?" I ask as we pass a window with its curtain drawn. They're preparing for the next participant.

"A lot." He points ahead to where the tunnel webs off in other directions. "And they'll be occupied *all* night long."

A curtain pulls open just as we reach it, revealing a naked woman on her knees, bound in ropes, her hands tied behind her, clamps affixed to her nipples. A mask covers her face, save for her lips, painted a bright red.

A fit, naked masked man strolls up to her, stroking his remarkable length as he approaches. "Open," I hear him command and she does.

Fisting the back of her blond head, he jams his cock into her mouth, forcing her all the way down on him. He only relents when she gags, releasing his tight grip on her hair. She leaves a red ring of lipstick on his veiny flesh as she pulls back for a reprieve. It only lasts a few seconds before he makes her swallow him whole again.

"She's going to choke on him," I mutter.

"From what I hear, it's her thing."

From what he hears? But that would mean Henry knows her. I examine the man's mouth, his hair—rich brown hair tied back in a small ponytail. And gasp. "Is that—"

"No names here," Henry chides. "But yes."

Which means the woman with Warner's dick down her throat is Tatiana. The lipstick certainly matches.

"Maybe *this* is why she didn't eat anything tonight." She didn't want to puke up a seven-course meal.

Henry snorts.

Warner leans down to whisper something in her ear, his hand slipping between her legs to stroke her clit. She answers with a simple "yes," which earns his wicked smile.

They fall into a brutal, depraved pattern of Warner thrusting into her waiting mouth, only pulling away for brief moments when she makes a strangled sound, until Tatiana's face is red and spit dribbles out of her mouth. I'm sure her pristine makeup that she fussed with all night is now streaked beneath that mask.

I don't understand how Tatiana could enjoy this, but who am I to judge.

"This isn't *our* kind of thing," Henry whispers as if reading my mind. He kisses my temple and then leads me away.

Everywhere I look, people are having sex or watching sex. This event is drenched in it. I know who my future husband is. No wonder he never misses it. But it stirs questions. "Have you ever been in one of those rooms?"

"Yes."

"How many times?"

"Every time." He didn't hesitate to answer.

My stomach swirls as I try to picture that. I knew Henry enjoyed watching. I didn't think he'd be so eager to perform. Maybe there *is* a video waiting to be leaked. "And what happened?"

He looks at me and I don't have to see his face to know his eyebrows are arched in a "What the fuck do you think happened, Abigail?" way.

"Was it something like that?" I point to a man in the window, bent over as a mime pegs him.

Henry stifles his laughter. "What impression have I ever given that I would be into *that*?" He pulls me away by my hand. "I don't enjoy giving up control."

"You don't say." Henry Wolf *is* control. It could be a slogan.

I get a playful swat against my ass and a soft "brat" in response.

"Fine, then what?"

"I'll show you." It seems quieter along this hall, though the crowd is plentiful. We pass by half a dozen more displays, most with couples having sex, some of women in chairs, masturbating for an audience. "Mostly this." Henry points out as we pass a cluster of threesomes. He stops at a window with five people—two men and three women—on an enormous bed. "Once, like this."

My jaw hangs as I watch two women take turns sucking off a man while the third is on her hands and knees, allowing the other man to drive into her from behind, his fist gripping her blond ponytail.

She adjusts her arms for support and reveals a tattoo on the inside of her wrist, of three intertwined hearts.

My jaw drops. That's Kendra. But the man having sex with her is not Preston. I focus on the other man, his long torso defined but on the slender side. He grabs hold of both women's heads and holds them close to his cock as he tips his head back and lets out a loud, guttural moan. Streams of cum shoot out of him, hitting the women's lips, streaking over their masks.

That is Preston.

Did Kendra know what she signed up for when he brought her to New York? I mean, she certainly seems to be enjoying sex with a masked stranger. But is this why she was eyeing Henry so fiercely over dinner? Did she expect him to be joining them in one of these displays?

No wonder Henry disapproved of Preston inviting a coworker to this party. But what could she divulge about the big boss without outing herself? Sex parties and orgies isn't typical water cooler conversation.

Henry's dark chuckle curls in my ear. "This should not be a surprise."

"It's not. I just ..." Henry hasn't given me detailed specifics about every encounter he's ever had, but I know his tastes are risqué. He's been with multiple women before, several times.

But watching this now, and imagining Henry as one of *these* men, in this tawdry annual event he never misses, where he can do *whatever* he wants, with whomever he wants ...

He uses these rooms *every* time he comes here. He admitted it.

So what does that mean for tonight?

Just the thought of another woman with her hands—and other parts—on him like *this* makes my fists clench and my eyes blur with rage. Especially when he's declared that no one will be touching *me*.

"What's bothering you?" He asks suddenly. I've never been good at hiding my feelings from him.

I look around at the crowd of strangers watching the spectacle. "You're not going to make me do this tonight, are you?" I whisper. Or at all, for that matter.

The muscle in his jaw ticks. Grabbing my hand, he leads me at a quick pace down the hall and around a corner, this foreign object teasing my core with each hurried step.

It's different here—still dark and swathed in curtains, but there are closed doors and no viewing windows. A mime in a revealing French maid's outfit skips along the path with a spray bottle in her gloved hands. When she sees us, she blows a kiss. Even the cleaning staff is in character, and they're *all* naughty.

Henry stops at the first door with a glowing light above it, swipes his bracelet across a scanner, and then pulls me inside, shutting the door behind us.

"What is this?" A tiny stall—no more than five by five. It reminds me of a change room, except there aren't any hooks or chairs, nothing save for a small receptacle mounted to the wall for trash.

"Take off your mask," he demands, sliding out of his. The steady pulse of music from outside is muffled, allowing for easy conversation.

I follow his orders. As much as I appreciate the anonymity, the air on my skin feels good.

He sighs heavily.

Why do I feel like I'm about to be scolded?

"First of all, I've never *made* you do anything, have I? I've never *forced* you?"

"No, but—"

"And you've enjoyed everything that I knew you would enjoy, right?"

"Yes. But I—"

"Okay, good. I'm glad we have that out of the way. Listen to me very carefully, Abigail." Henry's tone is cool and calm. "When I said I'm not sharing you with anyone like I did that night with Ronan, I mean that *no one is ever laying a fucking hand on you ever again*. Is that clear?"

I swallow. "Yes."

"So that spectacle back there? Having someone else's cock inside you? You don't have to worry about me asking you for that because it's not happening. *Ever.*"

I hesitate. "And what about you?"

"*Me*? I plan on spending an excessive amount of time inside you. Every day for the rest of my life, if it's up to me—"

"No, that's not what I mean." I giggle, even as his words fan a wave of heat through the lower half of my body. "You're in those rooms every year you come here. You said so yourself."

"Every *other* year, yes. You weren't in my life then."

I falter. Okay, that's somewhat of a declaration, but it still doesn't ease my worries. "What about next year or the year after? What if you decide that's something *you want* to do again?" What if, as Merrick so bluntly declared earlier, he's bored? Why have one woman when he can have three? "I've never seen you so giddy. You've been like a kid in a candy store all night here. You're telling me you're just going to give up this lifestyle and not have regrets?"

He purses his lips, and I don't know what is going on in his head, but I'm equal parts afraid to hear it and dying to know. When he finally meets my gaze, his blue eyes are piercing. "You still don't get it, do you?" A strange look fills his face. "You have commanded my attention without pause since that interview video. I lied and manipulated to get you to Alaska as my assistant, I risked my entire future because I couldn't stay away from you, I came back even after you shattered my heart."

Henry's never been so direct about how much my mistake hurt him this past summer.

"I feel like I'm on a fucking leash, and I don't even care. There isn't a woman out there who has ever tethered me like this." His voice turns gruff. "You *own* me, Abbi. Everything that I have and am is *yours*, and that will never change. That, I can promise you."

I fold into his body, pressing my cheek against his chest to feel the steady hammer of his heartbeat. "I love you so much. I'm terrified that I won't always be enough for you." As soon as I admit the words out loud, I accept how potent my fear still is, despite the ring on my finger, despite our conversations about this in the past.

"That's not possible."

"How do you know?"

He wraps me in his arms. "Because I've already had everything else, and none of it feels a fraction as good as you do."

I sink into his warmth, reveling in it. I know what he means, the latter part, anyway. But will *I* ever feel like enough for him?

"Do you want to leave?"

"No. I *am* having fun."

"Good. Because my favorite part is ahead." He slides down his mask.

"Which part is that?" I would much rather stay in this little stall.

He grips my jaw between his thumb and forefingers and leans down to capture my lips in his. A whimper escapes me and he deepens the kiss, forcing my mouth open wide to make room for his tongue.

My hands smooth over his hard chest, reveling in his curves as I slide my palms downward, aiming for his belt buckle.

Just as quickly, he pulls away, stopping my fingers from their goal. "The part where I prove how I could never be bored with you."

I slide my mask on and follow him out, my pulse racing.

"I GOT LOST in a House of Mirrors when I was nine," I admit as we ease along the corridor of reflections. The maze is draped in tulle and illuminated by red lights, and I'm already confused which direction to go. "I was convinced I was going to die there." Jed didn't help any either, running off to ride the Gravitron.

"You obviously found your way out." Henry leads, one hand gripping mine.

"My father came and got me. I was sitting on the floor, bawling. After, he walked me around the structure outside and showed me how small it was, that they'd never lose me in there."

"This one is big, with a lot of dead ends, so you better stay close." He squeezes my hand.

"I'm also not nine anymore."

"No, you certainly aren't." He stalls a moment to regard our reflection—one of a hundred.

"We look good together." I'll admit, I've never had so much fun dressing up for Halloween.

"We do." He leans forward to plant a sweet kiss on my lips.

I jump as I feel his fingers prodding the metal base of the toy through my bottoms. The dull, needy throb between my legs is growing more difficult to ignore.

"And how's that feeling?"

"Barely notice it." I lie.

"Really?" His mouth is inches from mine as he slips his index finger under the seam.

I roll my hips against his hand.

With a knowing grin, he slips his fingers away, and then continues.

We round a corner and find ourselves facing Margo, Joel, and Merrick.

"Dead end," Merrick announces, gesturing the way they came.

"We came from there," Henry points behind us.

"Then we must go this way." Joel points in another direction.

And bumps into a mirror.

"Okay, *this* way," he corrects, moving forward cautiously.

After what feels like a dozen wrong turns, frustration is growing.

"How big did you say this maze was again?" My feet are aching from these heels.

"Not *this* big," Henry mutters. "I don't remember it being *this* complicated either."

"For fuck's sake." Merrick laughs as he leads us to another dead end. "But look, they left us a chair this time." Sure enough, a simple wooden chair painted in shiny black lacquer sits in a corner.

"Oh, thank God." I park myself onto it. "Can I please have five minutes? These shoes were the worst decision ever."

"Yes, but only if you share." Henry has me off the seat and sitting in his lap before I know what's going on, pulling me backward and against his chest. The move stirs an acute reminder of the silver toy. "Take them off."

"Happily." I kick off my shoes, letting them fall to the black floor.

He lifts one of my stockinged feet and rubs the center with his thumb, drawing circles.

I whimper with relief. If the House of Mirrors is Henry's favorite part, I'm happy to say we've seen it and I'm ready to go home now.

Merrick leans against one mirrored wall, his arms folded across his chest, watching us. "Didn't we get lost in here for half an hour last year?"

"Yes, and you swore you were done with the maze, so why are you here again?" Henry grins.

"Because *I* asked him to," Margo purrs, trailing her index finger down the center of his bare chest, bypassing a red kiss mark someone planted above his nipple.

Was Merrick in one of the display boxes already tonight?

He smiles at Margo, and I can imagine the dimples hiding behind that mask. "So it's your fault, then."

"It is all my fault. Let Abbi rest her poor feet and I can make it up to you." She presses her lips against his as her hand settles between them, shamelessly cupping him while her boyfriend stands only two feet away. In her sheer black dress and thong, she may as well be naked.

I avert my gaze, feeling my cheeks flush, but we're in a House of Mirrors and there is nowhere I can look without watching their tongues dance and Margo's palm rubbing against Merrick's erection.

Beneath me, Henry's cock hardens. "Watch them," he whispers, leaning in to catch my earlobe with his teeth. "I know you want to."

Margo fumbles with the waistband of Merrick's striped pants, unfastening and pushing them down his thighs. She drops to her knees, giving us all a good look at his carved body and very impressive, hard length.

My lips part with a sharp inhale as she drags her tongue over him, from root to tip, and I somehow feel it at my core.

Merrick's head falls back, his fingers seizing her shiny black bob. He guides her forward until she's swallowing him. They fall into a rhythm—nothing like the punishing one that Warner subjected Tatiana to—and the soft hums and sucking sounds escaping them have my heartbeat sprinting.

There's no need to wonder if Joel is okay with watching his girlfriend give another man a blow job—thanks to his costume, we can see just how much he's enjoying the view.

"What if someone comes here?" I whisper.

"What if they do?" Henry repositions me so I'm facing them, my back flush against his chest, my legs dangling over his knees, not touching the floor. His cock presses against that round metal base, the pressure an odd mix of uncomfortable and erotic.

Margo pauses long enough to give a command in French.

Joel tugs his costume down past his hips and moves closer. Margo reaches up to stroke his swollen length, her mouth never leaving Merrick.

Henry's grip on my hips tightens, his breathing in my ear shallow as he watches Margo pleasure two other men.

I grind against his lap, as much for his benefit as for mine.

With a groan, his fingers dig into my flesh.

I roll my hips again, and the silver plug rolls inside me in a delightful way.

"You like watching him fuck her mouth," he murmurs in my ear.

It's not a question, and yet I nod.

"How much?" He slips his hand beneath my little skirt and between my legs, sliding his fingers under the elastic band of my bottoms. His thumb circles around my clit as he glides his fingers around my entrance, sliding in next to the plug. I know what he's going to find—my body soaked.

I part my legs a touch to give him better access.

He inhales sharply. "I thought so."

It's dark under the red light and Merrick's mask hides all, and yet I sense his eyes on us—on where my skirt hides Henry's illicit touch. It doesn't bother me that he's watching, though. In fact, the thought that a man like him might watch Henry and me together—might enjoy it—makes my heart pound harder.

I open my thighs more, even as I tremble with nervous excitement.

Henry's hands move, grabbing hold of the elastic waistband of my bottoms. He tugs and shimmies them off, pushing them past my knees. They fall to the floor, and he guides my thighs to hang over each side of his lap, spreading me wide. My little skirt still covers me but barely, riding high enough to reveal the garter belt clips. His hand is back beneath my skirt in seconds, seizing the round handle of the plug. Ever so slowly, he pulls it out before running it through my slit. A glimmer of silver catches in the countless mirrors before it disappears inside me again.

Over and over again, Henry teases me with the toy and we watch as Margo deep-throats Merrick and strokes Joel. There isn't an angle in here where everyone can't watch what everyone else is doing.

There's no denying that I'm enjoying this show. The plug glides easily over my slick flesh now, slipping in and out with no effort.

A worry flitters through my mind—of strangers coming around the corner and discovering this depravity—but it's fleeting. The only people who can identify me are directly in front of me, and none of them will be fazed by anything Henry and I do. With that in mind, I let my body relax against him.

My skirt rides up, enough that it no longer hides anything.

Merrick curses and the reaction stirs a tingling at the base of my spine.

Margo releases her grip on Joel and demands something in French, and Joel drops to his knees next to her, facing Merrick.

A soft gasp escapes me as they both lean in, their tongues tangling over Merrick's tip as they kiss, lapping at it in between the strokes they share.

"Fuck." Merrick's head falls back, his Adam's apple a sharp jut along a deliciously thick neck.

The teasing lasts another ten seconds and then Joel slides his mouth down, taking Merrick in.

"Oh my God," I hiss, enthralled by the performance.

Merrick grasps the back of Joel's head and guides him up and down a few times before pulling him away with a fist of hair and silently commanding Margo to take over. Back and forth, the two take turns pleasuring Merrick as Henry teases me mercilessly with this toy.

I've never seen anything like this before. Maybe it's because Joel and Merrick are both attractive on their own or because they don't seem to have sexual hang-ups, or maybe it's because we're all wearing masks and under red lights surrounded by mirrors, but a strange electricity ignites every sense inside me. I feel like I'm about to explode. All rational thoughts vanish.

I roll my hips against Henry's hand as I drift into that place of lost inhibitions, my skirt riding higher until it's bunched at my waist. Suddenly, the ache to have Henry inside me is too much. I grind my ass into his lap.

"Fuck, Abbi," he growls.

"No names, remember?" I scold softly.

His free hand slides down my Lycra top, beneath my bra, to fill with my breast, collecting my pebbled nipple between his fingertips.

I don't know how we ended up in this situation and yet now that we're here, there's only one way I want it to end. I reach between us to fumble with his belt and zipper, blindly unfastening them until I can fist his cock through his briefs.

The metal plug clangs against the floor, cast aside as Henry wrestles his pants down his thighs and yanks my body back. I cry out as he sinks into me with a single thrust and then brace my palms on his knees as I ride him, feeling heaviness grow in my belly as he fills me over and over again, hitting that spot deep inside.

He peels the top of my costume down and unfastens my

bra. Cool air caresses my breasts as they're displayed for countless reflections around us.

Merrick's head tips back with a cry as he unloads into Joel's mouth. The moment doesn't last long before he pushes Joel off his dick. "Finish him," he orders. Without missing a beat, Joel stands and Margo takes him in her mouth. Meanwhile, Merrick's attention is riveted to Henry and me, his semi-hard length hanging.

"Do you like his eyes on you?" Henry growls into my ear.

I hesitate.

"Don't lie to me." His teeth scrape against my skin. "And before you answer that, know that it doesn't bother me. I like his eyes on us too."

"Yes," I admit breathlessly after a moment.

He kisses the back of my neck and I feel his lips in every nerve of my body. "Do you trust that I know what you'll like?"

"Always. You know I do."

"Good." Hooking his arms around the backs of my thighs, he pulls my legs back, locking me into a position I can't get out of, making me entirely defenceless. The lewd reflection in countless mirrors has heat flooding to my core, as Henry angles his hips. His hard length slides in and out of my sex, and there's nothing I can do but watch.

Merrick drops to his knees in front of our chair, reaching over to move my skirt.

"Don't touch her," Henry warns in a growl.

"I won't," Merrick promises. "Fuck, but I want to. Those tits are spectacular."

Merrick doesn't need to touch me, though. Just the feel of that intense gaze settled where Henry and I are joined is making my cheeks burn under my mask and my body react. I don't know which one of us he's more interested in, and the longer he kneels there, watching, the less that question matters.

"She's perfect," he whispers through pants, answering my unspoken question and stirring a heightened wave of arousal.

I no longer care that I'm half-naked in a semi-public place where anyone could enter, that Henry is fucking me in front of three people. *Friends*, not people.

I glance down to see Merrick languidly stroking himself with one hand, while his other has settled on Henry's bare thigh, gripping his muscle just above where his pants are pushed down to. His breathing is heavy.

The mental image Henry painted for me earlier—of these two beautiful men pleasuring a woman *together*—crashes into my mind like an avalanche, consuming all other thoughts. Henry may not crave dick as he so eloquently put it, but he knows Merrick does and he's not shying away, not growling at him to remove his hands. Henry likes testing his own boundaries.

He also likes testing mine.

I've never tested his.

"Can he touch you?" I hear myself ask in a whisper and, I swear, behind that lion tamer's mask, I see a glint flash in Merrick's blue eyes—of shock or excitement, I can't tell.

Henry's hips slow, lose their rhythm. "Is that what *you* want to see?" he asks with ragged breaths. He's close to coming.

I hesitate. "Just once." Just like I agreed to that time in the grotto with Margo, even though I don't crave women.

I want to know that Henry will bend for me as readily as I bend for him.

"Fuck," he curses, then swallows hard. "Just this once. And only because it's him."

I bite back the smile of victory. Henry's trying something he's never done before—a seemingly impossible feat given his sexual experiences—and he's not doing it for himself, he's doing it because I asked him to.

"You sure?" Merrick asks, his hand still on Henry's thigh.

"Make it worthwhile," Henry growls.

A sexy smirk curls the lion tamer's lips. "You know I will." Merrick fishes out something from the pocket of his sagging pants, tearing off the plastic seal with his teeth in one expert bite. It's a bottle of lube like the one the naughty mime gave Henry.

I watch in the myriad of reflections as he coats his fingers with the clear liquid, tosses the empty container, and then reaches forward to rub the spot behind Henry's balls.

Henry's breath hitches and I hold my breath, wondering how he'll react.

His hips pick up their rhythm again and he slips in and out of me.

Merrick's crooked smirk is intoxicating as he edges forward, his hip fitting in between Henry's parted knees. "Stop for a minute," he demands, his deep voice like honey.

Henry complies and Merrick's muscular arm flexes as he hooks it around one of Henry's legs and lifts. He slides his slick fingers farther back. "Not the best angle, but I can make it work," Merrick murmurs.

Henry grunts, and I realize Merrick's aim—which I should have when I asked for this. My skin ignites over my entire body and I can hardly breathe. Has Henry ever allowed anything like that?

"Relax for me," Merrick coaxes, his voice gravelly, and I frantically search the reflections for one that shows me the explicit scene. Unfortunately, it's blocked by Merrick's bare ass, so I lean forward, straining to see from this award angle.

"That's my girl." Henry chuckles. "I can't believe you talked me into this."

I barely notice the couple behind us—Margo's wet mouth making obscene noises as she pleasures Joel—as Merrick slowly works a finger past the tight ring and into his friend at my bidding.

Henry moans as Merrick adds a second finger, following the same painstakingly slow process until Henry's body accepts him.

"You good?" Merrick asks, his eyes locked on Henry.

Henry inhales sharply and then answers with a gruff "Yeah. I'm ready."

Merrick lowers Henry's thigh to the floor.

Henry's hips start rocking again, cautiously at first, adjusting to the intrusion. But it's not long before, with a soft groan and a curse, he finally picks up the tempo.

Merrick's muscular frame remains sandwiched between Henry's thighs, so close to where we're joined, his free hand resting on Henry's thigh. He doesn't relent, his lips parted as he holds his position, meeting every thrust of Henry's with his own as Henry comes down on his friend's hand. Soon, Henry's soft moans are timed with it as well.

"He's enjoying this, I promise," Merrick whispers, his breathing shallow as he settles on his haunches and watches. "And so are you. Fuck, you are so wet." He licks his lower lip, looking seconds away from leaning in to join in with his mouth.

I wouldn't mind that in this heated moment, even if his aim isn't for me. Just imagining his tongue on both of us …

Henry picks up speed and I lose control. With a high-pitched cry, I arch my back and let my climax overtake me, my body trembling as my sex spasms around Henry's length for what feels like an eternity, the sensation overwhelming.

Henry follows with a desperate sound that I don't recall ever hearing from him before, his hips jerking erratically as he throbs and shudders inside me. He's holding me against him so tightly, every muscle in his body seems to be constricting. I'm sure my skin will be marred by bruises tomorrow.

Merrick's throaty moans trail ours, and when I come down off my high, he's bowed forward, his shoulders heaving as he strokes out another orgasm.

"Holy fuck." Henry releases my legs and pulls down my skirt to cover me from view. "I *have* created a monster," he whispers against my ear.

I twist in his lap to meet his lips with mine. "Are you okay? You're not mad at me?" I can't read anything behind that stupid mask.

He chuckles through ragged breaths. "I'm fine."

I hesitate. "Did you enjoy that?"

"You made it hard not to."

I frown, unsure what that means. I open my mouth to ask when he cuts me off with another kiss. "But if you ever ask me for *that* again, expect Margo's tongue in your pussy immediately after because that is something *I* really enjoyed."

"One and done. Got it." I guess that's fair.

Merrick has already slipped his fingers out of Henry. He collects my black panties from the floor and wipes his slick hands on them.

"Hey!"

He grins. "Sorry, but I need these more than you do."

"You think you can get those shoes back on?" Henry whispers, handing me my bra.

"As long as we're heading home now." Between the

stilettos and the lack of anything under my short skirt, I'm ready to call it a night.

"Deal." He shifts me off his lap so he can pull up his pants. I fix my costume.

I was so wrapped up in us that I didn't notice Joel finish.

Margo pouts as she watches us all dress. "But what about me?"

Joel says something in French that seems to appease her.

"This way?" Merrick points and heads the way we came, giving Henry's shoulder a friendly pat on his way past. As if nothing that just happened was out of the ordinary.

Henry stoops to collect the silver toy off the floor, slipping it into his pocket. Leaning down to kiss my temple, he whispers in my ear, "And you think I'll get bored?"

thirteen

enry curses as the phone rings for a third time.

"It could be important."

"It fucking better be," he growls into his pillow. "It's ten a.m. on a Sunday."

A dull throb aches in my temples from the mix of hard liquor and wine. "Answer it and make them go away."

Henry paws at his nightstand for his phone. He answers with a groggy "Yeah."

I crack an eyelid and admire his muscular body as he lies on his stomach, my mind drifting to last night, to how he always pushes my boundaries.

And how I always let him. Happily.

After a few moments of listening to whoever's on the other end, Henry rolls and sits at the edge of the bed, his demeanor changing instantly. "When?"

Something is wrong.

My exhaustion evaporates as I sit up and listen, trying to guess what this could be about. His father and Scott are gone, and he holds nothing but loathing for his mother. Did something happen to one of the guys last night? We left on our own. I don't know how late they stayed. My stomach clenches with the very thought. He would be devastated.

But Henry's giving me no clues as to what this is about.

"And what was the issue with that?" he asks, his tone softer.

I slide closer and smooth my hands over his back as he listens.

"As far as I know, she hasn't. Security would call me if she showed up here again."

Violet. This must be about her. I'll bet that's Howard and Gayle calling. She must have run away again.

"She hasn't been gone long enough for the police to do anything ... Yes ... Please keep me updated, and if I hear anything, I will do the same." He ends the call and chucks his phone.

"What happened?" I ask gently.

Henry rubs the bridge of his nose. "They're getting Audrey's house ready to sell and the real estate agent came by yesterday with an offer, even though it's not listed yet. Violet took issue with it and stormed off to her room. When Gayle went to check on her last night, she was gone. Crawled out the window. They called her friends, and she didn't go there."

"What about her old house?"

He shakes his head. "She's not answering her phone either."

"That kid ..." I snuck out of the house a handful of times, but it was to meet Jed at midnight to swim in the pond between our properties and I was always back within half an hour.

"They thought maybe she came here. But considering how we left things, I can't see why she would."

Unless she came to New York and is working up the

nerve to face her father again. *Especially* after how they left things. A thought strikes me. "When she came to Manhattan last time, she hung out at a diner that she and Audrey had been to in the past. I'll bet she'd go there."

"A diner." He gives me a flat look. "This is New York City, Abbi. Not Greenbank, where there's one diner and it's owned by your aunt."

"She said it was near the train station, and I remember the logo on the coffee cup she was carrying. It had a monster on it. Howard did say she loves New York, and we already know she's not afraid to come here alone. If I were a confused and angry fifteen-year-old girl, I'd go somewhere that makes me happy and that I'm familiar with while I figured out what to do next."

He hangs his head, pushing his hands through his hair, sending it into further disarray. "A diner with a monster on its logo?"

"Yeah. It was red and blue. Cute. It wouldn't be too hard to find."

Henry bites his bottom lip in thought. "You feel like going for a walk?"

Five minutes ago, I planned on staying under these blankets. But for Henry? I press a kiss against his shoulder. "Yes."

My HANDS ARE TURNING red as I grip the collar of my fall jacket in a pointless attempt to keep the frigid breeze from reaching inside. "How does the weather always know to turn right after Halloween?" My winter things are still in Greenbank, and I have no plans to visit anytime soon given how Mama has been behaving. I guess I'll need to shop for a few staples, beginning with a scarf and mittens.

Beside me, Henry strolls with purpose, seemingly unbothered by the chill. We may have rolled out of bed fifteen minutes ago, but unlike me with my unkempt hair and cobbled outfit, he looks perfectly put together in black pants and a charcoal sweater, a camel-colored peacoat thrown over top. There's no hint of the playful ringmaster who dragged out a mind-bending orgasm from me in the House of Mirrors last night.

It took all of two minutes to find the address for Breakers, the twenty-four-hour diner three blocks away from the station. "Have you thought about what you're going to say if she's here?" I ask.

"Yeah. How about 'Stop fucking running away. Are you trying to kill your grandparents?'"

By his stern tone, I can't tell if he's joking. "Okay, but for real."

His answering stare confirms he is not joking.

"You know you can't say that to her."

"Why not? It's true. She needs to stop running away and she *is* going to kill them with worry if she keeps this up. You should have heard Howard on the phone. She's being a selfish brat."

"Maybe. But she's also being a girl who just lost her mother, then found out some rather disturbing things about her, which led to finding you. As difficult as this was for you to handle learning, imagine how much harder it is for her. And if she did come back here, then she's likely looking for more answers, or a connection, or ... *something.*"

"She's not going to get *anything* from me behaving like this." But he frowns as he seems to process my words.

I leave him to his thoughts as we walk another block in silence, following my phone's directions to the diner on the corner. "This is the address." The exterior is painted black and a neon sign above reads Breakers with a little monster holding pancakes on his fork. "And it's definitely where she came last time." It's a busy area, with cars crawling along the street and pedestrians rushing by.

Henry holds the front door, waiting for me. I step into the warmth, inhaling the delicious scents of brewing coffee and frying bacon. It's a simple and clean place with a mix of brown leather-wrapped booths and white tables, the sections divided by half walls. Glass globe lights dangle to cast a warm glow. Several TVs are mounted on a back wall clad with white subway tile, the screens playing football highlights ahead of the day's games.

I nudge Henry and point to the dark-haired girl sitting by herself at a booth by the window. "That's her." I recognize her profile immediately.

Henry moves to charge forward.

I grab his forearm. "Maybe give her grandparents a call first so they can stop worrying?" And so Henry has a moment to collect his calm.

His jaw tenses but he doesn't argue, retrieving his phone from his pocket. He hits redial on Howard and Gayle's home number. "Hi, it's Henry. We found her and she's safe ... yes ... yes ... I'll let you know." He ends the call.

"She came here for a reason," I remind him, giving his arm an affectionate squeeze, but also one of warning. And I have a sneaking suspicion that reason is him. "*Listening* first might work better."

His chest rises with a deep breath but when he heads for her this time, he doesn't look like a charging bull. "Mind if we join you?"

His voice is calm but Violet jumps, anyway, her wide eyes darting from Henry to me, and back again. "How did you find me?"

He takes that as acceptance, gesturing at the opposite bench. I slide in, and Henry sinks in beside me, his thigh pressed against mine. The booth isn't meant for more than two people, but we can make it work. At least this allows him to face his daughter.

I hold my breath, equal parts curious and dreading how this exchange will go. I can't see Henry handling teenage rebellion well.

"So what? You're so rich, you have someone following me?" she mutters, the initial surprise at seeing us fading quickly, replaced by snarky armor. She jabs at a pancake with her fork. Based on the countless holes through them, she's been at this for a while.

Henry stalls for several seconds before answering coolly, "Yes. A robotic eye that tells me everywhere you go."

"I haven't seen it." *Stab, stab, stab.*

"That's because it's invisible. And it flies."

She matches his stony expression. "An invisible flying robotic eye. That's creepy."

"So is you suggesting that I've paid someone to spy on you," he retorts, with more than a hint of annoyance.

Violet's lips twitch. If I didn't know better, I'd think she was suppressing a smile.

"Your grandparents called me this morning, looking for you. They're beside themselves with worry."

She tugs at her collar, but she doesn't respond.

"You can't take off like that and you definitely can't take a train to New York City whenever you damn well please. You're fifteen."

"And remind me, what were *you* doing at fifteen?" Her beautiful blue eyes—the same color as his, though not the same shape—flash with challenge.

He grinds his teeth, and I'm afraid of what will come out of his mouth next.

I smooth a hand over Henry's thigh beneath the table. "They told us about your house going up for sale," I cut in, hoping to steer the conversation back to safety. "That's the house you've grown up in, right?"

After a beat, Violet nods.

"It must be hard for you to have to give it up."

"It's not like I didn't know it was coming." She goes back to her pancake stabbing.

"But you were still upset when the agent came by."

"You mean *Barbara*?" She scowls. "Some friend."

"The real estate agent was Audrey's friend?" Henry asks, calm again.

Violet hesitates, as if deciding whether she wants to acknowledge his question at all. "Her best friend. Back when things started to go downhill for my mom, Barbara offered to sell the house when the time came." She focuses on a strip of crispy bacon, twirling it this way and that between her fingertips. It looks like she's touched—or stabbed—everything on her plate, but I don't think she's eaten any of it.

"Well, isn't this snug." A waitress with round cheeks sidles up next to our table. "Can I get you something?"

"Coffee, please. One black, one with cream and sugar," Henry orders for me.

"Coming right up, cutie pie." She winks at Henry and strolls away, her hips swinging.

"Cutie pie?" I echo, unable to hold my grin. Henry's been called a lot of things. Anything referencing *cute* is not one of them.

He spares an eye roll for me before returning to the conversation. "Selling the house fast is a good idea. It makes it easier for your grandparents, who are dealing with a teenager who likes to sneak out and cause them stress they don't need at their age. They're in their eighties, Violet." There's that hint of a scolding tone, but not the exasperated one he's used with me. No, this one reminds me of the time Daddy literally caught me with my hand in the cookie jar before dinner, a fistful of chocolate chip cookies in my grasp.

Henry sounds almost ... fatherly.

Violet averts her gaze. At least she's showing some guilt for what she's put them through.

Henry sighs. "Houses cost money to maintain. The longer you guys hold on to it, the more Audrey's estate must pay out in costs. Utility bills, taxes, that sort of thing. Barbara is trying to make sure *you* walk away with as much money as possible once the estate is settled."

Violet seems to process his words, but I see the moment she rejects them. "No, but that's not it. She doesn't care about making *me* money!" she bursts, earning glances from several tables around us.

"And why do you say that?" Henry asks with eerie calm.

"Because my grandparents wanted to get the house painted and change the bathroom and, I don't know ... other stuff. You know, because people do that when they sell their house and want to get more money for it."

"They do." There's a hint of humor in Henry's tone, as if he's amused that she, a fifteen-year-old girl, feels the need to explain this to him, a thirty-two-year-old billionaire business tycoon.

"Then why has Barbara been talking them out of it? She said it would go fast without any of that done."

"She might be right. I didn't go into the house so I can't

say. It's a nice area, and the house is on a cul-de-sac. It's likely in high demand."

"No, that's not it." Violet shakes her head. "The person who wants to buy the house is Barbara's sister."

"Her *sister*." That has piqued Henry's interest.

Violet straightens her back, seemingly emboldened. "Yes. And a few months before my mom died, Barbara brought her sister over and they were walking all over the house, looking at things. I don't think they knew I was there. I overheard them talking about moving walls and stuff. And then she shows up yesterday with this offer before the house is even on the market, and Barbara keeps telling my grandparents how stressful putting a house on the market is, and how her sister is willing to buy it as is." Violet grips the fork in her hand. "It feels like they were just waiting for my mother to die so they could take it from us."

I'm beginning to see why Violet acted out. She's not wrong to be suspicious. Why else would Audrey's best friend be touring the house with her sister, talking about renovations, unless she had plans to buy it even then? How long have they been planning this? Like Henry said, it's a charming house in a cul-de-sac, in a nice, quiet neighborhood.

"Is that allowed? Selling your client's house to your family member?" I ask instead of voicing my other questions.

"Agents are supposed to protect their clients. That's hard to do when both the buyer *and* the seller are their clients, and that might be the case here."

"And the buyer's her sister," I emphasize.

"Exactly. She's more likely to work for her best interests than Audrey's." Henry strums his fingers across the table. "I don't like the sound of it."

"No," I agree.

"See?" Violet throws her hands up in the air. She hesitates. "*You*'re the big-shot businessman. Do *you* think my grandparents should take the offer?"

"What's the offer?" Henry asks.

Violet shrugs. "Does it matter?"

"Yes, it does. At fair value is a good offer, and one without any conditions attached is a great deal if there are issues that an inspection will turn up."

Violet seems to shrink with his words, her second of hope deflating.

"What did your grandparents say when you told them about what you overheard?" I ask.

"They said that I must have misunderstood. They've known Barbara her whole life, and she would never do something like that. But I know what I heard." She watches Henry, and I don't miss the silent request there.

Was this her plan when she ran to New York? To gather up the courage to seek out her rich and powerful father and ask for his help *without actually asking for his help*? Obviously, she didn't anticipate us showing up at the diner, but she recovered quickly.

"We wouldn't want to see Howard and Gayle taken advantage of." I find myself holding my breath too, waiting for Henry to do what he does best: take control.

Henry bites his bottom lip in thought. "The first step is to understand what the house is worth on the market, so we know if what this agent is coming to them with is fair."

"Okay ..." I prod, trying to convey my pleas with my eyes. *Come on, Henry, do the right thing here. Get involved.*

He twists his lips in thought. "I have a guy. I trust him to get us a good number. I will make the call. But *only*"—he holds up a finger as if to hit pause—"if you go back to your grandparents, apologize for taking off the way you did, and promise me that you'll stop causing them stress."

Violet purses her lips together as her head bobs.

The waitress appears then with our coffees. "Some breakfast for you two today?" she asks, sparing Violet's mauled plate of food a glance.

"Yes! I'd love an order of French toast, please," I jump in before Henry can decline, raising my eyebrows expectantly at him. His daughter is sitting across from him. This is a real chance to get to know her while he's playing the white knight and her defenses are down.

"Make it two. And if she's done murdering her food, perhaps a fresh plate of something else that she'll eat?" He refers to Violet in third person, but he's staring at her.

Violet's face morphs with a grin as she sets her cutlery down. It's the first smile we've seen touch her face, and it transforms her from pretty to downright beautiful. "I like French toast."

"Three orders of French toast, comin' right up!" The waitress whisks Violet's plate from her and strolls away.

"I have a few phone calls to make. I'll be back."

"Okay, *cutie pie*," I tease.

He leans in to whisper, "You'll pay for that one later." With a quick kiss on my cheek, he slides out of our crammed booth.

Violet watches over her shoulder as Henry strolls toward the door with a graceful stride, digging his phone out of his pocket. "Is he calling my grandparents?"

"He did when we got here. Now he's calling his real estate guy." On a Sunday morning, no less, and Henry will expect the man to answer.

"*Already?*"

That makes me chuckle. "He doesn't waste time."

"But he'll do what he says he's going to?" There's doubt in her voice.

I take a long sip of my coffee. "If he says he's going to do something, he'll do it." I can't believe I'm sitting across from Henry's *child*.

She watches me with unabashed curiosity for a long moment. "So you work for ... *him*?" She falters on *him*, as if she doesn't know what else to call Henry.

I decide not to push the father thing just yet. "I was Henry's assistant for a bit while we were in Alaska this past summer, but I don't work for his company anymore."

"Did you like working for him?"

I consider my answer. "It had its benefits." None that I'll ever admit to. "But it's better this way."

She chews on the inside of her cheek, as if holding back questions she's dying to ask.

So I share information about myself freely. "I'm a few credits away from finishing my college degree, which I'm doing by correspondence, and I'm starting my own soap company."

"Soap. That's ... cool, maybe?" Her pinched face says otherwise.

I laugh. "I've been making soap and oils and things since I was, well ... your age, and I love doing it."

She fidgets with the cuffs on her sweatshirt. "When's the wedding?"

"Next spring."

Violet peers at my hand. "Is that your engagement ring?"

"It is." I hold my hand out, admiring the pearl. "It was Henry's grandmother's ring. The gold is from the Wolf mine." It dawns on me then. "This was *your* great-grand-mother's ring."

She nods slowly, as if she's connecting the dots to this

foreign new life of hers. How weird it must be to have an entire side of your family that you know nothing about. "It's pretty. Not flashy."

"No, it's elegant but understated. Henry said that's what she was like. Marianne Wolf was her name. I don't know much else about her."

Henry strolls past us on the sidewalk, his phone pressed to his ear, his expression stern as he makes his demands. He used to intimidate me so much when he was like this, but now my pulse stirs watching him. He's in charge and he will get what he wants.

"What if it isn't a good deal?" Violet asks.

"Huh?" Her question catches me off guard.

She trails him with curious eyes. "What if his guy says Barbara's trying to take advantage of us?"

"Then Barbara will be lucky if she can sell a Barbie house by the time Henry is finished with her." The woman has no idea who she's trying to swindle.

A few beats pass and then Violet's throat bobs with a hard swallow. "Thanks for listening to me when no one else would." She may not have had kind words for me the last time we met, but at least she doesn't seem to hate me.

"You're welcome." I remember being fifteen. Not yet an adult and yet not a child anymore. Then again, Mama still dismisses my opinions on things now. "But I'm not the only one who listened." I point toward the brooding man who paces outside, the blustering breeze fanning his hair. Henry is the one getting things done. I only nudged him.

She glances at him but stays quiet. Something tells me she'll be too stubborn to acknowledge his help, just like she was too stubborn to ask for it in the first place. She needs to see another side of him. Unfortunately, Henry isn't the easiest person to get to know.

I have a thought. I slide out my phone. "What's your number?"

She frowns. "Why?"

"So I can send you our contact info, and the next time you want or need to see your father, you can call or text us." Instead of showing up at the penthouse unannounced, which is what I think she has been debating while mutilating her breakfast.

"I didn't *want* to see him," she mumbles, but her cheeks flush, giving away her intentions.

Sure you didn't. "You should be able to reach us, Violet," I say more gently. "Just in case."

She bites her bottom lip, considering the suggestion until finally, she relents.

I stifle my smile of triumph as she recites her number and I punch the digits into my phone.

fourteen

"I'm nervous about this," I admit through a sip of my drink—a frothy cocktail named Beauty and the Beast for the decorative rose petals and bell-shaped glass. "A stranger is picking out my wedding dress for me."

"No, Emmanuelle is *designing* the precise dress for you," Margo purrs, elegantly draped in the teal leather wing chair across from me. She looks prim and regal, gripping her gimlet with a delicate hand. Completely opposite to the scantily clad fortune teller sharing Merrick's dick with her boyfriend last night. "She has a talent for these things."

"But *what if* I hate it?" They never asked me about my likes or dislikes. Puffy sleeves? A crinoline skirt? Lace? Bows?

"*Abigail*, have I ever led you astray when it comes to fashion?"

"No," I admit with a hint of reluctance. If I could have Margo dress me every day, I would be relieved. And how does she manage to use her accent to make me feel guilty for questioning her?

"I can already see it now, and it will be magnifique. And

Emmanuelle is not a stranger anymore. We spent all after-noon with her so you two could get to know each other!"

Yes, much of it with me standing in my bra and panties for countless measurements while Margo and the pint-size designer circled me, slipping in and out of their native tongue as they discussed past runway events and flirted with each other.

I tried canceling. By the time we put Violet in Henry's car so Victor could drive her home to Philly and we walked back to the penthouse, it was already time to go. I wanted to sleep. But Margo would have none of it, and Henry ushered me out, telling me he'd be busy with the guys, anyway.

"Fine. I'm trusting you."

"As you *always* should." She winks playfully.

My attention wanders around the interior of Lux, the Wolf Tower's restaurant and lounge, located on the fiftieth floor where the building changes shape, narrowing above us as it continues its climb to the clouds. One side opens to a terrace that's closed for the winter.

Given it bears the same name as the Lux fine dining restaurant at Wolf Cove, I expected a similar vibe—silky linens and a killer view—but, while New York City's skyline is incredible, everything else here feels different. It's dark and moody, and far more lounge-like, with a mix of tables and cozy seating areas. Heavy velvets and leathers drape the walls and cover the furniture, and pendant chandeliers cast almost too little light. In the center is an enormous fireplace.

Henry and I have ordered dinner from this restaurant several times, but I've never stepped foot here in person. Now that I have, I think I'll be dragging Henry down more often.

Joel is perched on a stool at the far end of a full bar. He wandered over there fifteen minutes ago to peruse the extensive high-end liquor along the wall, and now he's in deep conversation with two women that he may or may not be trying to line up for a tryst. The way he strokes an auburn curl off one's cheek tells me he likely is. The way she leans into his touch tells me he'll likely succeed.

"How serious are you about Joel?" I ask suddenly. I've never broached the subject with Margo. But after last night, I feel like I know him differently, better.

She shrugs. "He is good for me. He cares for me, and yet he allows me to do as I please with whomever I please. He does not try to dominate me."

"Do you think you'll ever get married?"

"To him?" She shakes her head. "But maybe one day, when someone comes along that I fall madly in love with and do not wish to share. Like Henry, with you. I could never be with a man such as your Henry, though. He does not give up control easily."

He did last night, for me. I smile into my drink. "You know Joel's at the bar, hitting on two women, right?"

"Is he?" Margo glances over her shoulder at him. "Oh, he won't fuck them. They're not his type. I'm sure he will ask to photograph them together, though." She says it so nonchalantly.

"And that doesn't bother you *at all*?"

"Why?" She waggles her perfectly drawn eyebrows. "I will watch."

I know she is one hundred percent serious. Her very open and carefree sexual lifestyle no longer fazes me as it once did. We've spent most of the late afternoon and early evening together. There's been no mention of our House of Mirrors escapades, but no awkwardness either. Not that Margo would ever feel any shame or embarrassment, but oddly enough, I don't either. Maybe it's because I was with

Henry. Or maybe it's because we have our own history and, through it, a bond some might consider unconventional.

I take a deep breath, suddenly nervous. "Margo, will you be my maid of honor?"

She claps with glee. "But of course I will!"

An odd wave of relief washes over me that she didn't laugh or dismiss my request. That I didn't otherwise misread the depth of this unlikely friendship I've forged with the supermodel who once slept with Henry.

"Can I tell you a secret?" She leans in, her eyes sparkling with humor. "I already assumed I was."

I laugh at her admission. "Why doesn't that surprise me." It's so very Margo.

"This is going to be *so much* fun." She claps again and I sense her genuine excitement. "Who else have you asked to join us?"

"My friend Autumn, who you met in Alaska. The concierge." I called her last week to ask and she squealed into the phone.

"Oui. She is a doll."

I smile sheepishly at my next choice. "And I want to ask Ronan, but Henry's not totally on board."

She waves a dismissive hand. "Ask him, anyway. It is your bridal party, not Henry's."

"I can't do that!"

"Why not? Ronan is important to you, non?"

"He is."

"And he helped save Henry from almost certain death?"

"He did."

"And just because he is in love with you does not mean he cannot—"

"Whoa." I giggle. "Ronan is *not* in love with me."

"Oh, of course not. I am *entirely* wrong in my observation. I don't know what I'm talking about." She's grinning as if she knows better. "Either way, Henry can be difficult. He likes control and he always has it. But there are times when you must *ask* his permission, and then there are times you must *tell* him what you want and how it will be. He is a smart man, and he wants to make you happy. He will bend when he knows it is essential to you."

"I hope you're right."

"I am. But just in case, tell him while you're on your knees for him. He will give you anything you want." Her wicked cackle draws curious glances. "Maintenant, to more important things. Where should we have your ... how do you Americans call it"—she snaps her fingers as she frowns —"bachelorette party?"

~

A WARM, drunken buzz courses through my veins by the time Henry steps through the doorway of Lux. My pulse races at the sight of him. He looks delicious tonight in a tailored, all black outfit, the top two buttons of his shirt unfastened, his cuffs rolled up to show off his forearms.

Trailing in after him are Merrick, Warner, and Preston, dressed equally sharp. All of them ooze wealth and confidence.

My heart pounds as I think of all that I saw of these men last night. Henry was right, the costume party was not the right venue to meet his friends, but it was certainly the place to move past polite "get to know you" conversation. I've seen all of them with their pants down. *Literally.* By now, that doesn't shock me. Still, I'm happy for my boozy glow as I face them again. Maybe it'll help squash any awkwardness on my part when I face Merrick.

But how have Henry and Merrick been around each other? Could last night have damaged their friendship?

"Have you ever seen a more attractive bunch?" Margo watches the four men as they stroll toward us. She's not the only one. They draw interest from all corners.

"Good evening, ladies." Henry lifts the half-empty bottle of champagne from its bucket, checking the label. "What are we celebrating?"

"Your beautiful bride asked me to be her maid of honor." Margo beams.

"Isn't that brilliant." Preston flops into the seat next to Margo. "Wolf just roped us all in. Guess we should celebrate too." It sounds like they've already been celebrating. Preston is louder than he was last night.

"Single malts?" Merrick gives Margo's hair a playful ruffle. It's friendly, almost brotherly.

"I'd like to see what they have." Warner moves for the bar, his lush hair flowing free again. He winks at a group of women at a nearby table. None of them would imagine he had his "date" tied up in ropes last night and was jamming his cock down her throat for an audience.

My gaze flitters back to Merrick to find him watching me with an enigmatic smile. My cheeks flush. At least he's not avoiding me, I guess. "What about you, *Daddy*?" he asks in a mocking tone.

"Lagavulin and fuck off." Henry sinks into the spot on the couch next to me. His cheeks carry a pinkish hue.

As Preston and Margo start a conversation, I lean into Henry's side, inhaling his spicy cologne, craving his touch. "I take it you told them?"

"I did."

"And?"

"They were as shocked as I was but supportive. More so

than I expected, to be honest. But they've also been calling me that all night," he adds.

"What? *Daddy*?" I tease, meaning it to be light and flirtatious. It stirs an unexpected feeling in me, though, one I can't quite put my finger on.

"Don't you start too," he warns.

"I would *never*. But out of curiosity, would you rather I call you *Daddy* or *cutie pie*?" I squeal as Henry seizes my hips and pulls me onto his lap, tucking my legs together against his hip. He grips the back of my head and pulls me into a hard kiss before whispering against my lips, "Which one would you rather be screaming tonight when I'm fucking you?" Beneath me, I feel him getting hard.

Henry's not normally this affectionate in public, so either he's drunker than I realize, or he's emboldened around his friends.

Or he's reached the point of not giving a damn how the CEO of Wolf Hotels should act.

I curl an arm around his neck and appreciate the closeness for a moment before asking, "Did you hear from your real estate guy about the house yet?"

"Alex? I did. He sent one of his Philly guys over to look at the house and run the numbers this afternoon. It needs some work, but not much. Maybe fifteen thousand. But they can get at least fifty grand more than what Howard told me Barbara's sister is offering. Possibly more."

My jaw drops. "So Violet was right."

"Violet was right." A pensive smile touches his lips. If I didn't know better, I'd say it might be pride.

"What happens now?"

"I shared the numbers with Howard and told him they're getting robbed. He's going to decline."

"Good." My shoulders sink with relief. "And Barbara?"

"They signed a contract with her, but it'll be easy to get out of it this early in the game, especially given her unethical behavior. They're going to sign with Alex's company to represent the sale and I'm going to handle her." There's a cold calm in his tone that almost makes me feel sorry for the woman. Almost.

"Have you told Violet yet?"

"No. Howard and Gayle will."

I shake my head at my beautiful, complicated man who can tackle multimillion-dollar business deals but hasn't figured out how to handle one teenage girl.

His forehead wrinkles with confusion. "What?"

He doesn't get it. "This is your excuse to reach out to her."

"I guess." But his lips are pursed. He doesn't look convinced.

"Go on, text her!"

"Right now?"

"Yes. Right now." I dig his phone out of his pocket for him. "I sent you her number."

"You did." He opens his phone and finds in her name— he didn't waste time adding it to his Contacts list, I note— and begins typing, but stalls immediately on the "Hello, Violet, it's … " introduction.

"*Daddy*?" I say in a sultry tone.

"Just for that, you're not reading this." He slides me off his lap and back onto the couch.

I miss his warmth instantly, but I don't push it, enjoying my champagne as he sends his message to his daughter.

"There. Done," he declares, tucking his phone in his pocket. "How did all the dress stuff go?"

"Good, I think?"

"Superb," Margo declares, butting into our conversation

as Preston takes a phone call. "You will have the most beautiful bride of the year."

"I'll have that no matter what she wears." He sets his hand halfway on my thigh, his thumb drawing slow circles over my skin. The same way he always teases my clit.

Margo's eyes trace the movement and mischief dances across her beautiful face. "Especially with Joel as your wedding photographer?"

Henry's hand stalls. He wasn't part of last night's conversation, and I know what he's thinking because it's the same place my mind went.

"He showed me his portfolio. Not *that* one," I add quickly. "He's *incredible*, Henry. His photos are magazine quality."

"He is the best," Margo chirps. "At *many* things, but capturing moments is a specialty of his."

"I've seen those moments," Henry says wryly. "If that's who you want, Abbi, then that's who we'll have."

My head bobs. "That's who I want." And that was easier than I expected. Maybe Margo is right. Sometimes Henry has to be told rather than asked. I set my jaw with determination. "And I'm asking Ronan to be my bridesman."

A low groan escapes Henry. "We'll talk about it later."

But the copious rounds of drinks have given me courage. I hook my fingers over Henry's leather belt, my thumb dragging along his zipper where his erection from a few moments ago still lingers. "It's important to me that I have my closest, most trusted friends there."

"*I* don't trust him."

"Yes, you do. You would never have allowed *certain things* to happen if you didn't." I arch my eyebrows pointedly, though I don't need to emphasize any part of that sentence.

His lips purse with reluctance. How can he argue with

that? Unless he suspects what Margo insinuated earlier, about Ronan's feelings for me. Even so, that doesn't change our friendship.

"*Henry*. He brought me back to you. I'm having him there."

He sighs heavily. "As long as he doesn't disrupt the ceremony."

"Why would he do that?"

But Henry doesn't answer me, his eyes narrowing on Margo. "I suppose I have you to thank for this?"

"And *so many other* wonderful things in your life." She blows him a kiss and then says something in rapid French.

"No." His tone is sharp. "Absolutely not." He fires something back at her and then glares at me with exasperation, his affectionate touch gone. "You've got to be fucking kidding me, Abbi."

"What?" What now?

"You are not going to Ibiza *with Margo and Ronan* for your bachelorette party."

"I don't even know where that is!" The emphasis on Margo and Ronan catches up to me. "And why not? You don't trust me?"

"Yes, of course I trust *you*." His nostrils flare. "Fine, go to the party capital of Europe, where everyone's high and groping everyone else. I can't wait to see what they plan for me." He nods toward the bar. "But don't worry, I'm sure it'll be *tame*."

I feel my face pale as I think about what kind of trouble Merrick, Warner, and Preston will concoct for Henry's bachelor party. While I trust him, I don't trust them, and I definitely don't trust the fifty naked women they'll bring in to hump his lap. "On second thought, I'd like to be placed in a coma for that weekend," I mutter.

Henry smirks. "Thought so."

Merrick returns with two crystal glasses, wedging himself in the space on the couch next to me as if we're old friends and this is completely normal. He passes Henry his drink. "Just how you like it ... Daddy."

I stifle my giggle.

Merrick winks at me before shifting his focus to Margo. "That is one smooth-talking Frenchman up there. The blond is about to hand him her panties."

The same Frenchman who sucked your cock last night? I watch Merrick for any sign that he feels at all awkward or jealous about Joel's conquest, but there's nothing at all. It's like they're just people who helped each other out.

Margo sighs heavily. "I hope so. He's been whining that he doesn't have anyone new to photograph lately. I'm tired of listening to it."

"For his *art*?" Preston's eyes light up, finished with his call. "I'd fucking love to be there for that."

"We will see if they're amiable." Margo reaches over to fix his collar before patting his shoulder with her palm. It's so innocent and yet something about the simple touch makes me wonder if Merrick isn't the only of Henry's friends she's hooked up with.

"And how are plans for turning your chateau into a Wolf?" Preston asks as they fall into casual, friendly conversation.

She pouts, her focus now on Henry. "Slow. Someone is dragging his feet."

"Don't be too hard on him." Merrick throws a brawny arm across the back of the couch, giving the space between Henry's shoulder and neck an affectionate squeeze. "Daddy's been busy."

Henry's molars grind as he sips his drink, ignoring his friend's taunts.

Meanwhile, the deep, gravelly sound of Merrick's voice in my ear and being sandwiched between these two again after what transpired last night sparks heat between my thighs.

God, I've had too much to drink.

Merrick has let go of Henry, but his arm is still stretched out against the back of the couch. "By the way, here you go." He sets his drink down. Slipping his hand into his jacket, he pulls out my black bottoms from my costume.

"Uh ... Thanks?" I grab them and stuff them into my purse, my face reddening.

Henry leans over me. "You mean you've been walking around with those in your pocket all afternoon?"

Merrick grins. "I'm impressed with the laundry service here."

Henry shakes his head. "Prick." They're both so at ease with each other. It's a relief to see after what happened last night.

"You *want* me to be a prick?" With a sly grin, Merrick leans in and whispers in my ear, "You're perfect for him. We're all happy to see him marrying you."

Warmth floods my chest with his endorsement, even as his lips graze my earlobe.

"Watch it, Mer," Henry warns as Merrick pulls away.

The golden boy winks at me.

Warner returns and, after handing Preston his drink, fills the seat on the other side of Margo. "That restaurant was excellent. What was the name of it again?" He pats his taut belly. "I need to remember it for next time."

"I think it was Daddy's Place?" Preston cocks his head at Henry.

"Secret Daddy," Merrick counters without missing a beat.

Warner layers on, "Secret *Wolf* Daddy?" They all laugh. Even I'm having a hard time keeping a straight face.

"You're all idiots. How the fuck are you guys in your thirties?" Henry snaps, giving them the rise they're fishing for.

"Look at him, thinking he's more mature than us because he's a father now," Warner throws back, earning another round of laughter.

Margo's jaw drops as she stares at Henry and then spouts something in French.

Finally, something that shocks her.

fifteen

I wake to the sound of Henry's throaty chuckle.

"What's so funny?" I roll over to find him staring at his phone.

Instead of explaining, he hands it to me.

Henry: *Hi, Violet, it's Henry Wolf. Your grandparents agreed to fix up the house to sell through my agent. You'll get a much better price for it. I'll deal with Barbara.*

It's the message he sent to Violet last night after I pushed him. Short and simple and lacking any affection whatsoever, but I remind myself that Henry is still learning to crawl when it comes to her.

I caught Henry checking his phone a dozen times last night and while he always had something work-related waiting for him, I don't think that's what he was looking for.

Violet *finally* responded this morning, likely after weighing her answer all night, and it seems they've been chatting while I blissfully snored beside him.

Violet: *Hello, Henry Wolf. My grandparents told me. What is that saying? Oh yeah ... I told you so.*

Henry: *What is that other saying? Oh yeah ... You're welcome.*

Violet: *If I give your invisible robotic eye the finger, will you see it?*

Henry: *Yes. Stop giving your grandparents a hard time.*

Violet answered with a saluting emoji.

I knew she would resist thanking Henry. She likely harbors a lot of confused feelings where he and her mother are concerned. "She knows what you did for her, even if she didn't say it," I promise him, handing his phone back.

I hug my pillow and watch him stand and stretch, his firm ass on display. "You should take the day off." It's seven thirty a.m. and normally Henry's already almost out the door, but this weekend was exhausting in the best way.

"Can't. Some of us have to work." He rounds the bed, leaning down to kiss my lips. "I've got interviews for the new team to head the metals divisions."

"Hey! *I* have interviews this week too." Just saying that out loud sounds so foreign, but Zaheera insists I need an assistant to help with the administrative things. Her team has already vetted a pile of résumés and selected the best three candidates for me to choose from.

I assume she'll also tell me which one I should hire.

"You should get up, then."

I burrow back under the covers, planning on sleeping until my hangover headache—the second day in a row —fades.

The duvet flies away with a yank. I howl as Henry slaps my bare ass. "Shower. Now." Henry's *giddy*. He's never *giddy* in the morning, especially not on a Monday.

I watch his perfect, naked body move toward the en suite. Seeing his friends this weekend definitely lifted his spirits, but I think this mood has more to do with a certain sassy blue-eyed girl.

~

"I HAVE to fly to Barcelona next week," Henry tells me through a sip of his coffee, his gaze on his phone as he reads through urgent emails. "I'll be gone four days. Let Miles know if you're coming with me?"

I try to hide my dismay at the idea of Henry gone for that long. "I can't. I wish I could, but I have way too much to do for this launch, including making the actual soap. *And* I'm meeting with Jill. *And* I have assignments to catch up on or I won't get those credits." Just listing out the warring priorities has me stressed. "I need Victor to drive me to my office today if you don't need him?" It still sounds odd to call the little commercial space across the Lincoln Tunnel in New Jersey that I've rented "my office."

Henry's smile is soft. "I like seeing you like this."

"Like what? Overwhelmed?"

"Busy with things that are yours and important to you. Don't worry, you'll manage it."

He's talking about my company and my education. Even the wedding, which is technically *ours*, but Control Freak Henry wants *me* to make the decisions so it's one hundred percent what *I* want.

My phone chirps with a text from Autumn.

Autumn: *Not to be the bearer of bad news on a Monday morning, but you did ask me to send you anything that comes up.*

I click on the celebrity gossip site link she included. And gasp in horror.

Wolf Heir and Assistant Spotted at Exclusive High Society

Sex Party with Friends Margo Lauren and Hedge Fund Playboy Preston Abbott.

"I thought you said it was a secret party!" My stomach sinks as I see a grainy picture of Henry and I stepping out of Victor's car on Saturday night, our masks firmly in place. But it's us—the black-and-white stripes of my tights, my red braid stretching down my back. They've circled my hand again, as if the barely visible ring is recognizable. They really love doing that.

Henry rounds the counter to look over my shoulder. "They can't tell that's us."

"But they can *here*." Another picture shows us outside of our building. We weren't wearing our masks then. More pictures show the others leaving our building in costume. Whoever wrote this story assumed—correctly—that we were all going to the same party.

"Whatever. Deny it."

"But look at the headline!"

"There's no proof of what went on inside that warehouse." He is too calm for my liking.

"Well, they obviously know *something*." Someone has talked to them about what goes on at these costume parties. "What if they have pictures from *inside*?" Just the thought of that makes me want to vomit. I scroll further, but there aren't any more candid shots of us, only advertisements.

"They don't have anything. Remember those metal detectors we went through? The organizers take their security *very* seriously."

Henry's vow brings me little comfort. Another dark thought stirs. "This means someone followed us. They sat outside, waiting for us to leave, and then tailed us all the way there." It took almost an hour with traffic to get to that warehouse. Was it this Luca/Frank/Hank guy who's been calling everyone I know? It's been weeks since that initial phone call.

"I know. That's what they do. They're vile cockroaches, but if they can make money off this shit, there's no getting rid of them." Henry sighs. "I'm sorry."

"It's not your fault." I smooth my palm over his forearm. "But why us? I can understand following Margo around, but you're not an actor."

"I don't know why the fascination, but they've always found a way to put me in their headlines. Don't worry, it'll die down soon."

Henry has dealt with these people for most of his adult life. He's learned how to handle them. Will I ever become unruffled by this violation of privacy? "Until then?"

"There's *no story here*, Abbi. You went to a costume party on Halloween, and that's it. Everything else? No comment."

I take a deep breath. "I wish they'd stop calling me your assistant."

He smirks. "Talk to Zaheera. See if they can put a PR spin on this."

"I don't see how she can." Or why she would want to.

My phone rings and I flinch as Mama's name appears. "See? She hasn't dialed my number since the day I told her our wedding would be in Alaska. There's only one reason for her to break her silence." She's as dedicated to online gossip as she is to her church. She's seen the headline.

"Remember. Just a regular costume party." Henry kisses my temple first, and then my lips, peeling away as I try to deepen it. "Don't avoid her. It'll only make it worse."

He's halfway across the kitchen when I answer, my teeth gritted as I brace myself. "Hello, Mama."

"A *sex* party, Abigail Mitchell?" she shrieks.

sixteen

"I don't remember 'liaison with jewelers' being in the job description."

"And *I* don't remember 'marry the boss' being in it either," I say through a mouthful of my sandwich.

"Better you than me," Miles mutters.

I laugh. "I just need his contact info. I'll call him myself." Henry trusted this jeweler with sizing his grandmother's ring for me and he's designing my wedding ring, so this man is the right person to craft Henry's wedding band. "And it's Wolf gold that they're using, right?"

"Yeah, of course."

"Okay, perfect. Send me the info as soon as we get off the phone, please?" Because otherwise, I'll have to answer to Jill. She sent me a lengthy wedding to-do checklist last week and a reminder that the wedding is less than six months away. Apparently, I'm already behind.

"Will do. How's everything going over at Farm Girl Soap?"

"I'm sitting in the closet."

"*That* bad?"

I giggle. "No, I'm kidding. Sort of." I lean back in my office chair and admire the floral wallpaper and freshly painted walls. When we did the commercial site visit and Zaheera suggested converting the tiny storage room into an office for me, I snickered. I mean, I already have this space rented, with an area for making soaps and another for packaging it, and then an office in the back where my new assistant, Annie, is set up. Wasn't that enough?

But I already appreciate the cozy little space with a door I can lock—especially when Henry is thirty-eight hundred miles away and seven hours ahead, and likes to FaceTime from his hotel room, naked.

Best of all, Zaheera hung a matte Abbi Mitchell, Farm Girl Soap Co. sign on the outside of the door. An office warming gift from Nailed It.

"I've been making batches of soap, day in and day out." We're limiting it to my most popular scents—lemon, thyme, sage, and lavender—for the first sale, so we have something new to offer for the next round. "How's Barcelona?"

"The city is great. Henry is ... Henry."

I smile. Belinda once called him a bear when he's away from me for too long. It shouldn't make me happy to hear that, but it does. "At least he's acting more like himself again?"

Miles snorts. "Yeah, that's one way to look at it. 'Kay. Gotta go."

I flip through the wedding invitation samples while I wait for Miles to forward the jeweler's info. Jill sent me a box to choose from. With Raj's help, I narrowed it down to four favorites, but no matter how long I stare at them, I can't seem to choose. I sent pictures of them to Henry, but I already know he won't be much help.

My phone rings, and I double-blink at Violet's name on the screen. This is unexpected. "Hello?"

"Uh ... Hi, Abbi? I hope you don't mind me calling ..." Her voice trails.

"Of course not. What's up? Is everything okay?" My mind immediately goes to problems. Is there an issue with the house? Did something happen to Howard or Gayle?

"Yeah, everything's fine. Um ... the painters are at the house. They're covering everything in gray. It's ... *blah*."

"Blah gray! I know that one well. I have it in my new commercial kitchen." It was there when we took possession and it seemed pointless to spend money painting it. "It's boring, but it'll help sell the place."

"Yeah, that's what Tony said."

"How is he?" Henry said Alex sent his best Philly agent to them.

"Yeah, he's okay. Gramps likes him."

"Well, that's important." Silence hangs over the phone for a few long beats. I wonder if she's heard from Henry, but I don't ask. There must be a reason for this call.

"So, I have this project for school. We have to design a business with, like, a whole plan."

"That sounds like a big project."

"Yeah, it's thirty percent of my grade and I'm kind of behind on it, because of my mom and all that. Anyway, do you think I could ask you some questions?"

"*Me?*"

"Yeah. You said you had a company, right? Soap or something?"

"Yeah, I do, but ..." I falter. "You know, Henry would be the better person to ask." If anyone understands the business world, it's him.

There's a long pause and then, "You know what, it's okay. I'll find someone else—"

"No, no! It's fine. I can help you with this. Or try, at least." This is Henry's daughter. She's going to be my stepdaughter, a reality I haven't wrapped my head around yet. The fact that she's coming to me—that she hasn't written me off as her father's much younger fiancée—is something. "How much do you have done already?"

"Um … well, it's kind of hard to say."

I see where this is going. "You haven't started yet, have you?"

"Define *start*." I don't know her well, but I'm sure there is a sheepish smile behind that voice.

"And when's it due?"

"The first half, on Monday?"

I flop back in my chair. How am I supposed to fit this in? It's already Thursday and I'll be in this kitchen all weekend, preparing for next week's launch. But it doesn't sound like Violet has time to spare.

"I have tomorrow off school," Violet says, as if that fixes everything. "I could take the train in and meet you somewhere?"

I don't have time to meet her in the city, but I want to make this work. An idea strikes me. "Why doesn't Victor pick you up and bring you to my office? You can spend the day with me and learn about what I'm doing." We spend a few minutes planning and by the time we end the call, I feel like I might be able to help her.

But I'm still overwhelmed. "Come on, Miles!" I rest my forehead on my desk. I'm desperate to mark *something* off this stupid checklist.

A knock sounds.

"Come in!" I roll my head toward the door.

It creaks open and Annie pokes her curly blond head in. She winces when she sees me. "Hey, the photographer is here for that PR campaign?"

"What photog—oh my God." The photo shoot. "I totally forgot. How did I forget I had that?"

"'Cause you have a lot on your plate right now?"

My phone chirps with the jewelry contact info from Miles, as if to punctuate Annie's point. "Okay, can you tell him I'll be there in five minutes? Ten at most. I need to make this call first."

"Yeah, of course. I'll get him to start setting up."

"*Thank you.*" I afford my new assistant a tired smile. She's a twenty-five-year-old college graduate and the last one I interviewed. We clicked right away. She, too, grew up on a farm in Pennsylvania with an overbearing parent—though, in her case, it's her father. She started on Monday and already I don't know how I'd live without her. "Can I ask your opinion on something?"

She cocks her head. "Sure. Shoot."

I hold up the four invitation samples. "If you had to choose one of these for your wedding, which would you pick?"

She bites her bottom lip as her green eyes—magnified behind glasses—shift back and forth, scrutinizing them. "Definitely the second one. It's modern but timeless."

"That was Raj's first choice too."

"I don't know who Raj is, but he sounds smart." She grins.

"Definitely. I'll be out in a minute." I take a picture of it and text it to Jill. *One down.* With a sigh, I dial the jeweler.

~

It's dark and well past normal dinner hours by the time Victor pulls up to the lobby doors of Wolf Tower. "Thank you for the ride." Will I ever get used to having a driver take me anywhere I want to go?

Victor meets my eyes through the rearview mirror. "You're welcome, Ms. Mitchell. We'll see you in the morning?"

"Bright and early." I slip out of the car, offering the doorman a smile before I stroll through the revolving doors and into the lobby. After hours on my feet, all I want is a long, hot bath.

Every single employee greets me as I pass. I wish I knew all their names.

"Ms. Mitchell," Sullivan calls out, his enormous frame eating up space as he closes in on me. "I was asked to give you this." He hands me a folded note.

I frown, wariness creeping in. "From whom?"

"Didn't say. But he's upstairs in Lux, waiting for you."

I gingerly unfold the paper.

And a thrill runs through me.

Ronan engulfs me in his broad arms, pulling me against his chest in a hug.

I inhale the familiar mixture of sandalwood and Marlboro cigarettes that every single one of his shirts smells of. "What are you doing here!" We texted this morning and he asked what I had going on tonight, but he always does that. "You never said you were coming to New York!"

"Thought I'd surprise you." His deep, raspy voice warms my ears, bringing me back to countless nights under Alaska's starry sky, laughing at his and Connor's antics. As happy as I am, occasionally I catch myself reminiscing about a moment here or there and feeling an ache for a special time of my life, gone.

"I am floored, so you win." With one last squeeze, I pull away and look up into those haunting green eyes of his. "You look good." Casual, as always, in blue jeans and a plain charcoal shirt—long-sleeved, on account of the cooler weather, and clinging to his lean, sculpted body. His dark hair is buzzed as short as I remember it being. "I was going to call you this weekend."

"Sure you were," he teases.

"I was!" I give his biceps a playful smack. "Time just kind of got away from me."

"Where's Wolf?"

"Barcelona. I told you that, didn't I?"

"Oh right, I forgot."

I laugh. "No, you didn't."

"No, I didn't." He grins, and his gaze flitters over my mouth for the briefest moment. He's no less appealing than he always has been, but I feel nothing, save for friendly affection. "Hungry?"

"*Starving.*" I haven't eaten since lunch. Raj left a mixed green salad in the fridge for me, but now that I smell steak, a salad is the last thing I want.

"I was just about to order." With one of his signature crooked smiles, he slides into his chair.

I collapse into the other. "Okay, so seriously, what are you doing in New York?" It's a long way from Miami.

"Goin' back to Indianapolis for the weekend to visit the folks. Thought I'd grab a layover and visit you. You seem stressed lately."

"It's fine. All good things." I wave away his concern. "I'm

so glad to see you. Where are you staying? Do you need a place? We have plenty of room."

Ronan smooths a hand over his nape. "Yeah ... Even I'm not that big of a dick. And I'm not getting on Wolf's bad side. Don't worry about me. I'm crashing at a friend's place."

"I'm a friend!"

"A friend I plan on fucking." He chugs back his beer, the corners of his mouth curving upward.

Ronan hasn't changed.

Our waiter comes by then and so I quickly scour the menu, landing on a burger and fries.

Ronan relaxes back in his lounge chair, his thighs sprawled. "So, Red, tell me what's new?"

~

"*Fuck*." Ronan smooths a hand over his jaw. "You're gonna be a stepmom?"

"I know." I cringe around a french fry. I didn't hesitate to tell Ronan all about Violet—and Henry's scandalous past with Audrey. After all, he knew about Henry long before anyone else did. He's already proven I can trust him to keep a secret, and I don't have to tell him to stay mum. "She asked for my help with a project. I told her she could come to my office tomorrow. It's either a great idea or a stupid one. I mean, I don't know her at all."

"How's Wolf taking it?"

"He was shocked, to say the least, but I think he's starting to warm up to the idea."

"What does *that* mean?"

"I'm not sure." What does playing the role of Violet's father look like for Henry? "I'll let you know when I do. But we're keeping this on the down low, Ronan. To protect her, mostly. Henry's closest friends know, and now you."

He gives me a "Come on, are you kidding me?" look. "I'm not gonna say anything to anyone, including Connor." He hesitates. "I told him I left and went straight to the cabin, that last night in Alaska."

He means the night Ronan, Henry, and I were together, while Connor and Margo were defiling the hot tub. "Why?"

He shrugs. "You know me, Red. I don't kiss and tell."

"Yeah, but you and Connor share a brain."

He picks up a paper coaster and flicks it at me. "I don't know. I guess it felt too personal to share. You know what I mean?" In his eyes I see something raw.

"Yeah. I know what you mean," I say softly. "So, what about you? How's Miami? You already have a tan."

He pushes up his sleeves and stretches his arms out to study his golden forearms. "Yeah, it's good."

But he doesn't sound especially excited about being back there. "Have you decided about Wolf Cove next summer?"

He shakes his head. "Kind of reevaluating my whole life right now. Figuring out what I want to do with the rest of it."

Back in Alaska, I sensed Ronan was running away from something. It didn't take me long to figure out that it was a bad breakup. We were similar in that way—running to the remote wilderness to escape having our hearts smashed by people we trusted. But where Ronan guarded his feelings, I fell headfirst in love with Henry.

"What about for my wedding? Will you still come to that?"

His eyes flash to mine. "I already promised you I would."

I gather my nerve, suddenly doubting myself for even

considering this. "Actually, I was going to ask you if you'd do something for me." I hesitate.

"Spit it out. It can't be any worse than what you've already asked me to do for you."

My cheeks flush. "*I* did not ask you for that."

"You didn't complain about it either." He chuckles, but it dies off quickly. "Do you regret it?"

After a beat, I shake my head.

"Me neither." He picks lint off his shirt as if we're having a casual conversation. "So what do you need me to do?"

"Be in my wedding party?" God, we've come so far. There was a time, only a few months ago, that I pegged him as a depraved soul, raised by criminals and drug addicts and only after one thing.

He cocks his head. "What? Like a bridesmaid?"

"I think the technical term is *bridesman*." I hold my breath, and with each passing second that he doesn't answer, I worry he's going to decline. Maybe Margo was right about Ronan's feelings. Is it fair to ask him to stand beside me at the altar while I marry another man?

"Why me?" he finally asks.

"Because you're one of my very best friends, and you've been there for me through a lot of this." As a shoulder to cry on, a distraction, and a knight in shining armor when I thought I'd lost Henry for good. The most important people in my life—Mama, Jed, even Henry—have hurt me. But Ronan *never* has.

"Do I have to wear a dress?"

I giggle, sensing him shifting from a rare display of seriousness to the version of Ronan I recognize. "Yes, definitely."

"Are you asking Connor too?"

"No."

"That alone is worth it." He shrugs. "Sure, I guess I can do that."

"Gee, don't sound too thrilled," I mutter.

"I'll do it. Of course, I'll do it. I wouldn't want to be anywhere but there that day." Our eyes meet and it seems like a thousand thoughts are conveyed in that look. "Will you need me for the wedding night too?"

"No! *That* is not happening again." My cheeks burn with a new fury as I give him a playful kick. He grabs my foot, holding on to it for several long moments, his fingers searing against my ankle.

He releases me, his throat bobbing with a hard swallow. "I'm happy for you, Red. Really. You deserve the best."

"So do you." And I truly mean it. There's nothing I want more than for Ronan to find someone who deserves his loyalty. "You seeing anyone?"

"Nah. Same old. Rachel and Katie came down to party with us in Miami last weekend."

"I guess I don't need to ask how that went." I've seen firsthand how those three party.

He grins. "They asked me to give you a big fat kiss from them."

Mention of my cabinmates triggers other thoughts. "Have they gotten any calls from reporters?"

"If they have, they didn't say anything about it. Why? Have you heard from that douchebag again?"

"Nothing." It's been weeks. "Maybe I'm worried for nothing."

"I say fuck 'em all and enjoy your life."

"That's easy for you to say. There aren't pictures of *you* plastered on the internet with headlines about sex parties." It didn't take much to talk Mama off the ledge the morning she called about that. I spoon-fed her lies and she gobbled them up, happy to hear that the headlines are wrong and her daughter is not a deviant, though she had plenty to say about my costume and none of it was good.

The one positive that came out of it is that Mama is back to messaging me. She hasn't brought up the wedding or Henry once, sticking to talk of weather, Jed and Laura, Daddy's rehab. But at least she's talking to me again.

"Excuse me, have we met?"

I turn toward the sultry female voice and my mood sours instantly. "Roshani Mafi." As if I would ever forget that name or face.

The raven-haired beauty cocks her head. "So we *do* know each other."

"Not really. We met at the Wolf in Alaska. You were there for the grand opening." With aims to fuck Henry before her suitcase made it to her penthouse suite. I guess I can't blame her for that weekend entirely, though. Scott was the true harbinger, feeding off my insecurities. Still ... I hate her.

Her lips curve, but the smile doesn't reach her near-black eyes. "You're Henry's assistant." Still using his first name as if they're personally connected, I see.

"*Was* his assistant. That was months ago."

"That's right. Now you're engaged." Her gaze flitters to my left hand. "I would have expected something more extravagant from him."

I force a wide smile. "Clearly, you don't know him, then."

She makes a sound and then murmurs, "Congratulations," after a delayed moment.

"Thank you."

"Where is Henry tonight? I was hoping to see him." She looks around as if expecting him to appear.

"In Barcelona." Considering the last time they spoke when Henry threatened to notify her employer—*Luxury*

Travel, a magazine doing a special spread for the grand opening—of the things she was up to on their corporate dime, I wouldn't think she'd be eager to cross paths with him again.

"Sad about his brother, isn't it?" She tsks, as if Scott suffered some unfortunate event instead of embezzling funds from the company and conspiring to murder William Wolf to protect his inheritance, before dying while attacking me in his sick form of retribution. That last part, very few people know about, though.

Just mentioning his name has tension cording my muscles. "That's right. You knew Scott well." Three condoms well, according to what the hotel staff found strewn around her suite the next day. It's funny, the tiny details you remember when you've been to hell and back.

She makes a sound. "Not well enough to guess what he was capable of." Her eyes flicker to Ronan, where they linger. "And you are ..."

"Her friend." Ronan's never been one to flirt as brazenly as Connor does, which makes him seem standoffish. In Roshana's case, the unfriendlier, the better. I imagine she's not used to this reaction from men. I might hate her, but even I can admit that she's beautiful.

Roshana admires Ronan for another long moment before saying, "Have a wonderful weekend, and tell your boss I said hi."

"*Ex*-boss." And no, I don't think I will.

She strolls away, swinging her curvy hips.

"Who was that?" Ronan asks.

"A snake who will bite off your dick." Belinda was not wrong when she called Roshana a viper. Ronan's face fills with grim amusement, and I sigh. "A catalyst for the worst mistake of my life." I reluctantly tell Ronan the abbreviated version.

"That's the one Andy was working for that weekend," Ronan says, putting pieces together on his end.

"Yeah." The Australian who happily claimed Roshana and her blond companion used his body for their amusement. For weeks, I had believed it was Henry who went home with them that night. He didn't do anything to dissuade me of that belief, but he already knew about the terrible blunder I'd made with Michael. In a twisted way, Henry lied to protect me from the truth: that I had cheated on him.

But how would Roshana Mafi recognize me? We met on her arrival and then I was nothing more than a shadow the rest of the weekend, while she did her best to try to win her way into Henry's pants. "That whole exchange felt weird. Didn't that feel weird?"

Ronan's gaze wanders to Lux's exit doors, but Roshana is long gone. "That was definitely something."

seventeen

Violet climbs out of the SUV, her eyes narrowed on the strip of commercial storefronts. I understand her wariness. I felt the same way when Zaheera brought me here. The area is street after street of rectangular buildings, no coffee shops or restaurants within easy walking distance.

"Who is she again?" Annie asks curiously.

"A friend. She needed help with a school project." The lie tastes bad, but it's not my place to introduce Violet as Henry's daughter until they've given their blessing, and I think we're a long way from that.

Maybe it's not a lie though. Violet seems to trust me, so could this not be some cliched "rich dad marries gold-digging woman barely older than his daughter" storyline? There's little about this situation that's stereotypical, so maybe we *can* be friends?

Annie merely nods. Why would she doubt my answer? She's never even met Henry. But how long before people look at this girl heading toward our front door—in her black bomber jacket and leggings, her dark hair capped by a poppy-red knit beanie—and see the family resemblance?

The door chimes. "Hey." She waves tentatively, her bottom lip pulled between her teeth as she takes in my commercial kitchen—the stacks of supplies in cardboard boxes, the bowls and molds, and metal tables. She stalls on Ashlyn, the quiet blue-haired temp worker we brought in to help with equipment setup and cleanup, so I can focus on making the soap. Another thing Zaheera insisted on and I resisted, and now I'm so thankful for.

"Hey, Violet." I make quick introductions. "How was the drive from Philly?"

"Fine."

"Weird having a driver pick you up?"

"Yeah, kind of," she admits sheepishly.

"I'm still getting used to it too." She and I, we're not all that different. Neither of us grew up in Henry's world. "There's a coat hook over there. Get comfortable."

Violet drops her backpack on the floor in the corner and then sheds her outer things, save for the knit cap. She's swapped her usual hoodie for a more stylish chunky white cable-knit sweater.

"I like your hat. Where did you get that?" I ask.

"Um ... I made it." She fidgets with the cuffs on her sweater.

"Really? You know how to knit?"

"Yeah. Gramma taught me how. I sat around a lot over the last few months, so at least this way I had something to do."

Sat around next to her mother's bedside, watching her slowly die, she doesn't have to say. My heart aches for the girl, for what she had to witness. Something like that changes you forever. "Well, it's very cute and it looks great on you."

Her eyes roam the boxy space until she points to the wall. "Blah gray."

I laugh. "See? I wasn't lying." The walls are bare, devoid of personality.

"So ... this is your office."

"Actually, my 'office'"—I air quote with my fingers—"is a literal closet in the back that we decorated. But here is where the magic happens. Doesn't look like much, does it?"

She shrugs. "And that's all soap over there?"

"Most of the first batch, yeah." My nerves flutter. "We go live on the website Monday, and I don't know if anyone is going to buy any of it." It's one thing to have Peggy Sue demanding that I have a batch of sage soap for Greenbank's church bazaar. Is award-winning Nailed It Branding going to see Farm Girl Soap Co. as its first epic failure?

And I didn't mean to dump my insecurities on the poor girl within a minute of her walking in.

Violet picks up a packaged bar from the nearby table and holds it to her nose, inhaling. "I'd use it."

"Yeah?" I smile. That's a good start. "Come on. Let me show you around."

"It looks like homemade fudge." Violet leans over the counter, propped up by her elbows, as she watches me slice a block of mint-scented soap into measured rectangular chunks.

"Funny you should say that because a little kid back home bit into a peppermint chocolate bar at the Christmas market." I'd been experimenting with new scents for the holidays and found a chocolate fragrance oil online that I liked.

Her blue eyes widen. "What happened?"

"He spat it out and told me my fudge tasted like soap." I laugh. "It's all natural and nontoxic. Wasn't going to hurt him."

"He'll never look at fudge again without remembering you."

"Probably not."

I was nervous about how today with Violet would go, but within no time of her arrival—after the five-second tour, five-minute mockery of my closet office, and an overview of all that Nailed It and I have been working on these past months—she seems to have stepped out of her hard shell, revealing a quick-witted, curious girl who asks a lot of questions and smiles far more than she scowls.

"And you've been making these since you were my age?"

"Maybe even younger, I think? This lady in our church used to make vanilla-scented gingerbread men soaps for the Christmas bazaar. I thought they were the cutest things, and I wanted to make something like that to give to friends and family. Homemade gifts are always more special, right? So she showed me how. From there, I started reading up on how to use herbs and flowers from around the farm. I experimented with scent ideas, learned how to layer scents, what worked and what didn't." I laugh, shaking my head. "Once, I mixed lavender and eucalyptus. Bad idea. My mother complained about it for weeks, even though my father and I couldn't smell anything. Anyway, there's this little tack room in my family's barn back home, so I moved out there and kind of took over."

"The pictures on your website."

"Yes. That's the room." Violet actually paid attention.

"An indie business magazine did an article on me this summer. They dressed it up a bit. It doesn't look that nice in real life." I smile as I remember that day. Margo arranged for it all through her friend, Ryan McCleary. Jed tried to impress my supermodel friend by farming in a button-down shirt and tie, and then Margo showed Ryan her brand of appreciation in the pond out back. "I've only ever sold these at the local church bazaars and farmers' markets."

"What made you go big?"

I pause. Compared to the path I was heading down—supplying a major department store—a little rectangular rental space in New Jersey isn't much. But it's mine. "Henry did."

She picks up a broken sliver of soap, holding it to her nose. "What? He's not rich enough already, he wants his future wife to make bank too?" There's a hint of something I can't pick out in her tone, but it feels like a slight. My urge to defend Henry sparks.

She doesn't know him at all, though, I remind myself.

"He *is* rich," I admit because there's no point denying it. *And you will be, too, once that trust fund opens to you.* "But he doesn't care if I make a dollar doing this. Well, that's not true. He wants me to make money because then it means someone's buying my soaps and I'm not a giant failure," I correct. "But he pushed me because he wanted me to have something that I can be proud of." I smile softly. "He's encouraged me through this entire venture. I would never have had the nerve to do this." Nor the funds, but that's beside the point.

When I asked him why he pushed Zaheera and her start-up company on me, he said it was because he didn't want me to drown in his world.

I'm beginning to appreciate it now.

Violet watches me work for a few minutes. "How often does Henry come here?"

"He hasn't been here yet. He's not great at sitting back and watching. I guess that comes with the territory when you're as successful as he is, but he's trying to stay as hands-off as possible." He saw the listing before I signed the lease because I wanted his input, but aside from those first few weeks of hiring Zaheera's company, when he was blind-copied on all the emails between us to ensure they were doing what he expected of them, he's stepped away. "He said he'd come in next week, though, for the launch. Once he's back from Spain."

"Oh. So, he's not around?" She quickly adds, "Gramps said something about wanting to call him."

Maybe Howard does have reason to call Henry, but I didn't miss the hint of disappointment in her voice with that first part. "He comes home tomorrow. His plane takes off early so he should be home by midmorning."

She bites her bottom lip but doesn't say anything.

A—possibly stupid—idea strikes me. "You know, you could always stay over at our place tonight. Work on your project there. That way if you have any more questions, I can answer them."

"In Manhattan?"

"Yeah. We have plenty of room."

She hesitates. "I didn't bring any clothes with me."

"I'm sure I have something that'll fit you, and we can stop at the store on the way home for a toothbrush and all that."

"Um ..." She stalls. She may be looking for an excuse to avoid this, but my gut tells me she just doesn't want to appear too eager.

"No pressure at all, but I'm sure Henry would be happy to see you."

"I'd have to ask my grandparents."

"That's a change," I tease, my voice dry.

She bites down on a smile as she taps on her phone screen. But she's not texting Gayle and Howard. She's opened up Instagram and, with quick fingers, she has my profile open. "You haven't even launched yet and you have *that* many followers?" She holds up her phone, her eyes wide.

"That's thanks to Zaheera and the team's PR work, which is all stuff you should work into this project of yours." Their influencer campaign has brought a steady drumbeat of new followers each day. Margo's efforts seem to have paid off too. Dozens of the celebrity attendees at that party we made samples for have posted online, tagging us.

"Yeah, I think you're gonna do okay, Abbi." She snorts, as if my nervousness is silly.

"We'll see." I lift the wooden block of bars and carry it over to the packaging area.

Violet trails after me and watches as I wrap one in the simple brown paper packaging, binding it with twine. The round embossed label finishes it off.

"That's simple."

"It is. Henry helped me wrap bars once, after—" I cut myself off. No need to bring Scott into the day. "When I was running out of time. Here, try one." I set a bar in front of her.

She watches me wrap another before slowly mimicking me.

"Perfect."

She sets it aside. "You know, this feels suspiciously like free labor."

"*Or* fair trade for my sage advice. Plus, I'm buying you a toothbrush and underwear. I can throw in dinner?"

Her lips twitch. "Weird. But it's a deal."

"*After* you call your grandparents and ask if it's okay, right?"

"Right." She digs out her phone again and wanders over to a corner, her voice quiet as she speaks to either Howard or Gayle. In moments, she's back. "They're cool with it."

Unexpected giddiness bubbles inside me but I force it down and pretend this is no big deal. "Good." I move on to the next soap bar. "So, what's your business plan going to be for?"

She heaves a sigh, and the stress in that single sound is palpable. "Everyone's doing trendy things like food trucks and coffee shops and tattoo parlors. The only thing I can think of is this." She hesitates and then points to the beanie on her head.

I wide smile stretches across my face. "I think that is a *fantastic* business idea, and I'll tell you why."

I ROUND the corner to find Violet staring up at the string of egg white dangling from the ceiling. Saturday morning's sunlight streams in through the panoramic windows, highlighting the pancake powder spilled all over the kitchen.

"How did you manage that?"

"It takes talent, right?" She flashes a sheepish grin. "This is why my mom never left me alone in the kitchen for long."

"Wait until I tell Raj. He's gonna get a kick out of this." I grab a wet cloth and, climbing up onto the counter, I wipe away the egg. "There, you can't even tell."

"*I* can tell," she says with mock seriousness.

I giggle as I climb down. My time with Violet has been nothing short of enjoyable. We finished wrapping yesterday's batch of soaps just before five and hit up a few stores in the area to buy overnight supplies before having dinner at Lux.

The rest of the evening, we spent lounging on the couch in pajamas, a movie playing in the background while she worked on her assignment. Every so often, though, she'd slide in a question about Henry. Some of them were small and innocuous:

Does he play sports?

What does he like to eat?

And yet her inquiries tested my knowledge of the man I'm about to marry:

Yes, golf, and as I've just learned, he was very good at basketball.

(Besides me?) Sandwiches from Marcello's and cheesecake.

Other questions had me fumbling over my answers:

Did Henry like his brother?

Why does he hate his mother so much?

For those, I settled on a sanitized version of the truth:

Money and power do strange things to people.

She isn't a good person.

Henry will have to be the one to delve into those answers, decide how much truth he wants to share about his messed-up family.

I check my phone. "Henry should be home any minute." He texted an hour ago to say he'd landed. I was trying to figure out the best way to tell him Violet's here and decided it should be a surprise.

"How often is he gone for work?"

"Some months are busier than others, but quite a bit.

More than I'd like," I admit. "But he has *a lot* of responsibility, especially now that he's running it alone."

"Do you ever go with him?"

"A few times, but I was stuck in Greenbank for a while, helping take care of my dad after a tractor accident. Honestly, we haven't been together long enough for me to take advantage of travel opportunities. But I did meet him in France, and that was a great trip." Though it ended on a sour note, with us flying home to plan William's funeral, it also brought us so much closer. "I never traveled before this past summer when I went to Alaska. I didn't even have a passport."

"Did you know only forty percent of Americans have passports?"

"I knew it wasn't a lot." Henry said something similar to Aunt May when we asked for her help with Daddy—and dealing with Mama—for my trip to Europe. "What about you?"

Violet splashes a drop of water on the frying pan, testing its heat. "My mom and I went to California, right after she was diagnosed. Did the whole Disneyland thing, and the beach. It was so much fun, she promised we'd do it again."

From the sounds of it, though, that never happened.

As much of a royal pain in the ass Mama has been, it makes me want to pick up the phone and call her.

I watch Violet's back for a moment, wondering what she thinks of me, and of all this. It must be surreal for her. I'd like to think we've been getting along, but is it all an act? Will she talk about her father's irritating wife one day in a tell-all book? She's wearing the blue and red plaid pajamas I bought for her last night. They're so soft, I bought the same pair for myself. She laughed when I came down wearing them but didn't say anything.

227

Violet hums a tune as she ladles batter into the frying pan.

"That's a pretty song. What is it?" I ask as I check the sheet of bacon cooking in the oven.

"Oh, it's nothing. I'm taking drama and we're doing a play. We've been rehearsing a lot lately."

So Violet enjoys acting. Another tidbit into her life. "What's the play?"

"*Alice in Wonderland*."

"And who are you?"

"The Queen of Hearts."

My hand freezes on the bowl of fresh berries that Raj washed and prepared. "Violet! That's like the main character!"

She spares a glance over her shoulder to roll her eyes at me. "No, Alice is the main character. *Becca Taylor* got Alice." She sneers at the girl's name.

"Do we not like Becca Taylor?"

"She told people that the only reason I got the role was because my mom was dying."

"So we *hate* Becca Taylor." That might not be the mature thing to say, but I'm not trying to parent Violet, and besides, I kind of do hate whoever this snotty, jealous girl is. "Whatever, so you're the next main character."

"Most people would say that's the Mad Hatter. Or the Cheshire Cat."

"Okay, *fine*! But the Queen of Hearts is the villain. That's always the best role to play." At least, it's the most fun to watch. "Good for you, Vi. I've never had the guts to stand onstage." I didn't mean to shorten her name, it just happened. It's what everyone in the Outdoor Crew did if they didn't give you a nickname like Red. Connor was Con, Ronan was Ro. Some of the guys called me Abs.

Violet's cheeks lift in a small smile. If it bothers her that I called her that, she doesn't say anything.

"Abbi?" Henry's deep voice booms from the penthouse entrance.

"In the kitchen!" I call back, my heart skipping beats, both in excitement and apprehension.

"You've got five seconds to take off your clothes before I bend you over the counter and—"

"Look who's here!" It's nearly a scream, my voice up several notches with sudden panic. In hindsight, maybe my plan wasn't the best idea after not seeing him all week.

Henry appears then, freezing momentarily as he spots Violet, mid-flip with a pancake. "*Hi.*"

"Hi."

"I had no idea you were here," he says slowly. I'm not sure I've ever seen Henry blush, but his cheeks are flushed red.

"Obviously not." She wrinkles her nose as she returns to her pancakes. "I guess we're not eating at the counter. Is the table safe?"

He shoots me a "Thanks for warning me" look.

"Welcome back." I overcompensate with a wide smile. "I hope you're hungry!"

"So THAT's how you two ended up here, in matching pajamas?" Henry asks between mouthfuls. Violet may be messy in the kitchen, but she makes perfectly round and tasty dollar pancakes.

"Yeah. The first half is due on Monday. We worked on it last night. I think I'm halfway done?" She says it like it's a question rather than a fact. "As for the matching pajamas, that was all Abbi. Your fiancée is odd."

"What? I liked them! The material is so soft!" I emphasize that by smoothing my palm over my sleeve.

Henry smirks. "It's a little early for Christmas, isn't it?"

"*Christmas*?" Violet peers at her pajamas, not understanding.

I laugh. "They're red and *blue*, Henry." To her, I explain, "He has a hard time with blue and green."

"Huh. Really ..." She cocks her head and looks at him as if this tiny bit of information is fascinating.

"Why?" Henry pauses, his fork halfway to his mouth. "Do you too?"

"Nope. I'm normal." She bites off a piece of her bacon.

Henry snorts. "You like your school?"

"It's fine." She shrugs, chewing. "It's school."

"Violet is playing the Queen of Hearts," I chip in.

"Who's that?"

"You know, *Alice in Wonderland*? Girl falls down a rabbit hole?"

"Oh. Right. A fairy tale." Henry frowns, and it dawns on me that Crystal McGuire was probably too busy spending her husband's money and embezzling from a children's charity to read bedtime stories to her kids. "So you like acting?"

"I guess." Another shrug. Did I shrug so much when I was her age?

Henry studies her for a long moment as she eats. "Your mother was involved with the school plays at Hartley."

Violet nods. "She used to put me in drama camp every summer. She insisted I had natural talent."

"She played the piano." He says this more to himself, as if his memory is jogged.

Violet's eyes wander to the baby grand. "Yeah. She did the music for our plays when I was in middle school."

"Do you play?"

"Nope." Violet's mood is souring quickly with talk of her mother.

Henry's phone chirps and he reaches for it without hesitation. I've gotten used to this—his tether to his company—but I reach out beneath the table with my foot to nudge his shin. A silent plea for him to ignore it.

"It's important. Just a sec," he murmurs, his focus already on the screen.

As important as getting to know your daughter?

"So, when is this play?" I ask.

"Beginning of December."

"That's only a few weeks away. Are there tickets left?"

"Uh … I don't know. Why?" Violet stammers.

"Because we want to come. Right, Henry?"

He's scowling at his phone.

I nudge him under the table with my toe again. "Violet's play is in a few weeks. We'll go and see it, right?"

"Right, yeah," he says, but he's distracted. A curse slips from his lips. "Abbi, you and I need to talk."

The hairs on my neck prickle from his suddenly serious tone.

My phone rings then, and Mama's name shows up on the display.

"Don't answer that," he barks, spiking my anxiety.

"What is going on, Henry?"

Smoothing his palm over his mouth, he hands me his phone.

I read the headline, and my stomach drops.

eighteen

"How did they get these!" I scroll through the myriad of pictures from Wolf Cove, printed in the front-page tabloid article that's now gracing magazine racks all over the country. And here I was, wondering why I hadn't heard from Luca/Frank/Hank/Satan in weeks. It's because he was pulling together this story.

These are stills of security camera recordings, and there are *many*, all the way back to the very beginning, the night a bearded Henry carried my drunk ass back to my cabin.

There's a snapshot of Henry towering over me in the lodge's main hall the day he scolded me for showing my jealousy as Rachel served him drinks, and one of Henry with his hand settled on the small of my back while we're walking along the path—he was always so careful about touching me outside the cabin.

They aren't all security photos, though. There's one from the grand opening Saturday night, with me in my fabulous dress, standing morose in the background while Henry ignored me all night. Just below it is a still of me in Michael's arms that same night, and then one of him leading me into his cabin.

And another of me ducking out of the cabin in Michael's clothes the next morning.

More security pictures in the following weeks, after our ugly breakup and Henry's departure, show my relationships with Ronan and Connor unfold—the hugs and friendly leans against each other by the lake. It's all innocent enough, and yet it paints a totally different picture when paired with the *Wolf Hotel Billionaire's Innocent Farm Girl Not So Innocent* headline.

My eyes burn with the threat of angry tears as I graze over the first paragraph again.

Owner of artisanal Farm Girl Soap Co. start-up and assistant to Wolf Hotels billionaire Henry Wolf has had a busy summer, snagging the interest of her rich boss (despite the corporate policy against fraternization). But when the boss was away making those big bucks, the assistant played, falling into the arms and beds of several coworkers, including Wolf's personal masseuse and several hotel grounds workers. The question is, will Henry Wolf go through with the wedding now that we've uncovered his bride-to-be's dark secrets?

"Who even wrote this trash?" I mutter, more to myself. There aren't any blatant claims of my infidelity. Just a lot of choice words that make me look like a gold-digging whore and Henry look like a clueless sucker.

"These were taken from corporate property. They belong to *me*. Some asshole has clearly sold them to this shit mag!" Henry roars into his phone as he paces. Dyson is surely on the other side of that line. "I want the full list of *every* fucking security guard on staff this summer, and who was working the night of the grand opening. Get it from Belinda.

Find out where they live, their contact information. I'm going to make whoever did this pay!"

I haven't seen Henry this agitated since the night at the golf club when we discovered Scott had been lying about having seen William before he died.

Violet watches. What must she think of her father in this light?

"And this Ben Shaw? Who is he?" Henry barely listens before barking, "Find out!"

Here I was just two days ago, thinking that snooping reporter didn't unearth what he was digging for. But he had a bigger aim than releasing it on some hot-take celebrity scandal website that feeds a thousand clickbait offshoots. Not that those sites haven't jumped in to ride the magazine's coattails. I've already received texts from Autumn and half of Greenbank.

"How bad is it?" Violet whispers.

"Oh, you know, they've made it sound like I'm a habitual cheater, that I've been running around, humping every male's leg I can get near." Tears prick my eyes. Mama called twice and texted three times, but I'm avoiding her. Her judgment is the last thing I can deal with.

"But it's not true."

I avert my gaze because the reality is, there are many truths buried in this reputation-destroying smear campaign. "Does it matter? Enough people will believe it. I'm already getting DMs and comments on Farm Girl's social media."

Her face screws up. "*Already*?"

"Yup." Got my first "you slut" comment about an hour ago, before I even knew this article existed, and they're trickling in, gaining momentum. Everything from *whore* to *stupid*, plus a few comments directed at Henry.

"Dump her cheating ass, Wolf. I would never cheat on you."

"Her loss, our gain."

Annie texted to ask how I'd like to handle it.

I have no damn clue.

Violet bites her fingernail. "Don't people have anything better to do?"

"Clearly not."

My phone rings with a call from Ronan. I answer in a rush. "I'm so sorry you're getting dragged into this." I sent him screenshots of the magazine as soon as the initial shock wore off.

"I'm not getting dragged into anything. And don't fucking apologize to me, Red." He sounds annoyed. "Is Wolf with you?"

"He's here." And pacing while spitting out orders. "He's pissed."

"No shit." Ronan chuckles, but it's a mirthless sound. "I guarantee you it was either Corbin or Mark who sold those pics to the press. Those fuckers kept tabs on *everything* going on. Corbin has a hard-on for the boss. He's obsessed."

I vaguely recall those names and something about a Henry shrine. "In security?"

"Yeah. Mark was Aspen's roommate."

Oh no ... "Mark knew about Michael." He was there the morning after I hooked up with Michael. He also knew that Henry didn't sleep with Roshana and her friend that night, that Henry left and Roshana dragged in Andy—another of Mark and Michael's roommates.

Henry ends his call and offers me a curious "Who are you talking to" frown.

"Hey, Ronan, I've gotta go—"

"I'm flying back to New York. Be there by tonight," he says.

"No, don't be crazy. You're visiting your family."

"Shut up, Red. I'll see you soon." The line goes dead before I can object.

"What did he want?" There's no small hint of annoyance in Henry's tone.

The moment I relay the two security guard names, Henry's on his phone, barking orders again.

My phone chirped while I was talking to Ronan. I check my texts to see another link from Autumn. Doing my best to steel my nerve, I click on it. "You're kidding me!" The online edition of the magazine shared a picture from last Thursday night, of Ronan and me at our table in Lux, the moment he seized my foot in his hands when I teasingly kicked him.

It was innocent. Nothing. And yet it could easily look like *something*, especially when it's coupled with a subhead that reads, "Henry Wolf's Fiancée Seen Out With Love Interest While Future Husband and Boss in Spain."

And suddenly it clicks.

"Oh my god."

"What is it now?" Henry asks, dread heavy in his voice.

"Roshana Mafi is behind this." Of course, it makes sense.

"That travel magazine journalist?" Henry's face tightens. "Why would she bother with all this?"

"Because you turned her down and then threatened her if she took out her anger through her article on Wolf Cove. From what I've heard, she didn't take your rejection kindly." If what Andy relayed was true, Henry told her he was seeing someone, and she claimed to have had the better fuck the night before with Scott. "She was at Lux on Thursday night and then this shows up?" I hold up my phone for him to see.

His teeth grind.

"Roshana came by, pretending not to know how she knows me, but she's fully aware that you and I are engaged." Little bits of that conversation click into place. "I told her you were in Spain. She kept calling me your assistant after I corrected her and then told me to enjoy my weekend, as if she knew this article was going to drop. And then this picture releases? This is all *too* coincidental."

"Fuck, you might be right." Henry sighs heavily. "This is about her resentment for me, Abbi, not you."

"And yet I'm the one wearing the scarlet letter on my forehead!" I knew my misdeeds would come back to bite me.

He reaches for his phone again. "Roshana Mafi, a reporter for *Luxury Travel Magazine*. Find out how she's connected to Ben Shaw." He's oddly calm compared to five minutes ago.

"Who's he talking to now?" Violet whispers.

"Still Dyson. That's his fix-it lawyer. They're going to be doing this all day. I'm so sorry, Violet. Things are not going as I hoped." What that hope was, I can't say, beyond Henry getting to know his daughter. "You don't have to stay. If you want to get your things, I'll ask Victor to drive you home."

"It's fine." Violet waves me off. "I still have this assignment to do, anyway. I might have questions."

I falter. "Are you saying you *want* to stay for this disaster?"

She shrugs. "Yeah, I mean, if you don't mind. And if the *angry man* doesn't care."

"The *angry man* will be on the phone demanding heads for the next few hours."

"Oh, I can help with that! I've been practicing." Violet takes a deep breath and declares in a shrill, slightly British accent, "Off with their heads!"

Henry pauses midconversation to frown at his daughter.

Despite everything, I laugh.

"THESE NO-GOOD REPORTERS, hiding in bushes and making up stories. They're all a bunch of vultures!" Mama declares. "Why won't they leave you be?"

I stare up at the ceiling from my reclined position on the couch, still in my plaid pajamas. "Because people keep buying magazines and visiting their sites and making them lots of money." People like Mama. There was no fight, no questioning when I denied every shred of that article about me and my wanton summer. Mama lapped it up. I think she's happy to peddle that version—that it's a media-fabricated story to sell copies—to Greenbank, whether she believes me or not, and I'm happy to let her.

But Ben Shaw isn't any ordinary "hide in the bushes to get the shot" creep. Dyson called back within an hour with a full dossier. He has worked at reputable papers in New York, Chicago, and Boston. At one point, he was considered an up-and-coming star in the news world. The only problem? Ben Shaw himself isn't reputable. He got caught faking details. Another time, he created an anonymous source. Soon, there wasn't a single respectable paper that would buy his stories.

Lucky for him, the gossip magazine he sold to doesn't value integrity as much as money, and scandal sells as fast as bottled water on a hundred-degree day.

The biggest piece to this puzzle that Superstar Dyson uncovered for us is that Ben Shaw and Roshana Mafi went to journalism school together and are well acquainted. There are several pictures on each other's social media of them out to dinner with friends in recent years.

"Is there anything Henry can do about it?" my dad asks. I can almost see my parents hunkered over the kitchen table, the phone parked in front of them, my voice carrying over the speaker.

"He and his people are doing everything he can." Dyson flew to Chicago and tracked Corbin down. Five minutes into questioning, he squealed on everyone—Mark and himself, for taking and storing pictures on their phones that they sold to Ben; Andy, for approaching them within days of Henry and me going public, after Roshana hunted him down; and Tillie, who was more than happy to share as many sordid rumors as she could gather on me.

Dyson is working on their dismissal paperwork from Wolf as we speak.

As for Roshana, I'm not sure what Henry has in mind for her, but he's cooking up something and I doubt it will taste good.

Right now, though, he's leaning over the kitchen counter in a fitted white T-shirt and gray sweatpants, listening as Violet walks him through her knit hat business plan. She's worked on it all day, headphones on to drown out the commotion. Plates of half-eaten meals litter the counter behind them. Occasionally, one of them reaches for a french fry.

"Listen, Mama, I should go." A dark, gloomy sky looms outside. Ronan will be here soon.

"Of course, Abigail. You go and get a good night's rest. This will all blow over soon. Next news cycle."

"Thank you." At least I don't have to deal with her judgment on top of everyone else's.

"And when you're feelin' up to it, you and Henry need to come over for dinner again."

"Yeah, I'm not sure when that'll be." How much begging will it take to convince Henry to subject himself to Mama again?

"Soon, hopefully! We can talk all about this barn reception Henry suggested. You know, after the wedding, for the Greenbank folks."

I frown at Henry's back. "Right. That." *What?*

"Get some sleep, baby girl. Love you."

"Love you too. Both of you." We end the call. "Hey, Henry?"

"Yeah?" he hollers.

"Why does my mother think we're having a reception in the barn?"

"Because I suggested it when I called her yesterday."

My mouth drops. "You called her?" And she answered?

"I did. Figured a peace offering might make her a bit more amiable."

To be a fly on the wall during that conversation. How many times did Mama bring the lord's name into it? Regardless, it must have gone well. "That was actually ... smart." She gets what she wants without derailing our plans.

"That's why he makes the *big bucks*," Violet cuts in, air-quoting *big bucks*.

Henry spares a smirk her way before peering over his shoulder at me. He's still on Barcelona time. He must be exhausted.

"Thank you," I mouth.

"Thank me later," he mouths back, his blue eyes dragging over my body, reminding me that it's been five days since I felt him inside me.

The penthouse phone rings, which means Ronan has arrived and is being escorted up.

With a heavy sigh, Henry moves for the bar.

～

"You worked in the Wolf Hotel in Alaska too?" Violet tucks strands of hair behind her ear. She abandoned her school project to curl up in an armchair as soon as Ronan arrived.

The fireplace casts a warm glow throughout the vast double-story living room. Coupled with strategically placed table lamps and heavy knit blankets I found in a linen closet upstairs, there's an ease to this grand space I haven't felt before. Outside, freezing drizzle pelts the wall of windows. This morning's sunshine is long gone, but that seems fitting, given the dark turn of events.

"I did." Ronan swallows a gulp of scotch—a pricy bottle, not that Henry has anything cheap to pour him instead. "With Red for a while." He nudges my arm with his elbow.

"Was that before or after you were Henry's assistant?" She's trying to piece together our summer, but is it pure curiosity or is she wondering how much of today's shocking article could be true?

"After," Henry answers for me, sipping his drink as his free hand rubs my foot where it rests on his lap. I've stretched out along the sectional and have no plans of getting up again.

"Henry left Alaska after the grand opening." She doesn't need to know the disastrous reason why. "And I moved to what they call the Outdoor Crew, which is groundskeeping."

"So you were his executive assistant and then you ... cut grass?"

I laugh. "I mostly maintained the gardens because the guys were terrible at it. It was *very* different but also great. I love working with my hands and being outside."

"Abbi was the only woman in a group of degenerates," Henry adds.

"They were *fun*." I nudge Henry's thigh with my heel. "And when Henry was trapped in that mine, Ronan and

Connor—that's another one of the guys—went in to find him. They helped save Henry's life." Something I will be eternally grateful for.

"That's ... pretty cool." Violet's blue eyes meet Ronan's for a moment, long enough for her cheeks to pink, and then she abruptly announces, "Too much Coke!" And scurries off to the nearby bathroom. It's not hard for anyone to see that the almost sixteen-year-old might have a little crush on the gorgeous man sitting beside me.

"You even fucking blink at her in a way I don't like and I will end you," Henry warns as soon as the door shuts.

"*Come on.* She's a kid," Ronan snaps. "*And* she looks like you."

Henry turns his scowl on me. "*You told him?*"

"Of course, I did. How would I explain her here tonight? Besides, you should know by now Ronan can be trusted to keep quiet." He's kept plenty of juicy secrets, ones that would sell a lot more magazines. "I'd be more worried about who Preston's telling."

"Those guys won't say a word. They know how to be discreet." Henry returns to his foot ministrations.

"And she doesn't look *completely* like Henry. She showed me pictures of her and her mother. There's a good mix there." Her heart-shaped face and wide smile are, without doubt, Audrey's.

"Still, the more people see you two together, the more questions they're gonna ask. Eventually someone in the media will notice. You think they've been brutal with you, Red?" Ronan's eyebrows arch. "Wait until they get hold of this story."

My stomach churns with the thought. "She's only fifteen. They can't do that to her."

"And yet they will," he says through another sip.

"What happened today was because a conniving bitch couldn't take rejection and wants to play hardball." Henry adds quietly, "He's not wrong, though."

"What are we going to do, then? Violet's *in your life*, Henry. She's not going anywhere." If the past two days have taught me anything, it's that despite whatever Violet said early on, she wants to be here.

"I've already warned her about keeping this quiet. Seeing today's mess unfold will make her think twice about saying anything to anyone."

"People will still ask." Annie asked. It was an innocent question.

"Yeah, I know." Henry rubs the back of his neck. "What if we tell people that Audrey and my dad had a brief relationship, and she's my half-sister who I just discovered?"

"*Blame the dead guy.*" Ronan shakes his head. "That's *so* fucked up."

"Yeah, well, if you've got any other brilliant ideas, I'm all ears," Henry barks. "Because if the truth comes out, our lives will be hell, and both Audrey's and my father's reputations will be dragged through shit."

Maybe they deserve it, though. Audrey committed a terrible crime and William buried it from everyone, including Henry. Maybe they don't deserve to rest in peace. But no one deserves to make money off this story, which is what these tabloids will do.

Silence hangs in the living room, and my mind drifts back to thoughts of the *last* time the three of us were in a room together. My body flushes with the memory.

Henry's phone rings. "That's Dyson. Excuse me."

I move my feet and watch him stroll toward his office, his sweatpants hanging low on his hips. I can't wait to peel those off later and lick every inch of his skin.

"So?" Ronan leans into me until our shoulders touch. "How are you holding up? *Really*?" In his eyes is genuine concern.

I shrug. "There's not much I can do, is there? Henry's got HR and the lawyers preparing all the dismissal paperwork." Their security badges have already been suspended, with plans to haul them into a room the moment they show up for their shifts. *If* they have the nerve to show up. "He's calling in by video to fire them all personally. Theft charges are pending for the security guards." Tillie's going to get her wish of some face time with Henry, just not how she dreamed.

"*Damn.*"

"Yeah. They're looking into ways to punish the magazine for printing stolen corporate property. We'll see if they can make it stick."

"And this reporter?"

"Ben Shaw is a cockroach, but he didn't write anything in that article that is blatantly false. The last thing we want to do is have our business aired out in court during a lawsuit. They'll uncover *everything*." Which Ben surely knows.

"That wouldn't be ideal." Ronan rubs a hand over his short hair. "And that bitch from Thursday night?"

"I don't know what Henry has planned for Roshana yet." But I'm excited to find out. "If I didn't have this sale launching on Monday, I would throw my phone away and hide in here for the next *year*, until people forget."

"Attagirl. Face it head-on."

"They're attacking me, Ronan. Over a headline in a magazine they read in the grocery store." Or one they spotted as they scrolled aimlessly through their feeds. The "news" has grown legs, with dozens of secondhand basement-reporter sites regurgitating Ben Shaw's article for their own content. "Seriously, don't these people have lives?"

"No, they don't. Ignore them. Don't go looking for it."

God, he sounds like Henry. "That's the thing, I'm not!" I pull up Farm Girl's social media, something I've avoided doing for *hours*. Now? There are *hundreds* of new comments under posts from the past week. Annie wanted to go private, but Zaheera strongly advised against it. "See?" I pick one to read. "'I was going to try out this soap because Kendall McCoy said it made her skin feel so amazing, but now that I know the owner is a lying, cheating whore, I'm not giving her my money.'" My insides burn with indignation.

"Who the fuck is Kendall McCoy?"

"An influencer," I grumble, scrolling. "'Bitch not happy with her fine-ass man, she gotta get herself one for every day of the week.'"

He snorts. "Okay, that one's kind of funny."

I scroll farther. "Oh, this is even better. This person is psychoanalyzing me. According to her, I'm clearly working through commitment issues." I frown as I read another. "Apparently, I was handing out my soap at a party in Detroit last weekend and it gave her a terrible rash. Why would I be handing out soap at a party in *Detroit*?"

"People make shit up all the time. You can't trust anything on there."

"This one says she was in a sorority with me, and I slept with her boyfriend. Northgate doesn't have sororities! Oh, here's one defending me, I think? She says Henry's the personification of the patriarchal scourge upon society. He deserves to be cheated on. But then this one—"

"Okay, bad idea." Ronan yanks my phone out of my hand and tosses it to the opposite side of the couch. "Who has time to read a gossip article online, go search up the people, and then leave messages like that? People who have nothing good going on in their lives." Ronan raises his voice, a rare occurrence. "These people are fucking *losers*."

"Maybe, but they're losers who are trying to tank my business before it's even off the ground." I pull the blanket over my head.

Light footfalls approach. "What's going on now?" Violet asks, emerging from the bathroom.

"Abbi looked at something she shouldn't have," Ronan says with a sigh.

"Farm Girl," I moan into the soft weave.

"Did you see all your new followers, though?"

"What?" I peel the blanket halfway down my face.

"Yeah, you have ..." Violet holds her phone up to read. "Almost five thousand new followers since yesterday."

"Seriously?" Maybe Zaheera was right not to lock things down. "Why?"

"No such thing as bad publicity," Ronan says.

"They're just coming to watch me fail."

"Yeah, probably." Violet shrugs. "But some are curious. They want to know if it's true."

"Give them something to shut them all up, then," Ronan mutters.

"Like what?"

"You riding Wolf's lap."

"Eww!" Violet's face contorts.

Ronan chuckles. "Sorry, kid. I forgot."

"Forgot what?" Henry wanders back out.

"Nothing." I shoot a glare at Ronan. "What did Dyson want?"

He reclaims his spot on the couch, lifting my legs to drape over his lap. "To tell me that my acquisition of *Luxury*

Travel Magazine is underway. It's a great marketing opportunity for Wolf Hotels."

My jaw drops. "But that's ... You're kidding, right?"

"Don't worry. It's a boutique magazine. It wasn't *that* expensive."

Ronan curses under his breath.

Henry's plan is becoming clear to me. "You bought a whole company—*today*—so you can fire Roshana?"

"She couldn't stop singing its praises while she was in Alaska. Their compensation packages are top tier. Nowhere else is as competitive." He collects his glass and takes a sip of scotch, as if nothing about what he just did is out of the ordinary. "She loves her job and traveling. She's been moving up in the company, making a name for herself."

"And you'll be able to fire her?"

"After what she's done, I think she'll go quietly. And if she doesn't?" A vicious smile stretches across his lips. "Let's just say I can use my hotel security feeds too."

I don't think I want to know what those may have captured.

"Savage," Violet says, but she's smiling at Henry.

"Sends a very clear message." Henry sets his drink down and, grabbing hold of my ankles, drags me across to pull me into his lap. "Fuck with my loved ones, and I will come for you with everything I have." He leans in and skates his lips against mine in a kiss that feels way too intimate to be enjoying in front of his daughter.

"Later," I whisper, pulling away.

He frowns at Violet. "What are you doing?"

She has her phone aimed at us. "Taking a picture."

He gives her a flat look. "Yes, I understand that. *Why*?"

"It's like Ronan said. Give them something to shut them up." She shows us the shot she captured in the seconds after our lips pulled apart, our faces inches away. Henry's muscular arms wrapped around my curled-up body make me look so small next to him. It's sexy, and yet sweet.

"I love this." Henry and I have so few pictures together. At least, ones that sleazy photographers didn't take.

"You should post it on your Farm Girl accounts so people can see that you're together and that stupid article is all bullshit. You two wouldn't be kissing each other if Abbi was running around, sleeping with all these guys behind your back."

Am I supposed to scold her for cussing? Because I don't have it in me. And besides, Violet might be on to something. I don't need to be "riding Wolf's lap" for the message to be effective. "Would you be okay with that?" I ask Henry.

"With what?" His eyebrow arches. "People seeing me *kiss* you?"

I poke him in the ribs before asking, "Can you text it to me?"

Violet's thumbs move over her phone and moments later, my phone chirps from its resting spot across the couch.

Ronan fetches it and tosses it easily into my grip.

"I'll see what Annie and Zaheera say about that idea first. They might see a landmine that we don't."

"I think it's a smart idea," Henry says.

"Well, yeah, of course. *I* came up with it." Violet reaches up and pats herself on the shoulder.

"Actually, I think it was *my* idea?" Ronan jumps in.

"Uh ... *your* idea would get Abbi's accounts suspended," Violet retorts, rolling her eyes.

"Why does that not surprise me?" Henry mutters.

nineteen

Violet: *Just wanted to say good luck with the big launch!*

"What's that smile for?" Henry swoops in to pepper a kiss against my neck while he steals a glance at my screen.

"*Your daughter* is wishing me luck today." I punch out a quick reply.

Abbi: *Thank you!*

He hums, then snatches my phone from my grasp and quickly types out a message.

Abbi: *Get to class before I send you to boarding school.*

"Henry!" I glare at him. We are nowhere near making those kinds of jokes yet. How is she going to take that?

Three dots bounce almost immediately.

Violet: *Hey, Henry. I guess you graced Abbi's office with your royal presence? And do they have hot teachers at said boarding school?*

Henry's molars grind.

I tuck my phone into my pocket before Henry can grab it

to reply. "I think she won that round." But what's even more impressive is that she knew it was him.

"What kind of teacher allows her to text during class?" He frowns. "We need to investigate private schools in her area. She can start next semester."

"And have you asked her?"

"No, but she needs a good education. And to be with other people like her."

"What do you mean, like her?" It dawns on me a second later. "Oh, right. *Rich*." I roll my eyes. "Well, she's not. She's a kid who lives with her grandparents. Plus, you can't just come into her life and take over. She's not a company."

He scowls, but he doesn't respond.

That's a conversation for later. "What's the countdown?" I call out to Annie, who's sitting at her desk, watching the clock and pretending not to listen to us. Maybe I'm too trusting, but I don't think she would say anything about Violet if she did figure it out. That doesn't mean I didn't get her to sign an ironclad NDA, at Henry's insistence.

Annie grins and holds up her hand. "T-minus five minutes!"

"Okay." I take a deep breath as we wait for the clock to strike eleven a.m. and the shop to go live. "This is ridiculous. I don't know why I'm so nervous. We'll sell a handful of orders today."

"Either way, we're celebrating!" Annie holds up the bottle of Dom Pérignon Henry brought, already chilling in a bucket. Zaheera is on her way.

"Seriously, Henry, you don't need to stay. Today is going to be anticlimactic." Unless I drown myself in a vat of coconut oil.

He cocks his head and gives me an odd look. "Excuse us for a moment, please, Annie." Roping an arm around my waist, he herds me into my office, pushing my desk chair back and pulling the door shut behind him.

I know what this is about. Henry is attracted to confidence and right now I am displaying anything but that.

I look up to find him scowling down at me from mere inches away, our chests pressed against each other because there's no room to maneuver in here. "I know! My soaps are amazing and everyone who tries them loves them. Nailed It is the best at what they do. Margo has been talking me up to everyone she knows like some crazy soap pusher. I know all that!" I throw my hands up in surrender. "I guess I'm just trying to protect myself from disappointment. After this weekend, I don't know what to expect, and it's left me on edge."

Annie posted the picture Violet took with a caption that read, "The one and only love of my life. Can't wait to marry you" and then restricted the comments. It seems to have helped cauterize the flow of online hate messages, though we've seen a few comments dropped on old posts of this all being a publicity stunt for my product launch. That made me laugh. As if I need or want this kind of attention to help sell a few bars of soap when I'm marrying one of the richest men in the country.

Henry looms, his blue eyes searching mine.

I can't take it anymore. "Would you please say something?"

"Your office is in a closet."

I burst into giggles. "I know. I told you that already."

"I remember. I didn't fully appreciate that until now. But that's fine. I can make it work."

"For wha—"

His mouth is on mine before I finish my sentence, our lips meshed as a hand coils around my hair. He tugs it, forcing my head back. "No matter how today goes, you should be proud of yourself," he whispers against my lips, using his free hand to move my laptop out of the way before he urges me onto my desk. "*I'm* proud of you."

I match his tongue stroke for stroke, my hands clawing to gain access beneath his shirt, reveling in the smooth, taut skin over his muscles. But it's his words that pour through me like warmed honey, soothing the anxiety that's plagued me for days. "You're proud of your insecure, stupid little girl?" I tease, quoting something he said long ago.

He inhales sharply. "I've never thought that about you, Abbi."

"But you said—"

"And I regret it." I tip my head back as Henry's lips land on my neck, his teeth scraping deliciously across my skin. "I've *always* regretted saying that," he whispers into my ear.

But maybe it was true. I wouldn't call myself stupid, but I was certainly insecure, allowing other people to choose my life's path. Mama ... Jed ... And then Henry came along and bulldozed everything, pulled me out of any comfort zone I've ever known, made me question what I want.

His hands slide along the contours of my body, down to my hips. Seizing the waistband of my leggings and my panties, he wriggles them down to my ankles, where they're stopped by my hiking boots.

"You have to untie them."

"We don't have time for that."

I let out a squeal as Henry bends and forces his body through the space between my thighs, leaving my pants hooked around the back of his head and my ankles resting on his shoulders.

"This is tight." I laugh, falling back against the wallpapered wall, my body folded in half.

"Just how I like it." Henry fumbles with his buckle and zipper. In seconds he has his pants shoved down and he's prodding my entrance with the blunt head of his cock. "*Always* ready for me."

"These walls are thin—" My warning stalls on a scream as Henry thrusts into me with force.

"These walls are thin, Abbi," Henry mocks, punctuates his words with his hips.

I can't bite back another cry fast enough. "*Henry*, my assistant is right out—" My words are lost as Henry plunders my mouth with his tongue, my body nearly folded in half.

And then he slams into me again. And again, his beautiful arms bracing himself on either side of my shoulders as he drives into me at a relentless pace, his thighs slapping against mine, my little desk thumping against the wall as steadily and tellingly as a headboard. He's so deep at this angle, and each time he sinks in, a groan slips out of me, the mixture of pleasure and pain overwhelming.

All other thoughts vanish as I let Henry consume my body as he pleases.

I manage to prop myself up on my elbows, but with my pants bunched around his neck, I'm at his mercy. Henry takes advantage of that, pumping in and out of me. A rosy flush coats his skin.

"Fuck, I'm going to come now, Abbi," he growls, speeding up his pace. A moment later his body tenses and he releases a long, guttural groan as he pulses and fills me.

The sight and sound of him letting go has my orgasm chasing. I can't be bothered to hide my moans as my muscles seize up and ecstasy overwhelms me.

In seconds, my tiny closet office is quiet once again, save for our labored breathing.

Henry pulls out and collects a few tissues. "What was that you said about this day being anticlimactic?" he murmurs, cleaning me up.

I giggle. And then gasp. "Did we go live? We must have gone live by now!" Was that his intention? To distract me so I didn't go insane from the anxiety of the waiting game?

He ducks and slips my ankles over his head, settling them down gently onto the floor before pulling me up onto wobbly, Jell-O legs. "After you."

We redress, bumping elbows multiple times. I smooth my hair as best I can, but there's no hiding what just happened in here and by the time we emerge, my face is burning.

Annie is joined by Zaheera, who stands next to a bunch of rose gold balloons and cupcakes. They're wearing matching grins. "Guess what! We sold out!"

My mouth drops, my embarrassment instantly forgotten. "What do you mean?"

Annie laughs. "I mean exactly what it sounds like! You sold through everything. *Everything!*" She's bursting with excitement. "And there's a waitlist growing for the next batch already."

I gape at Henry. "Did you have something to do with that?"

"When would I have done that?" he deadpans.

"They're all individual orders," Zaheera confirms.

But how is that possible? I look back at my office door. "How long were we in there for?"

Annie looks at her watch. "The sale started fourteen minutes ago, so ..."

We listened to you two fuck for fifteen minutes, give or take, is what that long silence after says.

"This is ... I can't believe it!" A squeal of glee escapes me as I throw my arms around Henry's neck. None of that bull-shit from this weekend mattered. Not only did Roshana's attempt to punish Henry fail, but the visibility might have given me a boost.

He pulls me against him in a warm embrace. "I knew you could do it."

Annie pulls the champagne from the bucket. "What do you say, boss?"

twenty

"Can you imagine decorating this thing?" I stare up at the massive tree in awe, its countless Swarovski crystal lights a dazzling display for the thousands that huddle in the cold. A puff of my hot breath mingles with the frigid air.

Violet tugs on her periwinkle knit cap—another that she made herself during the long, quiet nights. Her blue eyes twinkle. They're even more vibrant in the cold. "I can't believe you've never seen the Rockefeller tree before."

"My parents aren't big on traveling. Or cities." When I admitted this fact to Violet, she gasped in horror, and then she insisted on coming to Manhattan so we could see it together. It was as good an excuse as any to get her here again.

She shakes her head. "We come *every* year. Well, except last year, obviously. Mom would read up on the tree so we'd know its history."

"Practically minutes away from me and I had no idea ..." Henry's jaw tenses. He stands on the other side of Violet, his stance solid, as if a barrier from the crowd. Looming not far behind us are Sullivan and Daniel, security guards for the Wolf who work as bodyguards off the hotel's clock. They're dressed casually, but anyone paying attention might question the two giant men moving in step, their heads on swivels.

So far, though, tucked in our winter coats and beanies, we're just part of the crowd.

Violet steals a glance up at Henry, likely wondering where he places his blame. Audrey? His father?

Her?

He can be intimidating when he's angry, especially if you don't know him, and especially if you're a teenage girl seeking his acceptance.

"What's this year's tree story?" I ask, hoping to keep the mood light. "Did you look it up?"

"Of course I did." She grins. "It's a Norway Spruce from Bainbridge, New York. It's eighty-two years old, it stands eighty feet tall, and weighs twelve *tons.*"

"Wow." I mouth, peering up at it again. "Can you imagine how much work it is to get it here and decorated?"

"There are videos!" Violet prattles on about the complex plan of security and cranes and trucks and five miles of light strands that wind around it. "Did you know that star at the top is worth *one point five million dollars*? And it's just sitting up there, waiting to be stolen."

Henry chuckles, his dark thoughts softening. "That thing weighs almost half a ton. I'd like to watch the fool try."

She shrugs. "Desperate people do crazy things."

"Speaking of crazy, have we seen what we needed to see?" He rubs his gloved hands together to emphasize his impatience. When I told him of this plan—standing in the cold with thousands of people to look at lights—he wasn't thrilled, but he made sure to mark it in his calendar.

"Yeah. Now we have to get street meat and a hot chocolate."

Henry cringes. "I'm not eating that."

"You *have to*! It's tradition!"

"I'll have one with you," I chirp before Henry can deny her. "What? I eat one every year at the carnival. They're good."

Henry shakes his head. "Do you two even know what's in those?"

"Deliciousness." Violet doesn't wait, weaving through people with ease, as if she was born and raised in the city. The girl is fearless.

Henry jerks his chin at the guys to move, but it's unnecessary. Sullivan's already using his massive frame to intimidate people out of the way until he's beside his ward.

She looks up at him and then spares an exasperated look over her shoulder for Henry.

"I've never had someone roll their eyes at me so much," Henry mutters, his arm roped around my waist. Daniel flanks my other side, a step behind us. It's been two weeks since that stupid magazine article hit shelves, and the online gossip cycle has moved on to a senator caught on video having his diaper changed at a sex party. I want to send him a thank-you card.

"She's a teenager. That's normal."

"Did you do that?"

"No, but I wasn't spawned by sin," I tease. "Seriously, I think it's a good thing. It means she's comfortable with you." As a person, and maybe even as her father.

"It's a highly annoying thing." But his lips curl with a smile.

⌇

Bishop Prep reminds me of my high school and every other high school I've ever stepped inside.

Same speckled vinyl floor that gleamed on the first day of school and hasn't since.

Same line of gray lockers, every fifth or sixth wearing a dent from a toe kick or a shoulder.

Same faint odor of stale sweat and dirty socks permeating the air.

Henry leans down to whisper dryly, "Remind me again why Violet isn't enrolled in the excellent private school seven blocks from here?"

"Because her friends are here, and this is *her* life." I smile sweetly up at him.

He flashes me an unimpressed look. I know he only wants the best for her, but she's had enough upheaval in her life. She needs *something* familiar, at least for now.

"Goodness, I haven't been here in ... well, since Audrey went here." Howard wiggles his fingers at a little girl bundled in head-to-toe pink winter gear, her thumb in her mouth.

The Sunday morning after we trudged to Rockefeller Square, snow began to fall and didn't stop for the next thirty hours, blanketing the northeastern states, wreaking havoc on travel, and earning these kids a day off from school. My flight to Chicago that Tuesday to write my exams was uncertain, so I ended up taking Henry's jet.

Violet warned us to arrive early tonight to ensure we found decent seats, but plenty of families must have had the same idea because the main corridor is busy, the floor stamped with boot prints.

A middle-aged woman's gaze stalls on my face, then moves to Henry's where it lingers even longer, and my stomach tenses. "*They read the article, they know what you did,*" that anxious voice in my head still whispers. But the average person wouldn't make the connection, would never expect us to be *here*, and even if they did, it's getting easier to deny it as trash and move on.

Henry is right—I could have fucked every guy in the Outdoor Crew, at the same time—and it's none of *anyone's* business. No one is entitled to my personal truth, despite how many people think they are.

"This place hasn't changed at all." Gayle shuffles along, leaning against her cane for support as we wait in line.

"Alex said the work on the house is done?" Henry asks, keeping pace with Howard.

"Yes. The photographer is coming in next week, along with some sort of stager?" Howard's wrinkled face crinkles with confusion.

"Yes, they'll rearrange things and furnish any missing pieces. It'll get you the best price possible for the house."

"Never needed those people before. Then again, I've never sold a house. We've been in ours for fifty-five years."

Henry whistles. "That's a *long* time." Nobody could guess who Henry is and what he does by listening to him now. He's just another ordinary man. One who's wearing a five-thousand-dollar suit and whose driver is parked outside waiting for the show to end.

But I think seeing Henry like this—chatting up a kindly old man while standing in a public school foyer—is my new favorite.

Howard smiles wistfully at his wife as she surveys the graduating class pictures along the wall. "We've been lucky."

"This is her year." Gayle pauses at one graduating class. "There she is." She taps the glass on a photo of a much younger Audrey. Violet has shown me enough pictures that I could pick her out of a lineup now.

I lean in to get a better look at the stunning senior. "I see a lot of her in Violet."

"I used to *only* see Audrey in Violet, but now that I've met her father ..." Her voice fades. Is she thinking of her late daughter's misdeeds? How does a parent wrap their head around something like that, especially when their child isn't here to answer for it? Audrey could have confided in her parents, regardless of the contract she signed with William. That she didn't is telling. She didn't want to burden them with that heavy truth.

Henry talks of hiding his true connection to Violet to protect Audrey's memory, but I'm more inclined to do it to protect everyone else it impacts, including this sweet woman who likely still sees her daughter as the girl in that photo, innocent, youthful, and full of dreams.

"We should get our seats now," I say gently.

"Yes." Gayle agrees, but I don't miss the light sheen in her eyes. "Before all the good ones are gone."

A woman at the door handing out playbills smiles wide when she sees us approach. "Mrs. Campbell, I don't know if you remember me—"

"Sandra Mack. Of course, I remember you. My goodness." Gayle explains to us, "I taught Sandra for two years in middle school. What grades were those again?"

"Sixth and eighth grade."

"Yes, of course. She was one of my favorite students."

"And you were my favorite teacher." Sandra clutches her hands to her chest. "We all heard about Audrey. I am *so sorry* for your loss."

Gayle's and Howard's lips press together tightly as they nod.

"She didn't suffer for too long in the end. I suppose that's a blessing." Howard adds quietly, "That's what they tell us, anyway."

Sandra's hazel eyes flitter to us. "Are you family?"

"Cousins," I blurt because her eyes are on me. "From out of town."

"Oh! Well, wonderful. Let me help you to your seats."

Sandra leads us into the cafeteria that's been transformed for the show, the rows of chairs facing the stage on the far side. Henry and I fall behind Gayle and Howard as we walk down the main corridor.

"Cousins from out of town?" Henry whispers.

"Better than the idea *you* came up with. And *you* should be carrying these." I thrust the bouquet of blush-colored roses into Henry's hands.

"Here you are." Sandra gestures to four seats at center right with sheets of white paper taped to them, labeled Reserved for Campbell Family. "We thought Violet might appreciate seeing familiar faces in the crowd, given all she's been through." She offers a sympathetic look before marching off the way she came.

We settle into our seats, with the men anchoring the ends, and Gayle and I beside each other. All around us, people pour in as the clock moves closer to curtain call, and a low buzz of voices grows.

"She is *so* nervous," Gayle confides in me. "She was practicing her lines *all night* and this morning, in the kitchen. Pacing around the table, yelling 'Off with her head!'" She chuckles.

"It's a big role for her. Especially as a sophomore. In my school plays, it was always the seniors chosen for the main characters."

Gayle drops her voice to a whisper. "I think it has more to do with *who's* in the audience tonight." She widens her eyes meaningfully at the solemn man sitting tall next to me, clutching flowers, his thoughts seemingly elsewhere as he takes in the chaos. "We know what a busy man he is. It means a lot to her that he came."

"He wouldn't miss it," I say with confidence, but the truth is, I never asked Henry how he felt about *any of this*. I never gave him a choice. I told him I'd bought four tickets and suggested giving Violet's grandparents a ride, and he merely said, "That's fine." But if he didn't want to be here, he wouldn't be here. He is Henry Wolf, after all.

I slip my hand into his, giving it a squeeze. "You good?"

He snaps out of whatever stupor he was caught in. "Yes." His eyes drift over my mouth. "You?"

I nod. "I'm excited to see her perform."

"You always know the right thing to do and say." A few beats pass before he leans in to kiss me. "I would be lost without you."

A lump swells in my throat. It's so rare for Henry to show vulnerability, and yet he's growing more comfortable doing so each day with me. "We'll figure it out together."

When the overhead lights dim and the spotlights hit the stage, a chorus of "shhhs" quiets the energetic crowd almost instantly. Henry's thumb strokes the back of my hand as we listen to the school principal and the drama teacher greet families, thanking the multitude of people who helped with everything from costumes to posters to a fundraising campaign.

The curtain finally draws open.

The classic tale begins as I remember, with an artfully painted backdrop of a forested scene that Violet said the art club spent three weeks working on. A senior male student—with the deepest voice in the school, according to her—sits on a stool, narrating the opening, just as she described he would.

Characters are introduced as the story unfolds in a quirky script with a few bows to today's times, bringing plenty of laughter from the crowd.

Henry's hand tightens within mine as Violet strolls out in a bright red ballgown and matching wig, her face a stony red, white, and black painted mask that reminds me too much of a mime's. She looks incredible.

I soon realize there's no need to be nervous for this girl. She fills the entire stage in an instant, as if she belongs there and the show is hers to lead.

Her gaze flickers out to the crowd, landing on us—on Henry—almost immediately.

With a deep breath, she belts out her first lines.

VIOLET EMERGES from backstage ten minutes after the play ends, still in her dress, but missing the wig. Her makeup has been hastily wiped off, leaving faint smears of red.

"You were the best Queen of Hearts this stage has ever seen!" Gayle exclaims.

"Thanks, Gramma." Violet towers over the old woman as she hugs her. "But I know you have to say that."

"Oh, shush, I certainly do not."

"She's right. You were marvelous." Howard hugs her. "Your mother would be so proud." Their hug seems to tighten over those last words.

When Violet turns to us, the corner of her bottom lip is pulled between her teeth. She does that when she's worried, I'm learning.

I beam. "That was amazing. *You* were amazing. Did you

hear the audience when you took your bow?" Tears pricked my eyes as she stepped forward and the crowd grew noticeably louder.

She gives a half shrug, like it wasn't anything.

"You should be so impressed with yourself." I throw my arms around her to pull her into a hug—the first I've ever given her.

She stiffens but only for a second before melting into my body.

"Also, Becca Taylor messed up her lines *three times*," I whisper in her ear.

Violet giggles as she pulls away, her smile turning sheepish as she looks at Henry. "So? I know it's not like your Hartley private school plays, but hopefully, it wasn't *too* painful?"

She's feigning indifference to Henry's opinion, but I know better. No matter where she was on the stage, she was checking the front row, as if monitoring his reactions.

Henry sighs heavily—he's too smart and perceptive to not have noticed this too. "You don't belong on that stage, Violet."

Her face falls instantly.

He settles his free hand on her shoulder. "You're *too* good. You made the entire show. There was no one else on stage when you were there." With one arm, he pulls her into his chest and whispers something in her ear that I don't catch but that makes my heart stutter all the same.

The moment is over as quickly as it starts, Violet breaking free first. She takes a deep, shaky breath.

"These are for you." Henry holds out the roses for her to collect.

"Thanks." She grins. "For the flowers, *Abbi*."

"Are you suggesting *I* can't be thoughtful?" Henry's face

is a mixture of amusement and annoyance. "Abbi, tell her how thoughtful I can be."

"He once rush-ordered a replacement vest for me when a grizzly bear tore mine apart."

Violet's expression twists with horror, making us both laugh.

"Excuse me." The drama teacher who stood on the stage at the start of the play appears next to Violet, her thick blond braid draped over her shoulder. "I'm Ms. Draper. I wanted to introduce myself and extend my condolences." She has a soft, almost airy voice. I can't picture her onstage, but Violet said she was on Broadway once, long ago. "I taught with Audrey at the elementary school for years before I moved here. It's a very sad thing, what happened to her."

Gayle and Howard offer their standard thank-yous.

"You two are cousins, is it?" Ms. Draper asks.

Word travels fast. As I expected. There isn't a room Henry can step into without garnering notice.

She frowns at him. "You look *so* familiar. I can't place it."

He smiles easily. "I guess I have one of those faces."

I stifle my snort. Yes, one of those stunning, enigmatic faces that makes people stumble on the sidewalk as they catch a long look. My insides are tightening as I hold my breath and wait for it to click in her head.

But it never seems to, and she dismisses it quickly, much to my relief. "Well! I'm sure you're all *so* impressed by the way Violet dominated the stage." She wraps an arm around Violet's shoulders. "I see big things in this one's future."

Henry gives her an arched brow with a "See? Told you so" look.

Genuine pride explodes inside me, not only for Violet but also for Henry, the father he's becoming before my eyes.

I NESTLE against Henry's chest as streetlights fly past on our ride home from Philly. "Mama called. She wants us there for Christmas."

"Didn't we already tell her we would come? Even though my vote was for the Maldives," he adds dryly.

"She wants us *there*, for Christmas. As in, waking up *in* the house, and staying the following night too." She and my father called earlier today to complain that they never get to see me. Well, Mama complained. Daddy stayed quiet, which is as good as an agreement from him.

"No. I am a thirty-two-year-old man, and I will not be told who I can and cannot share a bed with." He huffs a sigh. "However, to keep the peace, I *will* agree to stay at the bed-and-breakfast."

"There aren't any rooms available." I already called and checked, because the idea of Henry and my mother under the same roof makes my anxiety bubble.

"That weird place with all the cat themes?" His face pinches with doubt. "Did Bernadette book up all the rooms so we couldn't stay there?"

I laugh. "It's the *only* place to stay in Greenbank. And it's okay. Mama said she's willing to accept us staying together in my room since we're already 'living in sin,' and she knows it's the only way I'll agree to this idea." Apparently, she and the reverend have had long discussions and prayed deeply over the matter, asking the Lord for forgiveness. I could practically hear her teeth gnashing when she forced out those words. "The bed's small, but they said they can get an air mattress?" I press my lips together to keep from giggling as Henry glares. "She's trying. And it's our first Christmas together."

"And probably our last. I'm sorry, but that woman has pulled so many one-eighties, I would expect to wake up with her standing over me with a claw hammer."

"That wouldn't be very Christian of her. She does, however, have a special edition hardback Bible, and that would hurt." I rest my chin on his shoulder. "Please, Henry? She *is* trying."

He groans. "Fine. We'll drive there on Christmas Eve."

"Drive? Really?" I ask. Henry avoids long car rides at all costs.

"I gave everyone time off. Jack's got a toddler at home." He hesitates. "And this way we can stop in Philly on the way."

"Right." I should have known there was another motivation. "Are you sure you don't want to go there on Christmas morning, though? I can tell Mama you have family you need to see." She won't like it, but she'll have to accept it.

"Howard said they have cousins coming. *Real* cousins. It's best we stay clear of there on that day, to avoid questions. But it's the first Christmas without Audrey. I thought it'd be good to visit."

And the first Christmas Henry will spend without his father and brother, I must remind myself. So much has happened, it's easy to forget. The latter, Henry won't miss, but regardless of how complicated and confrontational his relationship was with his father—especially now that we've learned about Violet—I'm sure he will feel his absence.

"I think that's a great idea." I stretch up to kiss Henry's neck, reveling in the taste of his skin. A great idea that he came up with all on his own.

twenty-one

"This really is a cute neighborhood." Plump snowflakes float down, melting the second they land on the windshield of Henry's Porsche Cayenne—a vehicle I had no clue he owned until we walked up to it in the underground garage.

"Which is why that real estate agent tried to help her sister get it, and for a steal." Henry navigates the side street with one hand on the wheel, the other resting on the console. It's midafternoon on Christmas Eve, and the drive here was hectic, with all the last-minute holiday shopping. "Alex and Tony got them eighty thousand more."

My mouth gapes. Barbara should go to prison for that. "So, it's officially sold?"

"All the conditions passed yesterday. They close in early January."

And then Violet and Audrey's home, only three blocks away, will be someone else's. How hard must that be for Violet when she's already seen so much? I can't imagine the day my family farm no longer belongs to a Mitchell.

I reach over to squeeze his hand. "That was good of you to step in like that."

"As if you gave me much choice." But he wears a permanent smile as he pulls into Gayle and Howard's driveway, and we unload gifts from the trunk.

A festive wreath hangs on the door, but otherwise there isn't much in the way of decoration. I suppose it's too much for them to be climbing ladders to string lights at their age. Too bad they don't have a Jed next door to come over and help.

A set of eyes watches through the front blinds. "They're here!" comes a muffled shout.

We're not on the porch for more than two seconds when the door flies open, and we're met with a grinning Violet, Gayle behind her. Bing Crosby croons in the background and the scent of cloves and cinnamon permeates the air.

"Let them in!" Gayle ushers her granddaughter back into the living room and waves us through in her customary way, dropping her voice to whisper, "She has been watching that window like a hawk for the past two hours, waiting for you."

"I have not!" Violet retorts. "This is where the cookies are."

Howard pokes his head out of the kitchen. "Merry Christmas! Tea will be ready soon."

"My, my." Gayle admires the festive floral arrangement in my arms, bursting with red, white, and green flowers and foliage. "What is all this?"

I slip off my boots. "Just a little something for your table." My favorite part about enjoying Henry's wealth is buying gifts for others, and the fact that he never made a single comment about how outrageously expensive these were makes me love him more. Most people don't realize how generous Henry is.

Violet's curious eyes are on him and the armload of wrapped packages he carries. She trails him to the Christmas tree like a small, eager child while I follow Gayle to the dining room.

"Henry said you had family coming over?" Their table is set for eight with crammed placemats and folding chairs. I move a few things out of the way to fit the arrangement in the center.

"Yes, a cousin and her family. It's been a while since we've had Christmas here. We'd been going to Audrey's for years." Gayle adjusts a setting. "They're bringing the turkey and dressing with them, and Violet is helping to peel all the vegetables. It's a bit too much for us these days. Both of us have such terrible arthritis."

"Get out of here!" Henry scolds but his tone is pleasant.

We turn to find Violet hovering over his shoulder like a nosy cat as he stoops to unload gifts under the tree. She inhales deeply. "Farm Girl Soap!"

"I'm serious, I'll put them all back."

"Violet! Help Gramps with the tea," Gayle urges, waving her away with a shooing sound.

"Yes, Gramma." Violet skips past us, wearing an impish grin and not a hint of shame, disappearing into the kitchen.

Gayle shakes her head, but she's chuckling. "She's always been outgoing and energetic, but when Audrey's health declined, she seemed to lose that spark. I haven't seen her so full of beans in ... well, a *long* time."

"That's a good thing."

"Yes, I ... I hope so."

I frown, wondering what she means by that.

"Abbi!" Howard hollers from the kitchen. "Violet said you two were heading to your parents' today?"

I wander into the kitchen, leaning against the door-frame. "We are."

"Your first Christmas together. That's exciting."

"We'll see." I chuckle. "Henry doesn't know what he's signed up for when it comes to Christmas with my family."

Violet's eyes light up. "What do you mean? Like what?"

I steal a peek around the wall. Gayle is holding out a tin of cookies for Henry as he strategically tucks gifts around the tree. We might have gone overboard. "It starts with Christmas caroling around Greenbank tonight at eight," I whisper.

Violet slaps a hand over her mouth.

"*Him*? Singing Christmas carols?" Howard's bushy eyebrows furrow with doubt.

"Oh, believe me, *I* know." I giggle. "And then we go to a midnight service at the Finlays." Another upstanding family in our congregation. This part I'm most worried about given how Henry feels about the church. "They have this huge barn that they fill with bleachers and hay bales for people to sit, and on one side are the farm animals. They have an especially loud donkey named Boris who heehaws the entire time."

Violet hoots with laughter.

"And on Christmas Day, there are sweaters."

"*Christmas* sweaters?"

"*Matching* Christmas sweaters, with Bible verses." Mama asked for Henry's measurements.

"And he has *no* idea?" Howard asks.

"Who has no idea about what?" Henry suddenly looms around the corner, making me jump.

"Nothing." I smooth my palm over his chest in an affectionate gesture.

His eyes narrow on me and Violet, then move to

Howard, who clears his throat and keeps his focus on the teapot. "I don't like surprises, Abbi," he says evenly.

"Really? And I was so sure you did. You know, remember Halloween?"

He opens his mouth, but stalls.

"I thought so."

A slow, vicious smile unfolds on his lips. "You *really* want to play this game with me?"

My stomach flips. Somehow, I'm going to pay for this. I'll likely enjoy it immensely, but I'll still lose.

"My money's on Abbi," Violet says through a mouthful of cookie.

"Traitor." Henry glares at her. "What are they planning, Howard?"

The old man holds up the tray. "Tea, anyone?"

MY PHONE CHIRPS with another text from Mama, asking where we are and how long before we get to Greenbank.

"We should get going soon." Henry peers out the front window. "The snow is picking up and we have a few hours to go still."

Disappointment skitters across Violet's face. "But you haven't opened your gifts yet!" She dives under the tree, rifling through Henry's deliberately set piles, picking one up to shake it—while flashing a toothy grin over her shoulder at him—before pulling out two wrapped boxes. She drops one in each of our laps.

Henry eyes it. "You didn't need to get me anything."

She shrugs. "It's nothing big. 'Cause, you know, you have *everything* already. But you might as well open them together."

I steal a glance at Violet—with her bottom lip pulled between her teeth—as we peel away the tape and unwrap the boxes.

"I love it!" I hold up my olive-green knit hat, admiring the braided pattern.

"I thought that color would go with your hair."

I tug it on my head. "Thank you, Vi."

"She's been working on it every night for the past two weeks," Gayle exclaims.

Inside Henry's box is a simple beige knit beanie.

"You had a black one on at Rockefeller, so I thought something different would be good. You don't have one like this already, do you?" Violet waits for his response with her hands balled into tight fists.

"I don't have this color." When Henry meets her eyes, his sparkle with something raw I can't identify, and his jaw is taut. "It's perfect. Thank you, Violet."

She blushes and then averts her gaze as if uncomfortable.

I lean in. "And *I'm* thanking you, too, because your father looks hot in a beanie." It's the first time I've called him anything but Henry in front of her.

Violet scrunches her nose with disgust as Howard and Gayle laugh.

Henry shakes his head at me before holding up his index finger toward Violet. "Okay, you can open *one* today. The skinny, silver one in the tree."

I frown curiously at him as Violet bolts for it. I wrapped all the gifts we brought, but I didn't wrap that one.

"It's a surprise," he mouths with a knowing smirk.

She tears open the thin rectangular box and pulls out a plastic card attached to a lanyard. "A ski-lift ticket?" She frowns as she reads. "Colorado?"

"I thought the three of us could go there for a few days next week. I have a hotel there."

She reads the pass again and her face lights up. "That's my birthday."

A soft expression unfurls on Henry's face. "I know."

I hadn't even thought of Violet's birthday, so swamped with work and Christmas.

But Henry did.

I feel my pulse in my throat as I watch this exchange, the urge to throw myself at this man tremendous.

Violet looks at her grandparents, hopeful.

"Well, of course! He's already cleared it with us." Gayle's smile is broad. "You only turn sixteen once."

"I've never skied before," she admits, looping the lanyard around her neck.

"Neither have I. We can learn together," I say.

"I've already booked you both an instructor for the bunny hill," Henry confirms.

"And you'll be on—"

"The black diamond runs."

"Of course. Because there's nothing Henry wasn't born good at." I throw my hands up in mock annoyance, earning his amused snort and a round of chuckles.

We help clean up and spend a few minutes saying good-bye, with Violet diving into Henry's arms in a hug that makes my chest swell with emotion.

I find myself wishing we could stay. Or take her with us.

We're halfway down the path toward the SUV when it dawns on me. "*Aspen,* Colorado?"

"Took you long enough." Henry smiles. "Relax, he knows better than to come anywhere near you, trust me."

I hope so. That night with Michael is the only thing I

regret, and I regret it with every bone and sinew in my body. If I have to ever see him again, it'll be too soon.

I shed my coat for the long car ride to Greenbank and then admire Henry's handsome profile as he punches the address into the GPS.

"Why are you staring at me?" he murmurs.

"Am I?" I reach up to twirl strands of his hair between my fingertips. "I was thinking that you're going to make a great father. I mean, you already do, but you know what I mean."

"I do, and I think we should start trying now."

"*Now*?" My heart skips a beat, not expecting that response. "I'm still on the pill."

"Stop taking it."

I *could*. I'm supposed to start the next package tomorrow. "But what if it happens right away? The wedding is still four and a half months from now. I have to fit into my dress." Which I still haven't seen.

"I'm sure the designer could whip you up a new one in no time," he says casually, one hand resting on the steering wheel as he leans in to kiss me. "Let's start trying tonight in our new bed."

The king-size bed Henry had delivered to my parents' place last week, unbeknownst to me or Mama.

My stomach flutters, even though I've caught on. "Okay, now I know you're not being serious because we *can't*." I give him a look.

"I forgot."

"No, you didn't." He knows I'm on my period. Henry's always acutely aware of this time of the month because he turns needier.

He hums. "That's fine. The ways I plan on defiling your body tonight don't make babies, anyway."

Those flutters are quickly replaced by a hammering heartbeat.

"It's been a while since I fucked your ass." He flashes a sexy smile. A challenge. And I'm not sure he's joking.

"Henry ...," I warn.

"I just want to give my future mother-in-law something to pray for. It's my Christmas gift to her."

"Trust me, she already prays to the Lord for your salvation *every* day."

He throws the car into Reverse. "After this holiday, she'll be crossing herself for me until Easter."

I poke him in the ribs, but I'm laughing.

twenty-two

F *ebruary*

VIOLET ANSWERS the door with a wet mop of hair. "I'm sorry! I slept in!" She stumbles over the pile of shoes—all hers—backing up to let me into the house. "Give me five minutes. I just have to throw my things into a bag and I'll be ready." She trots off to her bedroom, leaving me to shut the front door.

"Good morning, dear." Gayle struggles to get up from the recliner.

I hold my hands in the air. "Don't get up on my account."

"This arthritis ..." She gives up on her effort, settling back in. She's still in her nightgown and housecoat, a blanket draped over her bottom half. "I thought I heard her stirring, but I guess it was something else. Maybe I should have my hearing checked."

"Don't worry about it. I built in lots of time and the roads are clear." Cold, but the Porsche SUV navigates well. I miss being behind the wheel, and Henry didn't argue with me too much about driving myself to Greenbank once he saw the clear weather forecast.

"So, this is your bridal shower you're going to?"

"Yes. The ladies at the congregation wanted to throw something for me." I resisted at first—showers are for, well, showering the bride with presents. Henry and I don't need anything—until Henry suggested I choose a charity to donate to in lieu of gifts.

He won *at least* a hundred points with Mama when I relayed that message.

"That's nice. And I'm sure your family is so happy to see you and Henry together."

I laugh and hope it doesn't sound too doubtful. "Where's Howard?"

"Resting. He's feeling under the weather lately. We both caught Violet's cold a few weeks ago and he hasn't been able to shake it. I'd like him to get checked out, but you know how men are."

I've seen Gayle a handful of times since we've met. She's never looked so frail and tired before. "We might be able to arrange a house call, if you'd like?" Do doctors even do that anymore? Regardless, there doesn't seem to be much Henry can't set up.

"Oh, that's sweet of you, dear, but we'll manage." She toys with a corner of her blanket. "And where is Henry this weekend?"

"Los Angeles, but he's flying to Pittsburgh to meet us at the hotel tonight." We have a suite booked at the same Wolf where Henry and I reunited after my father's accident.

"Gosh, that man travels a lot. He must be exhausted."

"He works hard."

She looks over her shoulder at Violet's shut door. "Ever since she came back from that ski trip, it seems like he's all she can talk about. Henry this and Henry that."

"He's a big fan of hers too. We both are." Colorado felt like the start of something special. We spent three days skiing, eating, laughing, and while Henry was there to check on hotel operations, we had his undivided attention. A rarity.

Violet's mood on the flight home was morose by comparison, but we didn't hold it against her. She didn't want the trip to end.

Gayle hesitates before asking, "You and Henry. Are you two planning on ... having children?" She flinches, as if just hearing herself ask the question pains her because she doesn't want to invade our privacy. So opposite to Mama.

"Yes, that is the plan."

"Soon?"

"Sooner than later. After the wedding, though." The topic hasn't come up since Henry's teasing on Christmas Eve, but each time I reach for a new package of birth control pills, I waffle over the idea of not opening it, of tossing them out.

Her eyebrows draw together. There's something heavy on her mind.

"What's wrong, Gayle?"

"Oh, nothing. We just worry about what will happen to Violet after we're gone. We can't help it, at our age. That's what you do. You don't worry about the inevitable. Instead, you worry about all your loved ones moving on with their lives when you're no longer here, and you hope everything will be okay." She chuckles softly. "And people move on. They have babies and get busy, they don't see each other as often, that sort of thing."

I think I see where Gayle's thoughts are gathering. "Violet is a part of our family now and she will always be Henry's daughter, no matter how many more children he has."

Gayle inhales sharply. "That's a relief to hear, dear. Thank you for saying that."

Violet's door flies open and she emerges, a duffel bag in her grip. "Does this work?" She poses to model the black leggings and red tunic sweater she threw on.

"Perfect."

"Great, 'cause I don't have anything else clean."

"Oh, I can wash your clothes for you while you're gone." Gayle smiles up at her granddaughter.

"No, Gramma, I've got it. You can't be going down to the basement. What if you fall?"

"I'll go slow."

Violet shakes her head. "Please don't make me worry about you while I'm gone. I'll do all the laundry when I'm back tomorrow."

After a beat, Gayle nods. "I'll leave it for you." But her shoulders slump.

"Do you need anything? Tea?"

She holds up a mug. "You already made me one, remember?"

"Or a sandwich?"

"Oh, don't fuss over me." Gayle waves her off. "We'll be fine."

Violet's brow wrinkles. "You sure?"

"Of course! Go and have fun with Abbi at the bridal shower. We'll see you tomorrow. Give me a kiss."

Violet stoops to kiss Gayle's forehead with a murmured "Love you, Gramma."

We wave our goodbyes and head outside, into the cold.

But Violet seems down.

"You okay?"

She peers over her shoulder at the house. "I feel guilty about leaving them alone overnight."

"Did you want to stay here? You don't have to come with me."

"No, that's the thing. I want to! And Gramma wouldn't let me stay, anyway. It's just hard, you know? She needs help getting out of bed. Her body's really stiff from the arthritis. Gramps is usually the one to help her, but with him being sick, I've been doing it."

My heart aches for her. And for Gayle. "Getting old sucks." Being sixteen and feeling like a caregiver to your elderly guardians isn't any easier. "I'll bet they love the extra time they're getting with you though." I open the tailgate on the SUV so Violet can toss her bag in.

"Yeah." She bites her bottom lip as she peers back at the house. "They were going to sell this place and move to a retirement home before my mom got sick."

I know. But I can't admit to knowing that because then I'd have to admit to Dyson digging into her grandparents and I'm not sure how Violet would feel about that, jokes of invisible flying robotic eyes aside.

"Oh, crap! I forgot something. I'll be back in a sec."

I get settled in for the long drive while Violet runs into the house, only to return empty-handed thirty seconds later.

"What'd you forget?"

She digs into her coat pockets to pull out a portable speaker and earbuds. "Hopefully, the walls are thicker at this hotel than the one in Aspen."

"Oh my God." My face burns as I put the SUV in Reverse and back up. "Don't worry, Henry made sure the bedrooms are far apart." He was visibly horrified to discover that his daughter heard us having sex, and Henry has never been bothered about having an audience.

Violet shucks her coat and adjusts the radio station. "Did I ever tell you that Becca Taylor and her friends cornered me with, like, a thousand questions after the play?"

"About what?"

"They asked who Henry is and if you're his wife, that sort of thing."

"What'd you tell them?" I ask warily. They must not recognize us.

"Don't worry, I stuck with the story. He's 'a cousin'." She air quotes. "But do you know what they started calling him?" She snorts. "The DILF."

"THAT'S MY GREAT-GRANDMOTHER'S RESTAURANT." I point at the Pearl, where a couple sits at a window table, giving their order to Ryleigh, the new teenage server Aunt May hired before Christmas. She wears too much eyeliner for Mama's liking. Garland still hangs around the door, a residual of the holidays.

"It's cute." Violet's curious gaze absorbs the many storefronts as we drive down Greenbank's bustling main street.

"My aunt runs it now. She offered to host the shower there, but it's way too small." It sounds like every female in the congregation plans on attending today, so Celeste booked the church hall. "May is *the best* cook. Seriously, her lasagna is to die for. Even Henry made a comment about it."

"Can we come back and eat there?"

"Yeah, definitely." My fists tighten around the steering wheel. "Listen, there are a few things you need to be prepared for. Mostly about my mother." We pass by the feed mill. Lloyd Hornback is out front, loading a bag of pellets into someone's truck. I wave at him, and he stalls before waving back. He didn't recognize me in this high-priced SUV.

"What about your mother?" Violet watches me expectantly.

"Right." Where do I begin? "For one, she has *very* strong opinions on things."

"What things?"

"*All* things." Even that which she doesn't understand, having lived a sheltered small town farm life. "And she's *very* devoted to her church and living a good Christian life."

Violet nods slowly. "I've been to church once. Somebody in our family was getting baptized or something. I don't know. It was a *really* long time ago."

Audrey and Violet would be labeled heathens by Mama's standards, but I keep that part to myself. "Mama goes *every* Sunday, without fail. And she reads verses from the Bible every night. Her best friends are Reverend Enderbey and his wife, Celeste. She is against drinking, cussing, and premarital sex. She thinks having too much money is a sin and wealth should be shared. She makes all her choices based on being in God's good graces."

"Wow. Huh." Violet seems to process my words. "What does she think about Henry?"

It didn't take long for Violet to connect those dots. "Mama's not his biggest fan. She *is* getting better." Especially after Henry suggested holding a second reception in Greenbank so the town could be a part of the celebration. And despite his worries, we did not wake up with her standing over our bed with a claw hammer on Christmas Day, but she did ask Reverend Enderbey to say a special prayer during the barn service for those who fall to temptations of pride, greed, and the flesh. His gaze was squarely on Henry while speaking the words. "But there are still a lot of things about Henry that she does not like and never will. She's still hoping that Jed and I will get back together."

"Who's Jed?"

"My ex, who is also the reverend's son." I give her the two-minute rundown.

"What a douchebag," she mutters.

"Yeah, but it doesn't even faze me anymore. I'm thankful." If Jed hadn't cheated on me, my life would be completely different. Unsatisfying. And I'd have no clue. "*Everything* happens for a reason." I've never felt that saying more than when I look at Henry.

"So, does your mother know about me, then?"

"*Noooo.*" I punctuate that with a shaky laugh. How do I put this delicately? "Mama has a big mouth. We can't trust that she'll keep it quiet, and we want to protect you from all the media stuff for as long as we can. Plus, it'll send Henry back five hundred pages in her good books. She's already called him the devil on earth several times."

Violet watches the houses pass. "Do you think Henry regrets what happened with my mom?" she asks quietly.

I hear the question she asks, but it's the one she doesn't ask aloud that lingers in the air between us. "The only regret Henry has where you're concerned is that he didn't know about you sooner."

After a few beats, her dimples pop with a smile.

"So, you're a cousin today, if you're okay with that."

"Oooh, can I be long-lost? Like, a brother and sister who came over from England only to be separated once they got here? Oh! Or maybe one of them died on the *Titanic*, leaving a child who was taken in by other survivors, only to discover their real lineage on their deathbed."

I laugh. "That is the exact kind of bait we don't need floating around out there for the media to pick up."

Her shoulders sink with exaggeration. "Fine. Just plain old boring cousin it is."

~

"WHO MADE THESE?" Violet asks around a mouthful.

"Those are Aunt May's famous Buffalo chicken pinwheels." Mama demands them for every church event.

Violet's paper plate is heaping with tea sandwiches, fresh-cut veggies, and home-baked treats. The hens—five church ladies who run all the social events around town—have been busy, helping organize this shower with the official host Celeste, who is at the food table, loading more pink lady squares onto a stand.

"Holy Christ, they are *really* good." She lays a hand over her mouth, her eyes flittering around the beige hall, stalling on the wall-mounted cross. "I mean, holy moly."

I laugh. "Don't worry, no one heard you." There are ninety-two guests at this bridal shower, and their collective chatter creates a steady buzz that can drown out any one voice from more than five feet away.

"Do you know *all* these people?"

"Pretty much, yeah." Most are churchgoers, and many were at Daddy's homecoming party. "Those are my cousins over there, who were *supposed* to be my bridesmaids." I jut my chin toward Joy, Diana, and Angela, huddled by the punch bowl. Angela's greeting was sour, but I let it roll off my shoulders. If she's offended, that's on Mama. Besides, they all should have known better than to accept an invitation to be in a bridal party from anyone but the bride herself.

"What happened?"

"Mama happened. Long story. I'll tell you on the way to Pittsburgh after this."

"Deal. Where *are* your bridesmaids, anyway? Aren't they supposed to come to these things?"

"Margo is literally strutting down a runway right now." She couldn't get out of that contract, and I would never ask her to. I had no idea the brat ordered two hundred bars of Farm Girl soap as shower favors until half an hour ago when I saw them stacked on a table. She swore Annie to secrecy. "Autumn had to cancel last minute because of a funeral, and there was no way I was subjecting Ronan to this. Plus, Mama has no idea that he's in my party, and she likely won't approve." She still doesn't understand why I'd choose friends over family.

Violet mouths "*Oh*" as she peers at Mama, standing among a group of ten women. She's wearing a new outfit—a green gingham dress crafted from the "fine fabric" I refused to use for my bridesmaids, she informed me. "She might not like Henry, but she seems to be having a good time."

"That's because she's the center of attention." After all, it's her daughter who's marrying the handsome billionaire hotel owner whom everyone is fascinated with—whether they'll admit to it or not.

Violet grins.

"Why do you two look like you're conspiring?" Aunt May sneaks up behind us, making us both jump.

"Violet was just saying how much she likes your sandwiches," I say.

Violet holds up a pinwheel. "These are delicious."

"You should try the feta and olive ones, then. They're

over on that table." Aunt May points to a corner. "They're a new recipe, but they seem to be a hit. They're going fast."

"On it." Violet trots off toward the table.

Aunt May laughs after her. "She's a sweet girl."

"She is."

"Henry's cousin, you said?"

"Yes. Distant." I hate lying to Aunt May, but this might be a secret too heavy for her to keep from my mother. It's best I not put her in that position.

"I see a resemblance there. It's nice she could make it." She gestures around the church hall. "Quite the turnout. I don't think I've been to a shower this big in a while."

"Yeah, I really didn't need all this." It was so kind of Celeste, especially given she pulled me aside to tell me that I'll always be a daughter to her, even if I'm not marrying her son.

"But you deserve *all this*." Aunt May smooths a loving hand over my cheek. She was fourteen when I was born, and I've always felt closer to her than to Mama. Maybe because she wasn't constantly trying to mold, scold, and judge me. "And Bernadette is enjoying the spotlight, which makes everything to do with the wedding easier on all of us."

I watch Mama a moment now, her her hands flapping dramatically. "What do you think they're talking about?"

"Oh, Janice McClellan probably brought up that gossip article because she can't help herself, and Bern's telling them about her fearless campaign to convince all of Green-bank's store owners to boycott them on account of them making up lies that only sinful fools believe."

I gape. "She is *not* doing that."

"Oh, you bet she is! Bernadette is on a mission, and you know what she can be like. I don't think she'll rest until she succeeds." Aunt May chuckles. "Peggy Sue said she saw Bern empty a rack of magazines at the supermarket and toss them into the trash."

"She's going to get herself arrested."

Aunt May snorts. "You kidding? Ten minutes in holding and she'd have Stewart convinced God will smite him if he doesn't let her out for doing the Lord's work."

"Oh, Mama." But my heart warms. No one can ever accuse her of not loving me enough. "She looks good."

"She's growing out her hair for Alaska, and that new dress fits her well. Wouldn't want that material to go to waste, would we?" Her crooked smile tells me she heard two earfuls worth about the good gingham I "refused" as well. "What colors are you going with for the wedding?"

"Black, white, and champagne."

"Very classy." She nods with approval.

"I hope so."

Mama pauses in her conversation, her head swiveling. When she spots me, she beckons me over with a frantic wave. "Abigail! Come and mingle with your guests!"

"MARVELOUS JOB FILLING in for the bridesmaids today!" Peggy Sue hollers at Violet from beside her baby-blue Parisienne, her thick glasses fogging in the frigid cold. "And make me one of those hats in red, like yours!"

"I'll have it to you by Easter." Violet waves before hitting the button to close the window and sinking into the passenger seat. "I really like her."

"Everyone likes Peggy Sue."

"Maybe not Mama." Violet bursts into laughter as my cheeks burn.

"Peggy Sue gets a kick out of riling her up." Most guests respected my wishes for a charitable donation, dropping their envelope into the card box, but there were still wrapped gifts on the table with my name on them. The majority were personalized—beveled picture frames engraved with Henry's and my name, matching crystal candlesticks with our initials, his-and-her bath towels—but that old coot not only wrapped up a racy white lace lingerie set for me to open in front of everyone but felt the need to note that my-stud-of-a-future-husband won't be able to keep his hands off me.

Mama's face puckered from biting her tongue so hard.

"Thank you for taking all those notes. It makes it so much easier to send thank-you cards."

"Yeah, no worries."

I check the dash clock. Henry should be landing in Pittsburgh soon, and it'll take an hour for us to get there, especially on the dark roads. "So, I was thinking ..."

Violet reaches back to fish out a cookie from the box Celeste insisted we take with us. "*Yes?*" She croons in a mock deep voice.

"What would you say about being one of my bridesmaids?" It dawned on me halfway through the shower that, if Violet were younger, we'd have made her a flower girl. It wouldn't be a question.

Violet pauses midbite. "Are you serious?"

"Of course I am."

She chews, giving herself time to process. "But won't your numbers be uneven?"

I shrug. "So what? I also have a man in my bridal party. And you should be in our wedding. It's *your dad* getting married." More and more, I've been dropping that word into our conversations to try to make it a familiar one.

She bites her lip. "Is he okay with this—"

"Yes." Or he will be when I tell him.

"Okay." A slow smile stretches across her face. "Yeah, that'd be cool."

"Good." A swell of emotion hits, telling me that while I might have made that decision only hours ago, it's the right one. "We'll get your measurements to the seamstress this week."

She reaches back to collect the wooden card box. "This is pretty." She traces the letters of Henry's and my name with her fingertip before easing it open.

"Celeste does calligraphy. She painted that by hand."

Digging inside, she pulls the top card out to read aloud. "'Dear Abigail, we are so thrilled for you. As requested, we've made a donation to—'" Violet's voice cuts off as she reads the rest silently. "You asked for donations in my mom's name?"

"Toward ALS research, yes. Henry and I felt that was the most meaningful charity for our family." Which now includes Violet. I lied to Mama, telling her Audrey was one of Henry's staff members. I wouldn't even share a last name.

I watch the dark roads for a moment as the silence in the car stretches. When I dare steal a glance next to me, I note the tear rolling down Violet's cheek.

twenty-three

M*arch*

"BUSY AFTERNOON, LADIES?" Sullivan holds the elevator door for us, our arms laden with shopping bags.

"Spring is coming soon, right?" Because we bought a wardrobe of clothes we can't wear until it does.

"A few more weeks."

"Lies," I moan, falling back against the elevator wall. He might be right, but with that early March blustering cold wind that churns through the streets, burning our cheeks, warmer weather feels an eternity away.

"At least you're going somewhere hot for your honeymoon, right?" Violet says.

"I have no idea. Henry won't tell me anything." It's the only part of the wedding that he's taken control of, and he's already said he won't even tell me what to pack.

"Miles would know. He knows all."

"Miles wants to keep his balls intact."

"Understandable." Violet met Henry's assistant the last time she was in the city and wanted to see her father's office. They took to each other in an instant.

"Margo knows because she's in charge of packing for me." Which means my daytime attire will be respectable enough, while my nights will likely be filled with public indecency and sex toys. "But she won't tell me either."

"Sounds like you're SOL, then."

The elevator feels like it's moving especially slow today, either because my arms are about to fall off under the weight of all these bags or because I'm dying for time to hurry up and for Henry to come home tomorrow night. He's been in Tokyo all week, and I'm regretting not going, but it was a last-minute trip and I'm elbow-deep in all things Farm Girl Soap Co.

"Okay, so if you were stranded alone on a deserted island and you could choose to have one of the following, which would you pick: a knife, a ball, or a book?"

Violet's question comes out of left field, but in the months since we met and the time we've spent together, I've grown to expect—and love—that about her. "What kind of ball? Like a Wilson, that I could turn into a friend to talk to?"

She shrugs. "Sure."

I consider the other options. "Are there animals on this island that I could use the knife on?"

She pauses for a beat. "Puppies and kittens."

"Aww. An island of puppies and kittens?" But then I wince. "So I'm going to starve, is what you're saying. Not even a chicken?"

"No chickens." Her face lights up. "But there *are* coconut trees."

"Ugh. I hate coconut, but fine, I can work with this." The elevator doors open into the penthouse lobby. "What's the book?"

"Does it matter?"

I unceremoniously drop my bags to free my hands, and punch in the code. "Well, yeah. If it's *Lord of the Rings*, that's over a thousand pages I could first read for entertainment and then burn for—"

"Surprise!"

I shriek as I take in the small crowd of familiar faces and the enormous "Happy Birthday" balloon archway that stretches across the living room.

Henry steps forward wearing a satisfied grin.

I burst into tears as I dive into his arms.

"YOU SERIOUSLY HAD NO IDEA?" Connor towers over me, his cornflower-blue eyes sparkling, his Miami-tanned skin making mine look especially pasty. "Because I totally fucked up last week and said 'See you on Saturday' in my text."

"I didn't even notice," I admit sheepishly.

"Huh. So, Abbi doesn't read our messages anymore." Connor smacks Ronan in the chest, nearly knocking his beer out of his grip. "Good to know."

"No, that's not it. I've just been *so* busy with work."

"How's all that going, anyway?" Ronan asks.

"Amazing. We keep doubling our special-order inventory and selling out. I've had to hire full-time staff for production, and we're already looking at a larger location to lease out. We're going to rent land from my parents to grow the herbs." Mama and Daddy will make money while the

Mitchell farm supports their daughter's business. They're onboard.

"See?" He clanks his glass against mine. "Told you that magazine didn't matter."

I don't want to talk about work, though. "I can't believe Henry pulled this off from the other side of the world." He said he made reservations for a birthday dinner tomorrow night.

"He has reliable minions to do his bidding." Ronan juts his chin toward Raj, Miles, and Violet, who are laughing about something at a dessert table loaded with candies and cakes—apparently, Violet's contribution to the party planning with Sasha.

"Either way, I'm so glad you guys could come." I haven't seen any of them, save for Ronan, since I left Alaska. My face hurts from all the smiling and laughing, catching up with Connor, as well as Katie and Rachel, and seeing Autumn in person. Even Jed and Laura made it here. Shocking, that Henry would extend the invitation but it's also rather big of him. For Jed's part, he's been friendly.

Henry reappears, a fresh champagne glass in hand. "For the birthday girl." He leans in to give me a deep kiss that's far too intimate for the current audience. But I think that might be the whole point—a reminder for the two men I'm talking to that Henry won and I'm taken.

"Thank you for the drink." I sink into his side.

"Oh, look, all my favorite people in one place again," Margo purrs, her lanky arm coiling around Connor's waist as she smiles up at him.

The last time the five of us were together was complete debauchery. In fact, *every* time I'm with Margo—save for the night after the Halloween party when Henry and I left early —depraved things happen.

"There are people under the age of eighteen here," I remind her.

"Ah yes, you mean Violet? I just spoke to her. She is *precious*, Henry."

Connor peers over my head with interest. "Yeah, who is that girl you came in here with? 'Cause *damn*."

Beside me, Henry's entire body stiffens.

Oh no. "Connor, that is Henry's—"

"Daughter," Henry cuts me off before I can say *cousin*. "And she's sixteen," he adds through gritted teeth.

My stomach leaps. It's the first time Henry has ever openly admitted to their real connection outside his inner circle. I wonder if he'll regret it later.

Connor lifts his free hand in the air, genuine shock filling his face. "Got it. Say no more."

Henry's phone rings. "Excuse me for a minute?" He presses a kiss against my temple, throws another daggered look at Connor, and then leaves to answer.

"Dude." Ronan shakes his head. "You really stepped in it."

"Fuck. How would I know? You knew?"

"*I* knew." Ronan smirks around a sip of his beer.

"Why didn't you warn me?" He snaps, and then his handsome face scrunches. "And how is that even possible? How fucking old is Wolf?"

"It's a long story, but we're keeping it out of the news as long as we can, so *please* don't say anything." I give him my best pleading stare. "We don't want her going through that."

"I won't say a word to anyone." He shakes his head to emphasize his promise, and I don't think I've ever seen Connor wear such a somber face.

"Are you staying in the hotel tonight?" Margo asks, swaying against his body like a cat in heat.

Connor gives his head a shake and then as quickly as the seriousness arrived, it fades. "Depends." He flashes that signature cocky grin. "Where are *you* staying?"

Not in this penthouse with Violet here, that's for sure.

"Abigail." Henry's voice pulls me away from the overt display.

"Yes?" I don't even note that he's used my full name until a beat later. My smile falls off instantly. "What is it?" What has made Henry's face look so grim?

"It's Howard."

twenty-four

Violet snores softly in my ear, her head resting on my shoulder, as I sit and watch Henry and Gayle speak to the doctor on call.

The ambulance brought Howard to a nice hospital, at least. It looks new, built within the last ten years maybe. And it's quiet at this late hour.

But it's still a hospital where people die, and Howard still had a stroke.

Henry thanks the doctor and waits a beat for Gayle to maneuver with her cane, going so far as to extend his arm, which she accepts with a smile. They slowly make their way over.

"How bad is it?" I whisper.

"Not great, but it could have been much worse," Henry says. "They got him in and on the clot-busting drugs quickly."

"That's good news." My shoulders sink with relief.

But Henry's brow is furrowed.

"One minute we were talking about a character on the

TV show, and the next, Howard was saying gibberish. Nothing made sense. Thank goodness that cell phone was within reach." Gayle shakes her head. "I'm so sorry we ruined your celebration, Abbi. I was going to wait until tomorrow to call, but—"

"No, we're glad you didn't wait," Henry cuts her off, a slight reprimand in his tone, as if even suggesting that Gayle not calling us would be offensive.

"Absolutely," I echo. We left everyone in the penthouse, telling them to stay as long as they wanted. I'm sure they've found a way to entertain themselves. Hopefully, it's not in our bed.

Violet stirs with a sharp inhale. "Gramps?" She peers up at Henry with sleepy eyes.

"He's going to be okay." He leans down and brushes hair off her forehead. "Come on, let's get you home."

"Wow." Henry looks around the penthouse. Aside from the multitude of candy jars, the flower arrangements, and the enormous archway of balloons, all evidence of a party is gone.

"Sasha's people are good."

"More likely Raj, even though he was here as a guest." Henry sinks into the couch, his head falling back. He must be exhausted from the travel, considering he flew in from the other side of the world this afternoon. "Remind me to give him a huge bonus."

I tumble down next to him, molding myself against his side. I haven't seen him all week. "Thank you for the party." I lick the sharp jut of his neck. "And for bringing my friends

299

here." I trail my lips along his jawline. "For everything." I end with my lips against his in a tender kiss.

"There's nothing I wouldn't do for you, Abbi. You know that." His voice is scratchy, as if he just woke up. "That reminds me." With another kiss, he peels away. "I'll be back in a sec." He pulls himself up and disappears down the hall, to his office, I assume, and then returns with a red jewelry box. "Happy birthday."

I gingerly slide the cardboard off. And gasp. "*Henry.*"

"Violet said you two were out shopping and you really liked this one."

"Yes, but this is too much." I remember the strangled sound I made when I asked the man behind the Cartier counter for the price.

He ignores me, sliding the necklace out from the box and fastening the clasp around my neck. The diamond pendant nestles against my chest.

I test its weight within my fingertips. "It's beautiful. Thank you."

"You're welcome." He smiles wryly. "Violet said to tell you that *I* picked it out, but *she* paid for it."

I snort. "She cracks me up."

"Yeah. She does that." His smile fades.

"What's wrong?"

His chest rises with a deep inhale, as if preparing himself. "We need to have a serious talk about Violet." In his blue eyes, a flurry of unreadable emotions swirl.

Tension cords through my body as I prepare myself. "I'm listening." But will I want to hear what he has to say?

"What she's been through the last few years, watching as Audrey slowly died, and then getting shuffled to Howard and Gayle ... They are good people, don't get me wrong, but they're struggling. Have you seen all the pill bottles in their kitchen?"

"I noticed." I didn't think Henry did, though. "Violet's doing all the laundry and grocery shopping. She's had to help Gayle out of bed to use the bathroom because Howard's a deep sleeper and Gayle struggles to get up on her own."

"And Howard just had a stroke. Even if he makes a full recovery, the doctor said it's going to take months of physiotherapy. Back and forth every day. Gayle doesn't drive anymore."

"So we can help with that, right? Hire a driver for them?"

"Yes, we can." His jaw tenses. "But I think Gayle and Howard should move into a home where they can get the help they need, just like they'd planned."

"Okay." I nod slowly, trying to read where Henry's thoughts are going. "And what about Violet?"

He swallows. "You're twenty-two years old and you have been incredible through all this, but you didn't sign up for a sixteen-year-old stepdaughter when I asked you to marry me."

"No, I signed up for anything that comes our way."

"And what if that means Violet moving in here? Us, responsible for her—"

"Oh my God, shut up, Henry." I punctuate that with a hard kiss and then, maybe it's my exhaustion, but I start to laugh, and it's a delirious sound. "*Of course*, Violet can live with us. *Of course*, I'm okay with that. I love her. Truly. And I love you. In fact, I don't think I've loved you more than I do at this very moment." I shake my head at him. "Did you think I might have an issue with this?" How long as he been searching for a way to bring up the topic?

"I didn't want to make decisions for us without asking

you." He smiles. "Isn't that what you're always scolding me about?"

"And I appreciate that." I lean in, kissing his jawline. "But you need to ask Violet if this is what *she* wants." My guess is she does.

His chest heaves with a deep inhale. "After we talk with Gayle and Howard. They might not be okay with this plan."

I think back to the conversation with Gayle. "I bet they'll be okay with it. More than okay with it." I stroke his cheek with my palm. "And you should look at having yourself named as her legal guardian. You don't have to announce who you *really* are." It's best that he doesn't.

The urge to erase all distance between us is overwhelming. I climb onto his lap, straddling his thighs. "I guess our days of doing whatever we want, wherever we want are coming to an end?"

His chest lifts with a deep, shaky inhale. "Is this really happening?"

"Yes. And it makes you happy."

He bites his bottom lip. "It does."

"It makes me happy, too." I pause. "But we'll give her the farthest bedroom from ours."

He winces as if still pained by the trauma of Aspen. "Definitely." Warm hands smooth over my backside as Henry pulls me closer to him until I can feel his hard length between my thighs. He captures my lips with his and our tongues brush against each other in a slow dance.

"Better take advantage of our freedom while we still can," I whisper, pulling away to remove my sweater and shuck my bra. The cool diamond pendant settles against my bare skin.

Henry's tired eyes flare with desire as he reaches up to fill his hands with my breasts. "How did I get so lucky?"

Leaning forward, he closes his mouth over one of my pebbled nipples.

My fingers weave through his thick mane of hair. "Remember? We have to thank Jed."

My nipple slips from Henry's mouth as he tips his head back and bellows with laughter.

twenty-five

"Grab your hat and mitts. It'll be cold."

"Where are we going again?" Violet jams her foot into her boot.

"To show you the house your great-grandfather built, and then I thought we could go and cut some wood." Henry slides on his red and black plaid jacket.

She frowns. "Don't you have people for that?"

"Yes. And today one of them is named Violet. Start making your way down the path toward the main lodge. I'll catch up in a minute."

She rolls her eyes as she tugs open the penthouse cabin's door. "What are the chances I'm going to get eaten by a bear?"

"Slim to none. You make too much damn noise. Now get out."

She grins, pulling the door behind her.

I lay the garment bag with my wedding dress across the dining table. Emmanuelle has designed me a masterpiece. It is neither puffy nor plain nor too heavy but molds to my body in all the right places and is layered with the most exquisite lace. I can't wait for Henry to see it. "You're taking her to that spot where you took me that first time?" Before I had any clue about his intentions to hire me as his assistant.

"Yes." Henry's gaze rolls over Penthouse Cabin Three— the only one with two bedrooms. It's almost identical in style to Penthouse Cabin One. "Are you sure you don't want to come with us?"

I slip my arms around his waist, falling into him. It feels so good to be back in Alaska. "I'll stay here and feed the fire. Jill and I have a bunch of last-minute things to go over for the wedding, anyway." Almost everything is taken care of, save for a few changes to account for minor glitches like half-spoiled strawberries and a shortage of white tulips. Mama, Daddy, and the rest of our guests arrive the day after tomorrow, but Henry and I wanted a couple of nights alone with Violet at Wolf Cove before we're pulled in twenty directions, with no time for each other.

Besides, I think this is a conversation best had between father and daughter.

"Don't worry." I smile up at his handsome face. "It's going to be fine."

His jaw tenses. "Maybe I should wait until after the wedding?"

"As we're leaving for our honeymoon?" I shake my head. Howard is home now and improving with daily therapy and help from a nurse Henry hired. According to the doctor, he'll make a near-full recovery, which is fantastic news. But the reality is they'll both be eighty-five this year, and the struggles will only get worse.

Henry and I sat down with them one day when Violet was out with friends and broached the subject of their granddaughter moving to Manhattan to live with us. I mean, it's the next logical step. We text every day, and we've seen her nearly every weekend since Christmas—either her coming into the city or us driving out. The reality is, Violet's as big a part of our lives as we are of hers.

Gayle and Howard weren't surprised, and when Gayle cried, she promised it was with delighted tears. She's been so afraid of becoming a burden for their granddaughter, who has a whole life ahead of her and shouldn't be saddled with taking care of her ailing grandparents, especially after what she faced with Audrey.

"She won't have to worry about Gayle and Howard anymore. You've found a wonderful place for them to move to, *way* nicer than the one they were waiting for before they pulled their names off the list." When we brought Gayle to see the assisted living home, I'm not sure her mouth was closed for more than a minute total, too busy hanging open in awe as we toured the one-bedroom suite they would move into, complete with a fireplace and a private garden, and then the many on-site facilities, including a therapy pool, an art studio, and a library. Of course she insisted they couldn't afford it and they didn't need this type of luxury. Henry would have none of it and told her to consider it fair trade for Audrey raising the perfect daughter for him.

My heart melted for the thousandth time for this man that day. He continues to amaze me with his generosity and thoughtfulness.

Henry frowns. "And if she says no?"

"She's going to say yes."

"How do you know?"

I stretch onto my tiptoes to kiss him. "Because how could anyone say no to you?"

～

I HEAR their boots stomping on the doormat outside before the telltale beeps of someone entering the code. The door swings open.

"How big do you think it was?" Violet asks, her arms loaded with firewood, her cheeks rosy from the chilly air.

"At least five hundred pounds. Maybe six." Henry trails in after her, carrying twice as much wood. He hip-checks the door shut.

"You saw a bear?" I ask.

"Bear *tracks*." Violet kicks off her muddy boots and carries the wood over to the fireplace.

"Did you cut all that?"

"No, but I did almost cut off my foot." Violet holds her hands out in front of the flame for warmth.

"It's too wet. We got this from up near the lodge." Henry stoops to unload and begins stacking.

Neither reveals anything about how their talk went.

Does that mean it went poorly?

Did they even talk?

I've been on pins and needles all afternoon. This is going to drive me nuts.

"*So* ... I ordered food. It should be here soon if you want to wash up and change?"

Violet looks down at her pants, speckled in mud. "Oh, good idea."

I wait for her door to shut before I pounce. "How did it go?" My whisper sounds like a hiss.

Henry stands, his gaze transfixed on the flames that dance in the hearth. Finally, his lips curve. "She said yes."

"Yes!"

"She asked if she could finish out her school year at Bishop Prep, which I said was fine. That's what we were planning on, anyway, given we won't be home for a few weeks."

I sigh with relief. "See? I told you."

A wistful look fills his face. "She called me *Dad*."

A small gasp escapes my lips.

"She also called me Henry, and Dude, and Wolf. And apparently, I'm officially a DILF." He shakes his head, chuckling. "What have we gotten ourselves into?"

"A family." I sink against his broad chest, reveling in the strength. "How are you feeling now?"

He inhales. "Whole, if that makes any sense."

"It does." It's how I've felt since that day Henry and I reunited, as if a missing piece of my heart returned to me. And, while Violet was never missing—because I had no idea she existed—now that she's here, I can't imagine our lives without her. "I'm so proud of you, Henry."

"For what? Doing the right thing?"

"No, I always knew you'd do the right thing eventually." I tip my head back to meet his eyes. "But you're doing it because you want to, not because you have to."

He searches my face. "Do you know what I want more than anything else right now?"

My body ignites with interest that I need to dose quickly. "We can't do that until later." The days of stripping off our clothes and fucking whenever we wish are coming to an end.

"Not *that*." He rubs his thumb over my bottom lip, his voice turning husky. "I can't wait to call you my wife. Saturday can't come soon enough."

My heart stutters as he leans in to kiss my lips. It begins sweetly but turns frantic in seconds, his tongue plunging into my mouth, while his fingers weave through my hair and his body is pressed against mine.

Violet will be out any moment. She doesn't need to see her father and me mauling each other's faces.

I break away from him, my breathing ragged. "So, did she call you *Dad* or *Daddy*?" I say the latter in a sultry tone.

I squeal as Henry tosses me onto the couch, before climbing on top of me, pinning my arms above my head. "What did I say would happen if you started up with that again?" He pitches forward to drag his tongue along my bottom lip.

Violet pokes her head out of her room. "Oh God, is this going to be like Aspen all over again?"

twenty-six

I watch John steer the ferry toward Wolf Cove's dock through a billow of my breath. The kindly old captain hugged and congratulated me when we first arrived, bringing me to tears. He was the first friendly face I saw a year ago when I left the comfort of all I'd known for the terrifying unknown.

Now he brings everyone I hold dear to the place I love, where I found myself.

A small army of staff huddle in their hotel-supplied jackets and vests, waiting with smiles and empty hands to collect luggage.

"There's Mama!" Even with her longer curls, I can still pick her out of a crowd. I wave.

I hear a faint holler of "Abigail! We're here!" and she waves back, as does my father who's standing beside her, free of his walking cast, healthy and strong again.

For all the fussing that Mama did about a wedding in Alaska, she's been buzzing around town with excitement since the bridal shower. By now everyone knows her full itinerary, from the glacier landing to the bear sightseeing trip we have planned for them and the Enderbeys in the coming days, as well as the fact that she refused Penthouse Cabin One for accommodations on account of not wanting to be eaten by wild animals.

I wave at Aunt May, Reverend Enderbey and Celeste, and Jed, who has come solo. Henry sent his jet to Pittsburgh and flew them all here together.

"Nervous?" Violet asks, sidling up beside me.

"Yes," I admit with a laugh. "I love this place so much, and I want everyone else to love it too. I think I'll be crushed if they don't." I know that sounds silly, and yet it feels like such a big part of Henry and me—who we are to each other.

"They'd have to be crazy not to love it here. I mean, come on." She points behind us, drawing my attention to the grandiose lodge that towers over the water.

"I know, right? But Mama could find fault in a newborn baby." And she'll point it out too. As far as Henry goes, she has hovered in lukewarm territory for months, which is better than that strange alien-abducted cheery version of her last fall and a thousand times better than the version who faked a heart attack to keep us apart.

Violet nudges my shoulder with hers. "Don't worry. They're gonna love it."

"They will." I nudge her back. "But let's try to get Mama drunk just in case."

"On it!" She rubs her mitted hands together. "And just so I have my stories straight, is Henry still my cousin?"

"Yes. We'd rather get through the next few days without her theatrics. But we will tell them the truth after the wedding." Less chance of Mama deciding Henry is the devil again and yelling her objections during the ceremony. Then we'll pray Mama can keep her mouth shut for Violet's benefit. Given her aim to rid Greenbank of all gossip magazines, there is hope.

Violet shrugs. "I like her. I think she's funny."

"She is *something*, all right." Henry is suddenly behind us, one arm slung over each of our shoulders. "But she's family."

Violet steals a bashful glance up at him before refocusing on the coming ferry, getting ready to dock.

I can see their faces clearly now—the awe filling them as they take in Henry's special place for the first time. I know that feeling. I stood in that spot, wearing that same look a year ago.

Had I known then that this place was nothing compared to the man behind it, who would capture my heart and become my *everything*.

"So, hey, does this mean I'll get a matching sweater next Christmas too?" Violet asks suddenly.

I grin as Henry's jaw clenches with annoyance. "Definitely."

epilogue

"I thought we agreed to no work," Henry scolds, watching me pull out my laptop and set it on the floor in front of my lounger.

I'm thrumming with excitement as I wave him over. "This isn't work. Joel sent the pictures." He promised to send them as quickly as possible, but I expected that would take weeks.

Henry strides leisurely across the deck to the shaded area where I lay, stomach down. His cerulean board shorts are settled low enough on his waist to show off the cut of his pelvis. "Why are you hiding here?"

"You're asking me that? Really?" His skin is a rich golden brown after almost a week under the Mediterranean sun. Meanwhile, I burned so badly on the first day of our honeymoon, the only touching Henry got to do for two days was rubbing aloe vera on my inflamed body.

"You'll be fine. You didn't put on enough sunscreen before." Henry pushes my legs apart to straddle my body just below my ass. "I need to touch land. I was thinking we could go to Monte Carlo tomorrow, if you're good with that? Preston's there. We could have dinner with him."

"Can Merrick come?" I tease, earning my left butt cheek a smack as I wait for the satellite reception to find a signal. Had I known Henry owned a yacht that he kept docked off the coast of France, I might have been able to guess his secret plans for our honeymoon. But I've never asked him to list his assets and, to be honest, being continuously surprised is more fun.

I already own the only parts of him I care about—his heart, his mind, his adoration.

"Ugh! Come on!" I tap the key repeatedly, wishing my computer would hurry up.

"Relax. It'll work." I feel a tug on my bikini string, and then another, and another.

"I really don't want the staff seeing me naked, Henry." I add quietly, "Again." Though the bikinis Margo packed for me leave little to the imagination anyway, but Captain Blain has already caught me straddling my husband's lap once on this trip.

"I told all of them to stay away from this side of the boat, unless they want to swim to shore."

"There! It's up!" I quickly punch in the passcode. Several folders appear. I select the one marked Wedding Day.

I gasp as the first pictures fill the screen.

Henry stretches his warm body out on top of me while keeping the bulk of his weight resting on his elbows. He presses his lips against my bare shoulder. "All right, let's see how good Joel really is."

I pause long enough to turn and steal a lingering kiss from his lips and try to ignore his growing erection against the crack of my ass. We've been on this yacht for six days, and he's had me in every position and countless surfaces and seems nowhere near sated.

But right now, I'm determined to relive the most perfect weekend of my life through a screen.

When Joel promised to capture *all* the moments, he wasn't exaggerating. There are *six hundred* perfect moments in this wedding folder, from my first sip of coffee, bare-faced, my hair in a clip, to our last moments at the lodge, as Henry helped me into the pickup truck. We spent our wedding night at the old house with the hearth burning and champagne chilled, our bodies rarely apart.

"Mama looked good, didn't she?" She was vehemently opposed to the idea of a black mother-of-the-bride gown. "Is this a wedding or a funeral, Abigail?" she'd declared. But when I sent her a designer satin dress to try on, she quickly changed her tune, allowing Celeste to make a few tweaks for sizing.

With her hair and makeup done at the Wolf Cove spa, she looked glamorous—a word I have never used to describe Mama. I noticed her stealing plenty of long, lingering looks at herself in the mirror. I guess the deadly sin of vanity wasn't a concern that day, and I'm glad for it.

Joel caught an especially perfect picture of us together, Mama teary-eyed as she helped zip up my dress—which she begrudgingly admitted was the prettiest wedding dress she'd ever seen and perfect for me. He also captured a candid shot of her smiling up at Henry during the reception. If I didn't know any better, I'd say the look of fondness was genuine.

Daddy was nothing short of dashing. I've seen him in his Sunday best plenty of times, but his Sunday best is not a custom-made tux courtesy of Henry's personal tailor—who Henry flew to Greenbank for measurements.

I think it's safe to say they will never forget their trip to Alaska and for all the right reasons. Mama was uncharacteristically composed when I sat them down the day after the wedding to divulge the whole truth about Violet. Shocked, but not cursing the ground that Henry walks on. And when I told them Violet was moving in with us, she nodded with satisfaction, declaring Henry might make a respectable father yet.

At least a third of the pictures are of our bridal party, and I can't fault Joel for that. Even Mama made a comment about their fine looks—including a debonair bridesman Ronan with a champagne tie to match the dresses. Preston wouldn't stop flirting with Aunt May, who was left flustered but not bothered in the least.

"Oh my God! I forgot about this." I laugh at one particular photo captured before the ceremony, down at the waterfront where Ronan and I used to sit watching the ducks and the sunset. I'm on one side of Ronan, while Margo is on the other, her body pressed against his, her hand conveniently hiding behind him. His face is etched in shock, while Margo wears a lascivious grin. "Do you know what she did to him there?"

"I have a pretty good idea." But Henry's voice is laced with humor. "I told her to be on her best behavior, for Violet's sake."

Joel was low-key obsessed with Violet, taking dozens of candid shots of her—alone, with me, with Henry. "She looks so grown up."

Henry's heavy sigh fills my ear. "I wish I'd met her when she was little."

I break to kiss his cheek. "But you know her now. That's what matters." And all because she had the guts to take a train and barge into our lives.

Henry rests his hand over mine, stalling my scroll as we work through the ceremony shots. There's a picture of Daddy walking me down to where Henry and Reverend Enderbey stood, my vibrant red hair styled in old-world glamor waves, my dress trailing gracefully behind me. Daddy and I wear matching tears. The camera doesn't show how tightly he's gripping me, it doesn't repeat the words he had just finished saying—that I'll always be his little Abigail, no matter what. And yet it somehow portrayed the emotion of that moment all the same. A lump swells in my throat as those same feelings rush back to me now.

"Okay, I'll admit it. Joel is good," Henry murmurs, nuzzling his nose against my ear. "I didn't think it was possible for him to capture how stunning you were that day, but he did. We're getting this one blown up for the wall."

I smile. I've never felt more beautiful than I did on our wedding day, emphasized the moment I reached Henry and he ignored all protocol, diving in to plant a searing kiss on my lips that left Reverend Enderbey clearing his throat and me flustered as we exchanged vows.

Every little detail that I lamented over these last months —from the silky invitations to the unconventional fig-and-blackberry-topped cheesecake to the dramatic black, white, and champagne table décor—will live forever in this folder. Joel missed *nothing* about the day, not even a shot of my diamond-laden wedding band next to Henry's carved matte gold ring.

We reach the end of the Wedding Day folder. "Can we ask him to print *all* of these?" Because I'll be revisiting them often.

"We can do whatever we want."

There are other folders too. One marked Pre-Wedding. "What are in these other—oh my God." I burst out laughing as Mama's terrified face fills the screen. A Kodiak lingers in the river maybe fifty yards away, more interested in the fish. "I knew they'd seen plenty of bears, but I didn't know Joel brought his camera with him." In another shot, Mama stands beside Celeste, looking halfway through crossing herself, preparing to die.

But back at the docks in Wolf Cove, they're all smiles for the camera, the yellow floatplane behind them.

The rest of the pictures in that folder are of our guests, enjoying all that Wolf Cove has to offer. Henry would not tell me what it cost, but he didn't balk at making sure every one of our friends and family had a memorable time.

"Your mother really liked Joel. Kept calling him 'that charming Frenchman.'"

"Yeah. Let's hope she doesn't look up his artwork." She'll never trust another person we introduce to her again. As it was, she nicknamed Margo "the Temptress" and kept a guarded eye on her whenever she was in the same room. Margo found it amusing.

Henry snorts.

"What's in this folder?" I click the one marked After-Party.

My laptop screen fills with pictures from inside the staff lodge, where it seems our bridal party relocated to after the formal reception shut down. I assume Ronan and Connor led that charge. By the bottles of hard liquor on nearly every table surface and the drunken embraces, it seems grace and virtue didn't follow.

My stomach drops as Connor's bare chest fills the screen, his beefy arm slung over Violet's shoulders. She's winking at the camera, holding up a shot glass filled with red liquid.

Henry's body stiffens.

Oh no.

"What the fuck are they doing?" he explodes.

"I'm sure it's not what it looks like." What else am I supposed to say? *Damn it, Connor.*

Henry scrambles off me and digs out his phone, takes a quick snap of my laptop screen, and then sends a text to Violet with one word: *Explain.*

"It might be a bit before she answers—"

"It's eight forty-two a.m. there. She's walking to school." He climbs to his feet and paces. "*What the fuck* was Violet doing there, anyway? She shouldn't be anywhere near the kind of shit that goes on around them. She's *sixteen* years old!"

"She's got to be messing with us." I shut my laptop, afraid of what else might be in that folder.

"If he touched her, there isn't a goddamn place in this world he can hide from me, and I don't give a fuck if those two crawled into that mine to—"

Henry's phone chirps with a text, stalling his rant. It's followed by a second message a beat later.

He reads them and his shoulders sag.

"Is that her?"

Henry hands me his phone without a word, his laughter a relief to my ears.

Violet: *Welcome to parenthood!*

Violet: *Chill, it was cranberry juice, and Ronan made me leave right after. Besides, they're too young for me. I'm going to make my move on the ferry captain.*

I can't help my giggle. "See? She's joking."

Henry's chuckle morphs into a groan. "This fucking kid is going to be a royal pain in my ass."

"Probably." She's already firmly entrenched in the penthouse, even though she doesn't officially move in until she's finished school in a month. Her room—the farthest one from ours—is being remodeled to her specifications while we're away. The security staff of Wolf Tower is all but wrapped around her pinkie finger, and Raj stocks the freezer with her favorite ready-to-bake chocolate chip cookie brand. We're waffling between two private schools for her to start in the fall—including one with an exceptional drama program—and will visit both with her when we're back from our honeymoon, right after we help Gayle and Howard move into their retirement home.

"Are you sure you want more?" I tease. I stopped taking the pill before the wedding, at Henry's request—but I was happy to dump the packages. Considering how many times we've had sex on this trip, I don't see how I won't return to New York pregnant, reproductive organs willing.

Strong hands seize my hips and flip me over onto my back. The scraps of my bikini fall to the deck floor, leaving me naked beneath the sunshade. Heat surges through my body with the promise of what's to come as Henry shucks his shorts and stands before me in all his masculine glory.

Around us is a brilliant azure sky and endless water, but I only have eyes for this man, every inch of him part of this dream I never want to wake from.

Henry strokes himself, his smile wicked. "Right now, Mrs. Wolf? *I'm sure* I want to make my wife scream."

∼

Did you enjoy Own Me? If so, please leave a review

∼

Learn more about Merrick in the Empire Nightclub series.
Continue for a sneak peek.

sneak peek: sweet mercy (empire nightclub, #1)

From internationally bestselling author K.A. Tucker comes the dark and sexy Empire Nightclub series.

~

Chapter One - Mercy

"Mercy Wheeler!"

My body, already rigid, stiffens at the sound of my name on the guard's tongue. I've been waiting in Fulcort Penitentiary's visitor lounge for over two hours now, long enough to leave me doubting whether I'd ever be let in.

Shutting my textbook, I collect my purse and rush for the counter with my stomach in my throat, afraid that any dallying could lose me my visit with my father.

The guard staff changed over at some point, because the thin older gentleman with the kind smile who took down my information earlier has been replaced by a burly oaf with beady little eyes and an unfriendly face. His name tag reads Parker. "Who you here to see?" he demands in a gruff tone.

"My dad." I clear the wobble from my voice. "Duncan Wheeler. It should say that on the log?" It comes out as a question, though I can see my father's name written in block letters next to the tip of this guy's pen.

"I like to double-check, is all." He smirks, then recites a long string of numbers and letters. My father's inmate ID number. "This is your first visit here?"

"Yeah." My father only began his sentence two weeks ago, and it took time to get me approved on his visitor list, which is bullshit. I'm the *only person* on his visitor list.

Parker the guard takes a long, lingering scan of my plain, baggy T-shirt. That, along with my loosest pair of jeans, is what I carefully chose to comply with the prison's visitor dress code policy. No tank tops, no shorts, no miniskirts. Nothing tight. Nothing to "provoke" the men serving time behind these bars.

His eyes stall on my chest for far too long.

I fight the urge to fidget under the lecherous gaze. He's at least twenty years older than me and unappealing, to say the least. Just imagining what kinds of thoughts are churning in his dirty mind makes my skin crawl. Then again, *everything* in this place—the barbed wire fences, the heavily armed guards, the long and narrow hallways, the constant buzzing as door locks are released, the fact that I'm about to sit in a room with murderers, rapists, and God only knows who else—makes my skin crawl.

"What's your old man in for?" Parker finally asks.

I hesitate. "Murder." Are prison guards even supposed to be asking these types of questions?

"Yeah?" His gaze drops to my chest again, and he's not

trying to be discreet about it. "And who'd your daddy kill, sweetheart?"

I'm not your goddamn sweetheart. My anger flares, at the invasion of my privacy, at the term he so casually tosses out, at the lustful stare. "Some asshole who wouldn't take no for an answer from me." A mechanic named Fleet who worked at the same auto repair shop where my dad worked, a slimy guy who smelled of motor oil and weed and apparently jerked off to cut-and-paste photos of my face atop porn mag bodies. Who cornered me one night with the full intention of experiencing the real thing.

My father didn't mean to kill him and yet here he is, serving twenty-two years because of a freak accident. Because the prosecutor was convinced otherwise and decided to make an example of him. Because we hired the world's most ineffective lawyer. It's the first thing I dwell on when my eyelids crack every day and the heaviest thing on my shoulders when I drift off at night.

I'm exhausted by guilt and anger, and it doesn't seem like it's going to let up any time soon.

Pervy Parker smirks. "Lock your things up in number seventeen and then head to security screening." He slaps a key onto the counter with his meaty paw. "Phone, car keys, coins, belt. Don't forget so much as a coin, unless you wanna get strip-searched." His mouth curves into a salacious smile. "And you won't get to say no to that if you ever wanna see your daddy again."

My face twists with horror before I can smother it. They wouldn't *actually* strip-search me for forgetting to take out a penny from my pocket, would they?

The prick laughs. "Welcome to Fulcort Penitentiary."

~

Who is she here to see? I wonder, watching the shriveled old lady fidget with her knuckles, her hair styled in tight gray curls, her wrinkled features touched with smears of pink and blue makeup. A husband? A son?

I've kept my eyes forward and down since I passed through the airport-level security screening process and was led me to this long, narrow visitation room. I've set my jaw and ignored the hair-raising feel of lingering looks and the stifling tension that courses through the air. My father warned me against attracting attention, that having inmates knowing he has "such a beautiful daughter" would only make his life harder in here. While I rolled my eyes as he said that, I also decided to heed his warning the best way I can, so as not to ruin his life further.

So, no makeup, no styled hair—I didn't even brush it today—and minimal eye contact.

Except this sweet-looking grandmother who sits at the cafeteria-style table across from me has caught my gaze and now I can't help but occupy my mind with questions about her while I wait. Namely, how many Saturdays has she spent sitting at Fulcort waiting for a loved one, and what will *I* look like when I'm sitting in this chair twenty-two *years* from now?

A soft buzz sounds on my left, pulling my attention away from her and toward the door where prisoners have been filtering in and out.

An ache swells in my chest as I watch my father shuffle through. It's only been two weeks and yet his face looks gaunt, the orange jumpsuit loose on his tall, lanky frame.

He pauses as the guard refers to a clipboard, his gaze frantically scanning the faces at each table.

I dare a small wave to grab his attention.

The second his green eyes meet mine, his face splits with a smile. He rushes for me.

"Walk!" a guard barks from somewhere.

I stand to meet him.

"Oh God, are you a sight for sore eyes!" He ropes his arms around my neck and pulls me tight into his body.

"I missed you so much!" I return the embrace, sinking into my father's chest as tears spill down my cheeks despite my best efforts to keep them at bay. "They made me wait for hours. I wasn't sure if I'd make it in today—"

"That's enough!" That same guard who just yelled at my father to walk moves in swiftly to stand beside us, his hard face offering not a shred of sympathy. "Unless you wanna lose visitation privileges, inmate!"

Dad pulls back with a solemn nod, his hands in the air in a sign of surrender. "Sorry." He gestures to the table. "Come on, Mercy. Sit. Let me look at you."

We settle into our seats across from each other, my father folding his hands tidily in front of him atop the table. A model of best behavior. The guard shoots him another warning look before continuing on.

"So?" I swallow against the lump in my throat, brushing my tears away. I've done so well, hiding tears from him up until now. "How are you doing?"

He shrugs. "You know. Fine, I guess." He quickly surveys the occupants of the tables around us.

That's when I notice that his jaw is tinged with a greenish-yellow bruise. "Dad! What happened to your face?" I reach for him on instinct.

He pulls back just as the tips of my fingernails graze his cheek. "It's nothing."

"Bullshit! Did someone hit you?"

His wary eyes dart to the nearby inmates again. "Don't

worry about it, Mercy. It's just the way things are inside. Someone thinks you looked at them funny.... Pecking order, that sort of thing. It's not hard to make enemies in a prison without trying. Anyway, it's almost healed."

My eyes begin to sting again. This is *my* fault. I should never have told him about what Fleet did that night. It's not like the dirty pig succeeded in his mission; a swift kick to his balls gave me the break I needed to run inside and call the police. Now, had the police done their goddamn job, Fleet never would have strolled into work the next morning with a smug smile on his face and a vivid description of how firm my ass is, and my normally mild-mannered father wouldn't have lost his temper.

Two weeks in and he's already been attacked? My father is one of the most easygoing guys I've ever met. The fact that he went after Fleet the way he did in the garage was a surprise to everyone, including Fleet, according to what witnesses said.

"Hey, hey, hey.... Come on. I can't handle watching you cry," my dad croons in a soothing voice. "And we don't have time for that. Tell me what's going on with you. How's school? Work?"

I grit my jaw to keep my emotions in check. We're supposed to have an hour, but the guard already warned me that Saturdays are busy and this visit will most likely get cut short. So much for prisoner rights. "Work is work. Same old." I've been an administrative assistant at a drug and alcohol addiction center called Mary's Way in downtown Phoenix for six years now. The center is geared toward women and children, and there never seems to be a shortage of them passing through our doors, hooked on vodka or heroin or crack. Some come by choice, others are mandated by the court.

Too many suddenly stop coming. Too many times I feel like we're of no help at all.

Dad nods like he knows.

Because he *does* know, thanks to my mother and her own addiction to a slew of deadly drugs. Heroin is the one that finally claimed her life when I was ten.

"And school? You're keeping up with that, right?"

I hesitate.

"Mercy—"

"*Yes*, I'm still going." Only because it was too late to drop out of my courses without receiving a failing grade. Though, given my scores on my recent midterms, I may earn a failing grade anyway.

He taps the table with his fingertip. "You need to keep up with that, Mercy. Don't let my mess derail your future. You've worked too hard for this, and you're so close to getting that degree."

I've been working toward my bachelor's degree part-time since I was eighteen, squeezing in classes at night and wherever I could find the time and money. At twenty-five, I'm two passing grades away from achieving it. Up until now my intention has always been to become a substance abuse counselor, to help other families avoid the same anguish and loss that my father and I live with. That's why I took the job at Mary's to begin with.

But shit happened, and now I have another focus, and it is laser-specific.

I swallow. "I'm looking at taking the LSAT."

"LSAT?" My dad frowns. "That have something to do with being a counselor?" My father isn't a highly educated man. He spent his teenage years working on cars and skipping class to get high. At some point he decided school wasn't for him, so he wrote his GED and then got a job in a mechanic shop. It took years, but he finally got licensed.

"No. It's for getting into law school." I level him with a serious gaze. "If you'd had a better lawyer than that shyster, you would have gotten involuntary manslaughter at most. Your sentence would have been a sliver of what you're facing now—"

"No, wait." He pinches the bridge of his nose. "What are you saying, Mercy? That you're going to give up on your plans and go to law school just so you can try and get me out of here? I mean, do you even wanna be a lawyer? I thought you hated lawyers." He chuckles as if the idea is amusing.

Nothing is amusing about this. "I want to be able to hug you without some guard breathing down our necks." My voice has turned hoarse. "I want my kids to be able to play and laugh with their grandfather." It's going to be years before there are actually tiny feet running about. But will my fifty-year-old father even live long enough to see the outside again?

"I don't like this at all." Dad shakes his head. "How many years of school is it, anyway?"

"A lot less than what you have to serve right now." Three full-time, plus articling. If I even get accepted anywhere. I've always excelled in my courses, but this is a new direction, one I've never spent a second considering. And then there's the whole "how do I pay for tuition and survive for three years while I'm going to law school full-time" question. All of our savings went to that joke of a lawyer who screwed my father.

It's a lot to figure out, but I *will* figure it out, because there is no way I'll accept coming here every Saturday for the next twenty-two years to watch my father slowly wither away.

"This isn't the life I hoped for you. But I know better than to argue with you." Dad sighs, his shoulders sinking. "So... what's the weather like? I haven't been outside yet today."

"Sunny. Hot."

"Shocking." He offers me a wry smile.

Despite my mood, I can't help but chuckle. It's always one or the other in the desert. A lot of the time, it's both, and in July, it's oppressively so. But the eternal sunshine is the main reason we moved to Arizona from North Carolina after my mother died. It's a natural mood-booster, my father says, and he has always worried about me inheriting her depression. "I had to change in the parking lot." The dented blue shitbox that I drive has never had working air-conditioning, so I pulled my T-shirt and jeans on over my shorts and tank top. "Figure I'll leave these clothes in the car for Saturdays. It'll be like my prison uniform."

He makes a sound. "Good call. Maybe bring a paper bag to wear over your head too."

"*Dad.*"

"Trust me, I've heard the way the men in here talk about women, especially pretty young women like you...." His eyes narrow on a guy three tables over whose dark eyes flitter curiously to us—to me—while a ready-to-burst pregnant woman sitting across from him babbles away. "I don't want anyone giving you grief when you come visit me."

"Nobody is going to give me grief." Except that guard, Parker, but there's no way I'm telling my dad about him. "And if anyone says anything, *ignore* it. They're just words."

He harrumphs. "How's the new place?"

I avert my gaze, dragging my fingertip across the table in tiny circles. "Fine."

He sighs. "That bad?"

"It's... lacking charm," I admit. Anyone who has lived in Phoenix for long enough knows which areas of the city to avoid, and when my dad's conviction was passed and we accepted the fact that I'd need to downgrade from the two-bedroom apartment we were sharing—a downgrade from the house we had before that—we started looking for cheap one-bedrooms closer to work and campus. We found one. A relatively clean, quiet twelve-unit complex with decent management and minimal needles littering the parking lot. A diamond in the rough, my dad called it.

Turns out it's more like a diamond in Mordor.

The couple two doors down—Bob and Rita—fight like they're sworn enemies. I've watched her launch glass from their fourth-storey balcony, aiming for his head as he runs to his car. The cops have been there twice that I know of. It's only a matter of time before an ambulance is wheeling someone out—my bet is it's Bob.

And then there's my next-door-neighbor, Glen, a hairy-chested guy who I hear every morning through the thin walls masturbating to the tune of my 7:00 a.m. alarm and who likes to knock on my door in the middle of the night, bleary-eyed and wearing nothing but his boxers. He always asks for Doritos. I tell him I don't buy Doritos—I *hate* Doritos—but he keeps coming back. I'm beginning to think Doritos is code for something else.

I don't open the door for him anymore.

And I'm not telling my father any of this. He has enough to worry about in here.

The guards come around, tapping several inmates on the shoulder to let them know that their time is up. That earns countless pained expressions from both prisoners and visitors alike. My dad and I watch as people embrace, some adhering to the rules while others hold on until they get a bark of warning.

That'll be us before long, and then it'll be another week before I make the hourlong drive up here.

My heart sinks. "So... what's your cellmate like?"

Dad smirks. "His name is Crazy Bob. And yes, they call him Crazy Bob to his face. Haven't asked what he's in for, and I don't think I wanna know. He likes the violin and NASCAR. Hasn't tried to shank or rape me in my sleep yet."

I frown my disapproval for the poor joke. "The violin and NASCAR. That's an odd combination, right?"

"Yeah. You could say that," my dad agrees. "But Crazy Bob is odd. He seems all right so far. Been in here over ten years now. Knows everything about everything. He's been giving me the lay of the land, so to speak. Where the mine-fields are, so I can avoid 'em."

"That's good. And the food?"

"The peas are mushy, the potatoes are grainy, and I've fixed tires that had more give than the meat they served last night." He chuckles. "So, kind of like your cooking. In fact, did you take a job in the kitchen that I don't know about?"

"Har. Har. Har." I roll my eyes. Leave it to my dad to try to make jokes in terrible circumstances. But he's always had a natural ability to defuse any tense situation.

So how did he end up getting punched in the face?

I bite the inside of my cheek, wondering if I should push. Finally, I can't help it. "Dad, why did someone hit you?"

He waves it off. "Aww... it was nothing—"

"So then tell me about it, if it's nothing," I challenge, wielding that sharp edge in my voice that Dad swears is like listening to a recording of my mother.

The longer he studies the smooth surface of the table,

the more I'm convinced that my gut is right and it's not just a matter of a pissing contest or a funny look.

"Dad...."

"Apparently Fleet's got family or something in here. He wanted me to know he wasn't happy with what happened to Fleet, is all." Dad shrugs nonchalantly. "So now I know. I'm just gonna stay out of the guy's way and everything'll be fine." His jaw tenses. He's more worried about it than he's letting on.

Rightfully so. My father is locked up in here with a family member of the guy he killed and he's already attacked him.

I think I'm going to vomit.

"We need to tell the guards—"

"No." He shakes his head firmly. "Trust me, *no*, Mercy. That won't do me *any* good in a place like *this*. Fulcort's known for.... Well, let's just say I'm a guy with no friends, no affiliations. I'm best to fly under the radar."

I frown. "What do you mean, affiliations?"

His gaze drifts around the room. I follow it, taking in the various men in orange jumpsuits. The population of Fulcort penitentiary is made up of every age and skin tone—short, tall, fat, skinny, clean-faced, scruffy.

How many of these men are like my father, I wonder.

How many of them don't belong in here?

Probably a lot less than the number of men who earned their cell.

My dad drops his voice to a murmur. "You see that guy over there? With the tattoo on his face? Don't be too obvious."

I shift my gaze to my left, spotting the guy in question easily. Half his face is marred with ink—a scaly dragon with talons—making him look downright scary. He's sitting across from a young pretty Latina girl with fake nails long enough to be used as a weapon in a place like this, I'd hazard. "Yeah."

"Crazy Bob says he's high up in some notorious LA gang. Anything that guy wants in here, he gets. Anything."

"So become his friend."

Dad chuckles. "That's not how it works." He glances over his shoulder at the group of inmates filtering in. "See that one there? The third in line?"

I watch a heavyset man with pock-marked cheeks and unkempt gray hair stroll in. He must be in his seventies, with a belly that strains the waistline of his prison garb. "Okay."

"He's got the warden and plenty of the guards in his pocket. Even dragon-face stays away from him. He could put a hit out on anyone and it'd be done in a day, inside these walls or not. That's what Crazy Bob claims, anyway."

I watch the man lumber along. Maybe it's the jumpsuit and shaggy mop on his head but I'm picturing him stretching pizza dough or selling car insurance from behind a chunky old desk circa 1970, not swimming at the top of the food chain in a maximum security prison, scaring LA gang-bangers.

"What's his deal?"

"Mob boss. Big into the drug trade."

I feel my eyebrows pop. "As in, like, Al Capone...?"

"As in, you betray him, he takes out your entire family and then you, and then he pisses on your ashes." Dad's voice drops to a whisper. "Crazy Bob told me that some clueless do-gooder guard came in here last year, stirring the pot against the corruption. He didn't last long."

"As in fired?"

"As in stopped coming in. His family hasn't heard from him since." Dad gives me a knowing look.

"I feel so much better knowing you're spending your days with these kind of people," I mutter, nausea stirring in my stomach. I study the mob boss as he passes. He walks with ease, as if he owns this room and he knows it. And maybe Crazy Bob isn't blowing smoke. Maybe he does own this place.

Curious about who he's here to see—one of his mobster minions, probably?—I let my gaze follow him to the four-person table in the far corner.

And find myself suddenly ensnared in a storm.

～

Chapter Two - Gabriel

I was fully prepared for two things when my eyelids peeled open this morning: one, that I'd be nursing a fucking epic hangover for most of the day after last night's festivities, and two, that I'd be in an extra-pissy mood by the time I made it up to this shithole.

What I did not expect was to be sitting in Fulcort with a raging hard-on for some chick visiting her old man.

But there you have it.

Fuck.

I've been coming here once a month for the last three years to see my father and I have *never* laid eyes on that woman before. I'd remember. Those sharp cheekbones, that thick jet-black hair. Those fat fucking lips, the kind that were made for wrapping around my cock and sucking slowly. She's hiding her body in baggy clothes—standard protocol, though she's taken it to the extreme; she's one step away from men's sweatpants—but her arms are toned, her neck is slender and long, her olive skin looks silky soft. I'm a betting man and I'd bet there's a tight ass and tits that sway when she's riding hard hiding beneath all that.

I didn't even notice her at first. I came in, settled into my dad's usual table in the corner of the room, and started surveying all the degenerates filling the room on this fine Saturday afternoon, killing time until Dad decided to grace me with his presence.

And then I spotted her over there, her pretty brow furrowed in worry as she leaned over the table to get as close to the man as possible without setting off the guards, and I haven't been able to peel my gaze away since.

It's been forever and a day since a woman has stirred my blood like this.

What's even more interesting is that she and the guy she's visiting—her dad, maybe?—leaned in to share a few whispered words and then those big, brown eyes of hers shifted to the inmates coming in.

To my father.

With wariness, she watched him stroll all the way over, and that's how, bingo, we're now eye-fucking each other. At least, that's what *I'm* doing.

Until I can get out of here, track her down, and switch to straight-up fucking.

My dad settles his girth into the stiff chair across from me. Somehow he's managed to pack on fifty pounds eating shitty prison food peppered with the odd steak dinner. "You're late," he mutters in his typical gruff voice.

"You have somewhere else you need to be?" I throw back before I can bite my tongue. If he wasn't going to complain about that, it'd be about something else. Still, he doesn't take too kindly to attitude, and Dad's bad side is not one you ever want to be on, blood-related or not. "Got caught up with work," I lie. "Who's that new guy over there? Number seven." I nod toward the table.

"What do I look like? Fucking four-one-one?" he snaps back, irritated.

I shrug, acting all nonchalant. "He seemed interested in you when you came in, is all."

Dad's bushy eyebrows furrow with the glare he shoots me before peering over his shoulder. "New fish. A nobody," he declares.

It's at that precise moment that my future lay glances our way. Her chocolate-brown eyes flare and then snap back, her face paling. Yeah, I'd say she got the skinny on who my father is, and it scares her. But will she be scared of me too? If so, what can I do to ease her fears?

My dick twitches with eagerness.

Dad shakes his head. "How's the club doing? You and Caleb haven't run it into the ground yet?"

I roll my eyes. "It's running smooth." Better than smooth, and he knows it. He likes to talk about Empire like it's his club, like it was his idea in the first place. He had nothing to do with it. My older brother and I purchased an old factory warehouse and converted it into a nightclub eight years ago. It's gone through several identity transformations but it's found its stride, catering to high-end clientele with cash to burn and people to impress. A one hundred percent legitimately run business, as far as any law enforcement is concerned. And, trust me, they've tried to prove otherwise. That's the downside of being the sons of Vlad Easton: you have the Feds and the IRS crawling up your ass on the regular.

"Peter was here last week." His cold gray eyes watch me.

"He said our *friends* have been causing problems for Harriet again."

By friends, Dad means the cartel, aka nobody's friend, and by causing problems for Harriet, he means venturing farther into US territory and encroaching on my family's foothold in the lucrative cocaine and heroin trade, a business that my father and his brother, Peter, have been nurturing for decades, originating with a supply arrangement from "our friends" down south.

A business that has amassed us impressive wealth and power.

"So what's Peter going to do?" I ask carefully. My uncle is a crazy fuck—almost as crazy as my dad, who isn't quite as crazy as the cartel.

His sagging skin contorts with his sneer. "What's *he* going to do? How about what are my sons going to do!" He stabs at the table's surface with his meaty index finger. "It's time you two stop fucking around like a bunch of playboys and act like you're ready to take care of the family business."

I bite my tongue against the urge to remind him that we've laundered millions through Empire for "the family business," and that it's Caleb and me who keep the highly lucrative underground fight ring going. We can't talk openly about it here, and besides, he doesn't want to hear that. He definitely doesn't want to hear the thoughts Caleb floated after the handcuffs landed on Dad's wrists almost four years ago—that it's time to let the cartel move in, wash our hands of the dirty drug business, and invest all this money in other, legitimate things. Things that won't land us in this shithole with him.

But it's like Dad reads my mind. "What do you think, that you two could afford any of your cars and your houses and your fucking club if not for all the sacrifices your uncle and I have made? All the blood and sweat that's poured. The tears?"

I highly doubt any of those tears came from my father. He didn't even cry when my mother died. The guy's tear ducts probably don't work. And I damn well know none of that pouring blood was his, though there's been more than enough spilled thanks to "Harriet."

He's right though: we've gotten filthy rich off junkies shooting their veins with heroin and partiers filling their nostrils with cocaine.

I sigh reluctantly. "We'll go talk to Peter."

"Good." He nods slowly. "Because I want things running smoothly for when I get out."

You're not getting out of here.

Read Sweet Mercy, Empire Nightclub #1 now...

also by k.a. tucker

Also by K.A. Tucker

The Wolf Hotel Series:

Tempt Me (#1)

Break Me (#2)

Teach Me (#3)

Surrender To Me (#4)

Own Me (#5)

Empire Nightclub Series:

Sweet Mercy (#1)

Gabriel Fallen (#2)

Dirty Empire (#3)

Fallen Empire (#4)

For K.A. Tucker's entire backlist, visit katuckerbooks.com

about the author

K.A. Tucker writes captivating stories with an edge.

She is the internationally bestselling author of the Ten Tiny Breaths and Burying Water series, He Will Be My Ruin, Until It Fades, Keep Her Safe, The Simple Wild, Be the Girl, and Say You Still Love Me. Her books have been featured in national publications including USA Today, Globe & Mail, Suspense Magazine, Publisher's Weekly, Oprah Mag, and First for Women.

K.A. Tucker currently resides outside of Toronto. Learn more about K.A. Tucker and her books at katucker-books.com